# CLASSIC MOTORCYCLE RACER TESTS

OSPREY
COLLECTOR'S
LIBRARY

# CLASSIC MOTORCYCLE RACER TESTS

Twenty track tests of postwar
road racing classics—from
Manx Norton to Ducati 600
TT2

## Alan Cathcart

Published in 1984 by Osprey Publishing Limited
12–14 Long Acre, London WC2E 9LP
Member company of the George Philip Group

British Library Cataloguing in Publication Data

Cathcart, Alan
    Classic motorcycle racer tests.—(Osprey
    collector's library)
    1. Motorcycles, Racing—Testing—History
    I. Title
    629.2'275        TL440
ISBN 0-85045-589-8

Editor Tim Parker
Design Gwyn Lewis
Filmset and printed in England by
BAS Printers Limited, Over Wallop, Hampshire

# Contents

# Acknowledgements

It goes without saying that I'm deeply indebted to the owners of all the bikes covered in this book for their faith and trust in allowing me to ride them. Without such confidence in my ability to return their precious, even priceless, machines in one piece at the end of the day, such tests would be literally impossible. And a big thank you too to all the mechanics who prepared the bikes for my use, and stood by without appearing TOO concerned while I sampled their handiwork.

Lots of other journalists have conducted racer tests down the years, though few are as fortunate as I have been to ride such a wonderful array of racing motorcycles all over the world. To the owners of the various circuits who placed their facilities so readily at my disposal, usually (except in Britain) without making any charge, I extend my sincere thanks, as well as to the freelance photographers in various countries with whom I worked to produce these stories. I'm grateful too to Mike Nicks of *Classic Bike*, who first gave me the chance as a neophyte scribbler to pro-

duce a racer test for his magazine, then kindly gave me a regular slot doing so in the largest-circulation periodical of its kind in the world. I'd probably never have made a niche for myself in bike journalism if not for his encouragement and support.

I am indebted to Peter Maskell of East Midlands Allied Press for the loan of some of their photographs, likewise Nick Nicholls and Don Morley for those of an historic nature.

Finally, a special thank you to the person who more than anyone else has supported my chosen profession of riding (and racing) exotic, sometimes fearsome motorcycles on tracks from Macau to Mallory, Misano to Montlhéry: my wife Stella. I'm very fortunate to be married to someone who countenances such a risky occupation so readily—and never once asks if my life insurance is fully paid up! Thanks, darling.

Alan Cathcart
Ealing, London
May 1984

# Editor's note

The idea of this book came after many hours' discussion as to how we could publish between hard covers a 'classic racing' story. Once stumbled upon the major problem was quite simply one of 'which bikes'? At the time of discussion Alan Cathcart produced his little record book and calmly stated he already had 60 tests under his leathers. Twenty tests seemed an easy choice, or so we thought (read 25 bikes as an actual total).

In the end we created six interesting and logical divisions and went on from there. Sure, we wanted to impress with the quality of the entry—couldn't leave out the Honda Six! We wanted to create technical interest—couldn't leave out the two little 125 Ducatis! We wanted topicality—Suzuki XR69? Soon we were back to 60 bikes. The final choice took more time and all that can be said in the last analysis is that there is something for everyone and there can always be a next time.

Each test used is an original. Some have appeared in journals before but not exactly as you will read here—here they are in full and all with comparable specification tables offering instant cross-reference. Some tests have never before appeared in English. Each test has high quality static photographs of the machine in question as well as classic contemporary racing shots and Cathcart in action. This collection is therefore both a permanent record and an exciting read.

No other author/journalist could have put this record on paper. Through considerable hard work, enthusiasm and dedication to the job in hand, and with no mean riding ability be it behind a pair of clip-ons or at an electronic typewriter, Alan Cathcart has forged a unique position in this business. He is the doyen amongst a tiny, select band of motojournalists who can race and write on the same day, on any machine, and anywhere in the world.

You'll read nothing like it anywhere else.

# 1 The postwar classics

## 1 | *350 Manx Norton* of Francis Beart

Francis Beart was one of the great men of British motorcycle racing for over 50 years until his sad death in March 1983, and he occupies a very special place in my own life on two wheels.

Though my connection with him began after he moved on to Aermacchis, Francis' reputation was founded on the remarkable achievements of a succession of much-modified Manx Nortons that passed through his hands, latterly all painted that unique shade of green (actually Ford's Ludlow green as used on their 1950s Prefect and Consul models!) which made his bikes stand out. An unsurpassed total of 11 Manx GP victories came his way, which coupled with ten 2nd places and three 3rds would be quite sufficient to mark Beart down as one of the Masters of Man, even without the solitary TT win (Denis Parkinson on a 350 Inter in the inaugural 1947 Clubmans TT) backed up by two 2nds and a 3rd in the June races. Francis preferred to concentrate on running his bikes in the longer, public road events such as the IoM races and the North West 200, where machine preparation and reliability counted for more than on short circuits, though the fact that he was equally adept at preparing bikes for the latter is indicated by the success of such as Joe Dunphy and Terry Shepherd on Beart-built machines in the 1960s.

Genuine Beart Nortons are few and far between, though Francis and his long-time assistant Phil Kettle, to whom much of the credit for the lengthy run of success is also due, worked

on sometimes as many as 60 or more customer engines over a winter close season. What made one of Beart's own bikes special was not so much the pale green livery but the superb and painstaking attention to detail in preparing the cycle parts. No customer could have afforded to pay for the countless hours spent carefully refining each of the components which went together to make one of Francis' own bikes, whose every aspect betrayed the Master's ceaseless quest for perfection. Each nut was carefully hollowed out to save precious grams, steel replaced with alloy wherever possible, then that alloy itself filled with more holes than a Swiss cheese if no weakening of the parts would result: the endless pursuit of weight reduction was one of the Beart passions—and he didn't let his riders spoil things by getting too plump, either!

The engines were rebuilt with a precision that not even Joe Craig could have surpassed, each setting and component used was carefully recorded in a logbook for future reference. Every opportunity to reduce unsprung weight and friction was sought—from mounting the rear units upside down, to replacing the wheel bearings after every race and carefully running them in on the bench, and using the narrowest possible tyre section and rim both to save unsprung weight *and* reduce the tyre contact patch for less friction while running upright.

Though at least one other genuine Beart Norton does exist in good condition in England, the finest monument to Francis' work had until recently been on view in the Stanford Hall Museum: he had actually rebuilt it himself to race-ready condition for the museum's founder, the late John Griffith, in 1974. I well remember watching the progress of the bike in the Beart workshop at his home at Shere, near Guildford, at the time. Francis fully intended it should be the last Manx Norton he ever worked on, and to make sure it was gave away all his special Manx tools to the Parris family at the end of the project.

There the bike sat, one of the jewels of the Stanford Hall collection, until the summer of 1983 when the majority of the exhibits were put up for sale. The bike was acquired by an American

*Left* **Joe Dunphy at Bedstead Corner on the 350 Beart Norton in the 1965 TT, when he finished 9th at 91·69 mph, winning a Silver Replica (Nicholls)**

*Right* **Shorn of its pale green Jakeman fairing, the many modifications Francis Beart carried out compared to a standard Manx Norton are evident on this bike (Barnwell)**

enthusiast, Bob MacLean, who in return for my services as intermediary, kindly (and trustingly) allowed me to track test it by riding it at the Classic Snetterton meeting in August before it was shipped to its new home. Needless to say, the chance to try what was effectively an as-new Beart Norton whose engine had literally only been fired up a couple of times and not ridden since Francis built it, had especial personal significance for me.

From the priceless details of the machine's life contained in the Beart logbook which accompanied it, it transpires that it was originally a 1961 machine which Francis bought from one of his customers during the winter of 1962/63, it having completed 1100 racing miles from new. In a way it's strange that he should have done so, since by that time the 7R AJS formed the backbone of the Beart effort in the 350 class, after he had struck up a close and fruitful friendship with Jack Williams of AMC. But in tandem with the 7R on which Peter Darvill was to win the Junior Manx GP for him that year (now owned and raced by Bob Warren), Francis rebuilt the 350

Manx to his own standards, and since MGP rules now permitted use of a fairing after the atrocious conditions in which the 1961 Junior had been run, fitted Jakeman two-piece streamlining with the rev counter mounted in a little 'dashboard' in the nose. Ernie Wakefield was commissioned to produce lightweight thin-gauge alloy oil and fuel tanks, the latter specially shaped to produce a recess in the top which permitted the rider to get his chin right down and so be completely shielded by the screen. The resultant protuberances caused the bike to be named the 'Sabrina' model by the paddock wags after a curvaceous starlet of the day, and to the bitter end Francis would never accept that with the filler cap on one side, the bulge on the other could not be made to hold anything but air. Ah well!

More to the point was the fitting of a highly effective 2LS Gilera front brake, one of two which Francis had acquired from Bob McIntyre's sponsor Joe Potts after the former was tragically killed at Oulton Park the year before: the brake had already been fitted successfully on loan to the

*Above* **Just as the Master restored her ten years before the test; note the abbreviated seat (Barnwell)**

*Right* **Oil and fuel tanks were specially made in light alloy by Wakefields (Barnwell)**

*Below* **Engine plates on all Beart bikes were engine-turned in alloy (Barnwell)**

Beart 500 on which Terry Shepherd finished second in the 1960 Race of the Year at Mallory after crashing in practice, so its effectiveness was proven in those pre-Fontana days, though it proved lethal till the right combination of linings was discovered.

The bike was debuted in Beart colours in the 1963 Manx GP by Jimmy Guthrie, who finished 20th after the specially-made front brake adjusters kept slackening: beautifully fashioned from light alloy and each drilled full of a dozen holes, they can be easily adjusted during a race with the thumb but depend on a sprung tensioner to stay in place: this must have broken or bent during the race.

The Norton was not used again until the following year, when Guthrie again rode it in the Manx, unfortunately writing it off when he fell at Rhencullen in the race, doing himself and the bike a power of no good. Rebuilt during the 1964/65 winter, Francis' log recounts that it required a new frame, swinging-arm, rear wheel, oil and fuel tanks, one front fork slider, a fairing and sundry other bits and pieces: Guthrie had been fortunate to emerge relatively intact himself. He made amends in the 1965 Manx by finishing 6th at 89·11 mph, but before this Joe Dunphy had ridden the bike in the Junior TT, finishing 9th at 91·69 mph en route to the Joe Craig Trophy which he clinched with a fine 2nd on the Beart 500 Manx in the Senior. Francis noted, however, in his log the performance of the pushrod Aermacchis in the Junior, Milani finishing 6th at 92·40 mph: 'worth looking out for' was the cryptic comment which contained the seed of an idea later to bear fruit. After this the bike was sold, before eventually finding its way into the hands of John Griffith.

With Francis sadly no longer with us to confirm that he had built the engine up to racing specification, two things had to be done before I could use the bike. Firstly, a perusal of the log showed that the 1974 rebuild included fitting a new Mahle piston, new big and little ends and many other new components. But having Ron Lewis check it over and replace all the perished oil and fuel lines seemed a wise move, as well as to clean off the surface corrosion on the magnesium cases caused by standing all those years in a damp and unheated environment. A check of the tyres showed them not to be the dreaded T1 compounds I'd feared, but a combination of as-new 472 on the back and that stickiest of triangular compounds, 398 on the front. An oil change and a new soft plug later, we were ready for Snetterton.

Gearing raised a question-mark, for since this Beart Norton had effectively only ever been used in the Isle of Man, Francis had fitted TT gearing of 21/45 when he restored the bike to the spec. it was in when Joe Dunphy rode it. Without any spare sprockets I was stuck with being considerably overgeared for Snetterton, but at least I was able to sample the bike as it would have been raced in the Island. Perhaps surprisingly, in view of the high bottom gear, it fired up easily on the line all weekend: nice not to have to start a TT by pushing halfway to Quarter Bridge before the plot chugged into life . . . .

Rigorously adhering to the Beart precept of warming the R40 lengthily and carefully, I changed to an RL50 (Francis always preferred Lodge plugs) and set off for practice on HMV (His Master's Vehicle). One lap later I was back in the paddock, the clutch slipping badly at anything more than 5000 rpm. Diagnosing that one more steel clutch plate would do the trick, I duly borrowed same from Joaquin Folch's G50 which was already sidelined with a cracked crankcase, and tried again.

This time all went well, and for the first time I was able to appreciate just how great the margin of improvement was between a Beart Norton and a standard, unmodified model. For a start all the controls are so light and sensitive, whether the featherlight throttle or the single-finger clutch and front brake: they don't come like that—only hours of painstaking assembly makes them that way. It's possible to ride the bike with a great deal of finesse and care, simply because each of the controls, including the beautifully balanced steering, can be operated with a fine degree of sensitivity. I didn't much care for the seating position though, which thanks to the Beart patented weight-saving seat (i.e. cut off the whole front half) tended to decant my precious bodily parts on to the unprotected upper frame rails once I started trying reasonably hard on the bike, and this was not only uncomfortable but also caused the very light alloy fuel tank to move about. It also made the oil filler cap flip up a couple of times till I got wise and taped it down. The stretched-out riding stance that the seat position forces one to adopt does, I admit, sit ill at ease with my more modern style of riding, but then Francis never cared for his riders to move about on the bikes, and especially not to stick knees out in the wind which he regarded as creating unnecessary drag. He never managed to cure me of the habit (though he did try!) but one thing I did learn from him was to keep my head down at all times as much under the screen as possible. The Norton invited such demeanour.

It also seemed to accelerate very smartly in spite of the handicap of the high gearing and 4-speed gearbox, doubtless because of the lower weight thanks to Francis' detailing: this turned out to be 296 lb with oil but no fuel, compared to at least 320 lb and probably more for a similar standard Manx with fairing and fittings. I've seen some weigh in at over 350 lb at Daytona.

In the Period 1 350 race I found myself embroiled in a dice for 2nd place with Angelo Guadagnino's presumably correctly-geared 350 Manx, and noted that even using my self-appointed limit of 7500 rpm I could pull away from him coming out of slow corners, but lost out in midrange before the Green Goddess got her skirts well gathered up and took over again at the top end. And I must admit to being able to outhandle him, especially in Russells where

the left/right high-speed flick could by the end of the weekend be taken hard on the stop in top—and I've never been able to do that on any other bike without getting into all sorts of terrible trouble on the way out. The Norton is beautifully set up for precisely this type of corner which abounds on the Isle of Man: knock it off just for a fraction in a corner where you shouldn't, especially going up the Mounain, and you may never see those 500 lost revs again before Brandywell.

The bike does give the impression of being very long-legged—a real long-distance stayer rather than a short circuit sprinter. You can feel the engine beating away reassuringly and seemingly unburstably beneath you, and without the performance of a 500 there's almost time to look around and enjoy the view going down the straight—till you realize that the next corner's looming up surprisingly quickly. It's a deceptively fast bike once into its stride. Getting it there can take a bit of doing, and there must be no fear in slipping the clutch coming out of even a corner as relatively fast as Sears to get it back on the boil: megaphonitis only clears at 5000 rpm, and with a 4-speed box there's a couple of gaps which need bridging if you're only using 7500 rpm as a limit. Respect for Bob MacLean's new purchase dissuaded me from trying out life at 8000. The gearchange is quite light and fairly positive, though I did find a false neutral a couple of times—coincidentally each occasion when I was involved in a tussle with another ex-Beart bike: Bob Warren's ex-Darvill MGP-winning 7R. With the Beart Aermacchi also out in another race in the hands of Dave Varney, there was much at Classic Snetterton that year to satisfy the disciples of the Master.

Two 2nd places and two 3rds out of four rides on the Beart Norton over that weekend showed the bike to have been superbly rebuilt to competition standards by Francis. A glance around the machine confirms this: there are those flecks of blue paint on so many of the nuts and bolts and other components large and small—all to

identify them as belonging to the 350 bike rather than the (yellow) 500. The dull nickle finish to most of the bolt-on components; the way each of the clutch springs and their cups are painted a different colour to make sure they go back together the way they came out; the engine-turning on the alloy engine plates. All this and more combines to echo another of Francis Beart's maxims: 'if it looks right, chances are it'll go right.' Though the fairies conspired to prevent it ever winning the race it deserved in the Manx GP, the 350 Beart Norton went as well as it looked.

| Model | 350 Beart Norton |
| --- | --- |
| Engine | Dohc single-cylinder 4-stroke |
| Bore × stroke | 76 × 76·7 mm |
| Capacity | 348 cc |
| Power output | 38 bhp at 7800 rpm |
| Compression ratio | 11·22 to 1 |
| Carburation | $1\frac{3}{16}$ in. Amal GP |
| Ignition | Bosch magneto and coil |
| Clutch | Dry multi-plate |
| Gearbox | 4-speed AMC |
| Frame | Duplex cradle Featherbed |
| Suspension: front | Roadholders |
| rear | Girling |
| Brakes: front | 210 mm 2LS Gilera drum |
| rear | SLS Norton drum |
| Tyres: front | 3·00 × 19 |
| rear | 3·50 × 19 |
| Weight | 296 lb |
| Top speed | 125 mph |
| Year of manufacture | 1961 |
| Owner | Bob MacLean, New York, USA |

*Above left* **Nothing handles like a Manx Norton—except another one (Barnwell)**

*Left* **Modern-compound Dunlop triangulars are fitted to the Beart bike now owned by American Bob MacLean (Barnwell)**

# 2 | The AMC duo—the AJS 7R and the Matchless G50

**Aussie Harry Hinton was one of the hundreds of riders all over the world who raced 7R Ajays with success. Here he is at Brands Hatch in September 1958 (Nicholls)**

Ask most racing enthusiasts what they consider to be the architype British racing single (what the French delightfully term the *Gromono*), and the mantle will almost certainly fall on the Manx Norton. Yet the history of the AJS 7R and the Matchless G50 is almost as long and honourable, and by the time the AMC factory ceased all production of racing machinery at the end of 1962, the two models in each class were very evenly matched. In spite of this, and of their longevity which sees many Seeley-framed G50s still in use in classic racing today, there is the feeling that the AMC single was never quite as good as the equivalent Manx. But as so often, a closer examination of the facts shows that, certainly as regards the ultimate development of each design, this is an illusion.

Although the designation 7R was first applied (in 1936) to a pre-war 'cammy' AJS, when revived postwar in 1948 it was applied to an entirely new design which bore little in common with its prewar predecessor, other than that it was a 350 cc single with a chain-driven single overhead camshaft. Designed by Philip Walker and intended to compete initially not with the Norton at all, but with the Mk VIII KTT Velocette, with whom it shared identical engine dimensions (74 × 81 mm), the first 7R looked remarkably similar to the last of the line produced in 1962. With its duplex cradle frame, telescopic front forks and large conical hubs cast from magnesium alloy, the cycle parts changed very little over the years.

However, the pool petrol in use at the time required a compression ratio of only 8·45 to 1 to be used, resulting in 30 bhp at 7000 rpm. Not surprisingly, this wasn't enough to cope with the Manxes and Velos, but the 7R quickly caught on amongst the clubmen of the racing fraternity at whom it was aimed. Though Jock West did some early testing, there is little doubt that most development work was carried out by the model's early customers—for the reason that AMC had allowed little or no budget for development testing! Notwithstanding, its popularity was such that it quickly received the epithet of the 'Boy Racer', and was gradually improved while raced with success, over the next five years: Matt Wright in particular must be credited with the successful early development.

In 1953 a major redesign took place, entailing a completely new frame with narrower cradle and much more rigid engine/gearbox assembly positioning: this effectively remained unchanged until the end of production in 1962. The engine too was modified, and given a narrower crankpin and more rigid bottom end. A development version was produced for the works team—known as the 'triple knocker' by reason of its 3-valve head (2 exhaust, 1 inlet)—the ultimate version of which (unfortunately never raced) had bevel

instead of chain drive to the camshafts. Though development costs persuaded the short-sighted AMC board to abort the project, it was on the chain-driven 'triple knocker' that Rod Coleman gave the 7R its only TT win, when he won the Junior in 1954. In that same year, the most significant event in the 7R/G50's life occurred when Jack Williams joined AMC to take over the racing department.

Jack Williams, father of Norton rider Peter, was always a development engineer first and a designer second. Working on a shoestring budget, and often fighting the whole of the AMC management in order to be allowed to do things his way, he wrought miracles with the two valve 7R, whose finest moment up until then had been in the Manx GP in 1952, when Bob McIntyre won the Junior, and finished 2nd later in the week in the Senior race on the very same machine. Jack Williams' development of the 7R engine in fact formed the subject, in 1962, of his paper for

*Below left* **Francis Beart modified the 7R's fuel tank slightly to allow the rider to tuck his elbows in better (Wallace)**

*Below* **A Peel fairing is fitted to Bob Warren's AJS, otherwise in the same trim as when Peter Darvill won the 1963 Manx GP on it (Wallace)**

*Above* **The male/female rear unit mountings were a trademark of AMC racers, and prevented experimentation without altering the swingarm (Wallace)**

*Above right* **The capacious fairing provides good protection from the elements (Wallace)**

his IMechE qualifications, and fascinating reading it makes too, even to a layman. Restricted by the tiny budget at his disposal, he overcame a major problem by constructing his own test apparatus, including a dummy cylinder with a detachable wooden head to which could be fitted a variety of ports, the shape of which he altered with plasticine. Similarly he also lined the inside of a cylinder with white cardboard, to find out what the flow of fuel was doing as it passed through the head: by mixing coloured dyes with the petrol he could see at a glance where the drops of mixture went inside the airstream. Years later, Dick O'Brien, the legendary Harley-Davidson engineer, updated this simple but effective concept, by constructing a clear plexiglass cylinder to observe the same function when working on the XR750 engine.

If ever the rival Gilera or MV factories—or even AMC's bitter competitors at Bracebridge Street—could have seen inside Jack Williams' race shop, they'd probably have died laughing at this home-made equipment. But Jack's feats in development were no laughing matter, and deserve the greatest admiration. From 37 bhp at 7500 rpm when he commenced work in the summer of 1954, Jack painstakingly and lovingly

developed the design, wringing a $\frac{1}{2}$ bhp out of it here and another $\frac{1}{4}$ bhp there, until in 1962 he had achieved 42 bhp at 7800 rpm with considerably increased torque and reliability, and a wider spread of power. The means by which he achieved this, especially when set against the financial and other conditions under which he did so, must rank as one of the greatest achievements in British motorcycle racing.

Suffice to say that the efforts of Jack Williams and his team resulted in an 'off the peg' racer, fast and reliable enough to take on the best of the Italian factories without being disgraced. It was thus doubly ironic that one of its greatest assets—reliability—should desert it at two crucial moments when a Junior TT win was on the cards: Bob McIntyre in 1959, when excessive

**Bottom Bend at Brands Hatch on the ex-Beart AJS 7R owned by Bob Warren (Wallace)**

vibration (later traced to the aluminium bridge piece connecting the gearbox to the frame) caused him to retire after giving a big fright to the MVs of Surtees and Hartle; and Mike Hailwood in 1961, when his engine's gudgeon pin broke on the way up the Mountain on the last lap while in the lead, after lapping only fractionally slower than the Italian four-cylinder fire engines.

The 2-valve 7R never won a TT, but its considerable success in the Manx GP and in the hands of private owners persuaded the factory to allow Jack Williams to produce a 500 cc version.

In 1956 the 7R engine dimensions had been revised to the near square proportions of 75·5 × 78 mm, enabling a safe rev limit of 7800 rpm (although in fact most riders used 8000 rpm and more regularly: Jack always discouraged this since peak power was achieved at the lower rev limit, yet with the 4-speed gearbox fitted to machines of that era it was inevitable that higher revs would be used in the lower gears to 'bridge the gap'). At any rate, when a 500 cc version was announced in 1959, it proved to have over-square dimensions of 90 × 78 mm, and originally produced 47 bhp at 7200 rpm on a 10·6 to 1 compression ratio. For marketing reasons it carried a Matchless badge, but it was surprising that AMC had not produced this version of their established 350 single sooner, especially in light of the mostly disastrous experiences suffered by owners of their G45 Senior twin. In the first couple of years at least, demand far exceeded supply for the new Matchless G50.

Although slightly slower on top speed than the equivalent Manx Norton, the G50 proved much more reliable, and above all easier to maintain, while some assiduous development work by Jack Williams soon had the machine fully competitive with the 500 Manx. Not surprisingly, he achieved this by following the same path as in developing the 7R, by meticulously researching and improving the engine's breathing characteristics. The prototype engine in 1958 had used 7R valves, but when announced in 1959, the exhaust size had been increased to $1\frac{3}{4}$ in.: for 1960, an even larger exhaust and $1\frac{7}{8}$ in. inlet were used, when at this stage the engine was producing 51·5 bhp at its peak revs of 7200 rpm. Weight was identical to the 7R at about 285 lb dry.

For the last year of production, 1962, a 2 in. inlet valve was used, and engine power went up to 52 bhp: however, this bigger valve resulted in a less tractable engine, and the small valve engine always gave better acceleration. Other modifications for 1962 included the use of a forged piston, using a 1 in. gudgeon pin (as opposed to the small valve 1961 engines, which used a sand cast piston and $\frac{7}{8}$ in. pin). Compression ratio was now up to 11·8 to 1. Although more powerful on the brake, these later engines in fact represented a step backwards, because the heavier reciprocating weight of the revised piston assembly resulted in a more difficult machine to ride, and a sudden loss of reliability in the form of several cracked pistons (usually around the gudgeon pin base) and broken crank pins (caused by an incorrectly hardened batch) meant that the ultimate development version of the Matchless G50 never fulfilled its true potential. At the end of 1962 the AMC board decided to discontinue production of both G50/7Rs and Manxes (Norton were by now part of the AMC group): spare parts continued to be supplied, but no new machines were constructed for the next four years. In 1966 the company finally went under, and the G50/7R patterns and rights became the property of ex-sidecar racer Colin Seeley. Although he completed a few machines from spare parts, as well as manufacturing a batch of engines to fit his own frames, production was very much on a limited basis. When Seeley in turn went out of business in the early 1970s, the supply of spare parts completely dried up. Given that fact, it's nothing short of astonishing that so many Seeleys and G50s should still be seen on the tracks of Britain today, since spares are not only so precious, but in many cases have to be specially made to enable the machines to continue running.

Precise factory records for the construction of 7Rs and G50s unfortunately no longer exist, but from talking to people who worked in the racing department at AMC, it appears that about 475 7Rs were constructed between 1948 and the end of 1962, and about 180 G50s during the four years of production from 1959 on: added to this of course are the 10 or 15 Matchless-framed G50s which Seeley constructed out of spares in 1966/67, and of course the 50 G50 CSR desert racers, which the factory constructed (and sold!) in 1960

The 7R handled beautifully, but the lack of 5th gear meant having to rev it hard to 'fill the gap' (Wallace)

as 'homologation specials' to enable them to race the G50 successfully in AMA competition in the USA. These production figures are however approximations only, and perhaps someone, somewhere has access to the factory records?

At any rate, 1961 represented the apogee of development of both 7R and G50, and it's by coincidence that the two machines I rode at Brands Hatch were both manufactured in this vintage year. The G50 was my own machine, while the 7R was the property of Bob Warren and has a famous history. It was bought new in 1961 by the legendary Norton (and later Aermacchi) tuner Francis Beart, who had been keeping his eye on the development of the AMC singles as they crept up on the Manx Norton in power and reliability. After the 1960 Junior TT, when Bob McIntyre finished 3rd at over 95 mph, Alan Shepherd 7th and three other Ajays in the first 12, Francis decided that a well-ridden 7R was by now more than a match for the equivalent Manx. He thus purchased a brand new bike for the 1961 season, with an engine specially prepared by Jack Williams himself, tested to produce 41·5 bhp at the engine shaft. A matchbox float bowl was fitted to the $1\frac{3}{8}$ in. Amal GP carb: car-

buration on this engine has always proved particularly troublesome, and a mysterious fault occasionally sets in which, while impossible to cure by any known means, suddenly disappears only to re-manifest itself at a later date.

At any rate, the 7R was ridden to 8th place in the 1961 Junior TT by Ellis Boyce, at 92·33 mph, and by Roy Mayhew in the 1961 Manx GP, in which he finished 7th in miserable conditions, after leading at one time and being forced to stop to recover from sheer cold and exhaustion. In 1962, Boyce rode the bike to 9th place in the Junior TT at 92·30 mph (highly consistent!), but in the Manx that year Joe Dunphy retired on the first lap when a brake cable broke. Over the winter of 1961/62 modifications were made to the cycle parts to enable Dunphy—who liked the riding position of a Manx much more than that of the 7R—to feel as much at home as possible, and recesses cut in the tank to give him a more comfortable racing crouch. Unfortunately Dunphy retired on the first lap of the 1963 Junior TT when the magneto failed (a common occurrence in those days). However, success came in the Manx Grand Prix that year, when Peter Darvill rode the Beart 7R to victory by over one minute, breaking the Junior lap record by over 30 seconds into the bargain, at 93·87 mph. An amusing Beart anecdote concerning that success is that—at Francis' suggestion—Darvill had painted a red line on the rev counter at 8500 rpm (instead of the normal 7800), realizing that Tom Kirby, at that time their greatest rival for honours, was certain to come nosing around the machine in the warming-up paddock. Sure enough he did, and animated discussion ensued about the dishonesty of using 'works specials' in a clubmans race! What neither Kirby nor his rider Roger Hunter knew was that Darvill and Beart had already decided to use 8500 rpm for the first lap to open up a quick lead—and did in fact do so, much to Jack Williams' horror! The engine did hold together though, and this was the first time that any of Francis Beart's numerous wins on the Isle of Man was scored by anything other than a Norton.

After a 6th place by Joe Dunphy in the 1964 TT, the machine was sold to Bill Scott, who rode it for a couple of years with a fair degree of success. In 1967 he took the engine out of the Beart frame and put it in his own, capping it with the cutaway tank and a Peel fairing, and sold it to Chris Neve; after passing through the hands of another Manx GP runner, Bill Gibson, Bob Warren bought it in 1972, and has campaigned it successfully ever since. Amazingly, Francis Beart rebuilt the engine himself before he died, and discovered that the piston was one of his own specially-modified Wellworthy examples—the piston is still there even now. It has been running reliably all these years, including in at least six Manx GPs!

Bob Warren rode the bike in the 1973 Junior Manx in which he gained a Finishers Award after achieving the distinction of dropping the bike on two occasions at Governor's Bridge at the same spot! The second time the Peel 'Mountain Mile' fairing fitted to the bike took rather a beating, so he purchased one of the last new examples of this all-enveloping streamlining, which adds a delightful period view to the machine. When I bought my G50 in 1975, it too had a Peel fairing, which served me in good stead during those early days of my racing career, when I seemed to spend even more time on my ear than I do nowadays! The rugged streamlining proved a great boon as I struggled to find not only the limits of the machine's capabilities, but also of myself as a rider. I'm ashamed to admit I fell off it at least half a dozen times, never with any worse result than a bent footrest or gear lever, because each time I went down, the fairing took it like a man and practically bounced me back up again! I grew very attached to the 'Matchstick' during the course of that season, particularly as I won my first ever trophies with it, and fortunately was sensible enough as a result not to sell it when I moved on to a Seeley (which I never got to like half as much) at the end of that year. After letting it languish in my garage for two or three years, I finally got tired of feeling guilty every time I looked at it, and had it restored to original specification to use in Continental and British classic racing.

Almost any G50 or 7R engine will have several broken fins: this is because the material used was basically too brittle an alloy, unlike on the Manx Norton where this problem rarely occurs. Ron Lewis, who rebuilt both the cycle parts and engine, and is basically responsible for restoring a very tired old racer into the usable classic seen in the pictures, managed to save the original head and barrel by the laborious but effective technique of welding up and machining down new fins. The result is as you see in the pictures—though I have to say that after our test day at Brands one fin had already cracked again! On Bob Warren's bike the fins have been pegged, to some effect.

Reacquainting myself with the G50 on the track proved a nostalgic and highly enjoyable experience. Although not possessed of anything like such a famous history as Bob's 7R (it was owned for some years by the Continental Circus rider Steve Ellis, and then passed via Manx GP rider Malcolm Deburgh to me) the Matchless' previous owners had evidently looked after it and updated it over the years. The cooling ring on the front brake was a period 'accessory', which apparently proved very effective offered by Francis Beart in his catalogue. The gearbox is fitted with a 6-speed Schafleitner cluster, which transforms the machine and enables you to keep the engine continuously on the boil. The only problem is that it works in reverse pattern to the normal 4-speed box (1 down, 5 up) and that does take a bit of getting used to—as I rediscovered on my second lap when I selected fourth instead of second coming into Clearways and almost shunted my sparkling pride and joy—from then on I was more cautious in changing gear. This was our third test session with it since the rebuild

**Fred Neville was one of many riders who switched from the faster but more complicated Manx Norton to the ultimately more dependable Matchless G50. Here he sweeps round Stowe Corner at 'Silverstone Saturday' in 1960 (Nicholls)**

and it was by now fully sorted: it's as much of a delight to ride as I remembered, with a willing engine that wants to rev well over the 7200 rpm limit—but beware of dire consequences if you do, because even with a small valve engine and meticulous assembly a bent valve awaits the careless or deliberately heavy-fisted.

Handling was superb and predictable over the twists and bumps of the Brands circuit, except on the descent to Bottom Bend, where the ripples caused the front suspension to patter when laid over for the left-hander—possibly a little more TQF hydraulic fluid was needed in the front forks. Surprisingly for a machine fitted with a (slightly reversed cone) megaphone exhaust, megaphonitis is practically non-existent, though the 6-speed gearbox does help you keep within the 5000–7200 rpm power band much more easily than would be the case with a standard 4-speed gearbox. I must say that the riding position seems much more comfortable on both bikes than on Manx Nortons I have ridden, but

perhaps that's a question of personal taste—certainly it was possible to get tucked well away behind the little fly-screen, even with the bulk of a full-face helmet, the chin bar of which acts as its own rubber pad on the tank! Apart from the gearbox, the only other problematic feature was the front brake: this still has the original linings that were on the bike when I bought it, having been fitted with Ferodo Green material by Joe Dunphy for the 1974 Manx GP, when Malcolm Deburgh retired after the first lap. Green linings are notably 'all or nothing', and this was always the case with this front brake, which had a very fierce action and tended to grab very easily: in contrast, the back brake is beautifully progressive and effective. Lastly, clutch adjustment is critical, and a constant eye must be kept on the end-float clearance.

*Above* **Alloy cooling rings for the front brake were a popular period addition which improved the effectiveness of the 2LS AMC unit (Wallace)**

*Below* **After the mostly disastrous experiences with the G45 twin, the G50 enabled the winged 'M' tank badge to stand proud again (Wallace)**

Externally almost identical to the 7R, the G50 engine is essentially an overbored version of the smaller sohc unit. Gearbox holds a 6-speed Schafleitner cluster (Wallace)

After 20 laps or so in the company of Martyn Ashwood's similar G50, I pulled in and took over Bob's 7R. This was fitted with an SU float chamber (a common modification in those days) during Chris Neve's ownership to attempt to cure the carburettor gremlins which this engine has always experienced. These had manifested themselves earlier in the day when Bob was riding, but fortunately they decided to absent themselves for my stint. Remembering to turn on the primary chain oiler (R30 oil is carried in the top frame tube, and issues via a drip feed to lubricate the primary chain), I pulled back on compression, a quick shove and away: the G50/7R was not fitted with an advance/retard mechanism, nor an air lever, and none is needed. They must, however, be warmed up carefully from cold with a soft plug, and the equivalent of RL50 Lodge or NGK q fitted for racing.

Pulling away on the 7R I immediately discovered the major inhibiting factor of the machine—the 4-speed gearbox. Even allowing for the fact that I was only revving to 7500, in deference to the elderly piston, the gap between

the ratios was quite pronounced: first gear particularly seemed very notchy and—when I was forced to select it for Druids—much too low. No wonder people experimented with all sorts of unsatisfactory Swedish 5-speed gearboxes to try to get round this problem, until the excellent Schafleitner clusters came on the market. A 5- or preferably 6-speed gearbox would transform this engine even more than that of the G50, whose bigger capacity and improved torque need fewer cogs. After a couple of laps I began to grow accustomed not only to the gear pattern (1 up, 3 down), but also to the considerably increased engine noise caused by the all-enveloping Peel fairing. Bob's bike was better set up than mine in the handling department, and in spite of oil on the track at Bottom Bend, I was soon down to a 60 second lap (as opposed to 57·6 on the faster G50).

Nevertheless it must be said that the machine did seem rather slow and almost vintage after the G50—megaphonitis was also quite pronounced, and encountered—because of the 4-speed box—between 4200 and 4600 rpm: no wonder riders of the day used to over-rev the engines deliberately to try to avoid dropping out of the power range. Even so, the Peel fairing allows you to travel deceptively quickly, because sitting so totally enclosed as you are, it's more difficult to judge speed and distance than on an unfaired bike, and a couple of times I had to use the excellent front brake quite sharply at Paddock to get round. Top speed incidentally on a good 7R was between 115 and 120 mph, and on a G50, 125 to 130 mph (though Selwyn Griffith's Cowles Matchless was once timed in the Island at 135 mph). When you compare that to the 145 mph of the 350 MV or Benelli, or the 150 mph plus of the 500 MV or Paton, the reason for the decline of the British single is readily apparent.

With their elegant, understated lines and beautiful detail work, the AJS 7R and Matchless G50 epitomize all that was best in British racing motorcycle design in the postwar period. To a certain extent too they represent the triumph of

development over design: Jack Williams would surely have liked nothing better than to have started afresh with a clean sheet of paper when he took over the racing department at AMC in 1954, but finance and company policy dictated otherwise. That the products of that department remained so competitive for so many years (Jack Findlay finished 2nd in the 500 cc World Championship on the McIntyre G50 in 1970) bears testament to his tenacity and ingenuity, and the Seeleys appearing in club racing today, as well as original machines such as the two depicted in these pictures, are a living memorial to the success of his work.

*Below* **A classic riding position, with conical Smiths rev counter nestling in the numberplate cowling's 'dashboard'. On its left is the feed hole for the primary chain oil supply, stored in the frame tubes (Wallace)**

*Right* **Getting down to it: the author has reaped much success with his G50 over the past ten years of ownership**

| Model | AJS 7R | Matchless G50 |
|---|---|---|
| Engine | Sohc, single-cylinder, 4-stroke | Sohc, single-cylinder, 4-stroke |
| Bore × stroke | 75·5 × 78 mm | 90 × 78 mm |
| Capacity | 349 cc | 496 cc |
| Power output | 41·5 bhp at 7800 rpm | 51 bhp at 7200 rpm |
| Compression ratio | 12 to 1 | 11·2 to 1 |
| Carburation | $1\frac{3}{8}$ in. Amal GP | $1\frac{1}{2}$ in. Amal GP |
| Ignition | Lucas magneto | Lucas magneto |
| Clutch | Dry multi-plate | Dry multi-plate |
| Gearbox | 4-speed AMC | 6-speed Schafleitner |
| Frame | Duplex cradle | Duplex cradle |
| Suspension: front | AMC | AMC |
| rear | Girling | Girling |
| Brakes: front | $8\frac{1}{4}$ in. 2LS AMC drum | $8\frac{1}{4}$ in. 2LS AMC drum |
| rear | $8\frac{1}{4}$ in. SLS AMC drum | $8\frac{1}{4}$ in. SLS AMC drum |
| Tyres: front | 3·00 × 19 | 3·00 × 19 |
| rear | 3·50 × 19 | 3·50 × 19 |
| Weight | 285 lb | 290 lb |
| Top speed | 120 mph | 132 mph |
| Year of manufacture | 1961 | 1961 |
| Owner | Bob Warren, Kent, England | Alan Cathcart, London |

# 3 | Giuseppe Pattoni's *500 Paton* of 1968

**Only eight of the handmade Paton twins are entitled to wear this distinctive emblem, denoting the use of gear-drive throughout the engine (Author)**

One of the most remarkable aspects of the Italian racing scene has always been the host of small teams and factories enthusiastically slaving away to develop a machine they've designed and built themselves, rather than simply buying a production racer from Normaha or Matchasaki and hoping they can squeeze a few extra bhp out of it than the next chap. It's as true today as it was 25 years ago; though sometimes of course what starts out as a small venture, often funded by a wealthy sportsman, eventually becomes a major racing—and road—manufacturer in its own right: Morbidelli, MV Agusta and Mondial are all good examples of this. Many teams however stay small, and produce a very limited number of hand-made, beautifully crafted specials, one of which they may occasionally succeed in selling to someone who wants to ride something different that might give him an edge, and isn't too worried (or else tries not to think about) the probable lack of spares. After all, when you blew up your Manx Norton in a street race in Spain, you could be sure of scrounging enough bits at least to put together a start-money special for next weekend's Continental Circus race in Germany; it was a different kettle of fish if yours was an ex-works racer or a toolroom special . . . .

In the late 1960s one Italian special stood out as a reliable and successful machine that was able, on occasion, to challenge the factory teams of MV and Honda, while at the same time proving consistently quicker than the brigade of British singles: the Paton. Pronounced as spelt (*not* Pay-ton), its origins in fact lie in the famous simultaneous withdrawal from racing at the end of the 1957 season of the Guzzi, Gilera and Mondial factories. Giuseppe Pattoni had been chief mechanic to the Mondial team, specifically to Cecil Sandford's championship-winning 250 which he looked after himself. Left high and dry by the Boselli family's abrupt about-turn, Pattoni teamed up with another famous name who runs through the history of postwar motorcycle racing like a golden seam: Lino Tonti, who'd been working for Mondial also as a development engineer, and was later to move to Bianchi to design their twins. Together PAttoni and TONti made the first Paton, actually a dohc conversion for the single camshaft 125/175 Mondial production racers; later, after the partnership broke up when Tonti joined Bianchi in 1959, Pattoni continued alone, producing new bikes from the Mondial spares stock, to which he had access.

Their first customer was none other than Stan Hailwood, whose 18-year-old son Mike made his TT debut on a 125 Paton in 1958; he was 7th, and had considerable short circuit success with the little bike although, as he once told me, 'it was so small I should have worn kneepads to stop hitting myself on the chin . . .'.

For the genial but shy Giuseppe Pattoni — 'Pep' to his friends — bikes were then but a hobby, to be pursued into the midnight hours after his daily work at a Lancia dealer in Milan. But fate was kind to him, for the company was purchased by a man named Giorgio Pianta, a successful racing, rally and test driver with Fiat/Lancia. In return for Pattoni's tender loving care on Pianta's cars, he gave him time off to attend bike races, plus use of the well-equipped workshop under the dealership, and it was thus that the line of twin-cylinder Paton GP bikes was born in 1964. Pep's first twin was a 250; in typical modest manner he says that Tonti designed it for him, but speaking to others who were involved in the project it's clear that

Fred Stevens made the breakthrough for Paton, scoring a double victory in the 1967 North West 200. Here he rounds Druids Hill Bend at Brands Hatch on the test bike later that year, ahead of a horde of British singles (Nicholls)

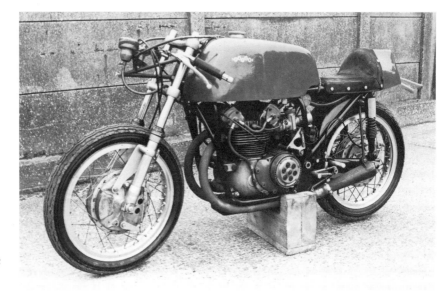

Three views of the 500
Paton twin, showing the
ultra-short wheelbase, dohc
unit and light but well-
braced frame (Author)

what in fact happened was that Pattoni took Tonti's relatively unsuccessful Bianchi twin design, improved and updated it himself and incorporated his own ideas. Whatever, the 250—though somewhat overweight for its class—set the mould for the rest of the Paton line, all of which were unit construction dohc parallel twins, with 6-speed gearbox, double cradle frame, geardriven camshafts and twin-coil ignition. The accent on gear drive, by the way, is repeated in the Paton emblem displayed on all the bikes since then!

Ridden by Alberto Pagani, the 250 proved reliable if not too fast; this was epitomized by its best result, 3rd place in the 1964 Lightweight TT, no less than *18 minutes* behind winner Jim Redman's Honda in a race of attrition that saw over 20 retirements by bikes from works teams. The use of Pagani—later an Aermacchi and MV works rider, but then just the promising son of a famous father—highlights one of Pattoni's greatest attributes: the ability to spot a talented youngster, and bring him along the right way. The list of riders who began their Grand Prix careers on a Paton is formidable: besides Hailwood (whom he didn't exactly choose!), those who did include GP car driver Vittorio Brambilla, Gilberto Milani, Bertarelli, Virginio Ferrari, Roberto Gallina, and MV riders Bergamonti, Pagani and Toracca. That was just the trouble: Pattoni would give them their chance—but was powerless to prevent a richer manufacturer such as MV from plucking a good rider from him after they'd proved themselves on his bikes.

But in 1966 help came from an unexpected source; England. The 250 had given rise to a 350 in 1965, and after a couple of races in Italy the latter was sold to Canadian Mike Duff, then on the lookout for a competitive ride to accompany his 250 works Yamaha. Mike took the bike to the UK, tried it on a wet day at Mallory, and as he later told me: 'It was little, light, had a good gearbox, but vibrated rather a lot—it was a 360 degree twin in those days. Still, it was as fast as my G50—but it was only a 350! I sold it after only a couple of races because I realized how difficult it wold be to keep such a one-off bike running on my own.'

The new owner of the 350 Paton—the only one ever made, incidentally—was Liverpool wheeler-dealer Bill Hannah, whose name became synonymous with the marque over the next few seasons. Hannah and his rider, Fred Stevens, were so impressed with the bike that Hannah flew to Italy to persuade Pattoni to make a 500 version. To Pep, this was manna from heaven: an apparently wealthy English sponsor prepared to back him in producing and racing his beloved twins. Stevens moved to Milan for the winter with his mechanic Ian Mackay (later Bel-Ray's man in Europe), learnt Italian, and set-to with a will. Pattoni was able to recruit another topline mechanic, Gianemelio Marchesiani, to help him build the bikes, as well as run a second one for new Italian rider Angelo Bergamonti. The Paton GP team had been formed.

'Bill Hannah bought Fred's bike outright,' recalls Pattoni, 'but he wanted his name on Bergamonti's as well, so he gave us a nominal sum towards travelling expenses, and since I've never been any good at attracting sponsors I didn't have anyone else involved, so all the years we raced in the GPs, they were Hannah–Patons. Bill was a nice man, but he wasn't always in touch with reality; he used to have these fantastic schemes which were as much a dream as anything, but to him they were real. It was sad, but I think he was always bound to finish up where he did.' The Paton bikes were real enough. Retaining the same stroke as the 250 (53 × 56 mm) and 350 (62 × 56), to avoid expensive changes to the built-up crank, Pattoni first produced a 463 cc version in 1966; after a season of development, all seemed set for a fairytale end to the season, when even after a pitstop Stevens held a secure 2nd place in the Italian GP at Monza, in front of the Paton's home crowd, behind Ago's MV. Alas, a slipping clutch dropped him to 4th on the very last lap—but the team had now arrived on the international scene.

1967 was a year to remember for Pattoni: 'We won the Italian Championship with Bergamonti—beating Agostini—and Stevens won both classes in the North West 200, came 3rd in the Belgian GP, 4th in the TT, and both riders finished 3rd and 4th at Monza—all in the 500 class: we were 3rd in the Manufacturers Championship. I lent a bike to Pasolini for the Rimini races in May, and he actually led Hailwood's Honda 500/4 till the end of the race when he had to stop with an oil leak; it was the same day as the North-West victories: I wish I could have been in both places at once!'

Fred Stevens surprisingly retired at the end of the season, to run a car business in his native Southport. Hannah replaced him by Circus regular Billie Nelson, who brought success almost at once, winning the Austrian GP at record speed. Over the next few years, Nelson and a succession of Italian riders raced the Patons round the tracks of Europe with great success, never challenging the might of MV, but usually occupying the runner-up slot. Engine capacity was gradually increased, to 476 cc in 1968, then 483 cc in 1969 and finally, with a 73·5 bore and 57·5 mm stroke, to 488 cc in 1970: the ex-Stevens bike was updated in this way for Billie Nelson to ride. A 4-valve head took three years to develop, appearing in 1970 and helping to keep the bike competitive long after Hannah disappeared from the scene: Patons scored 500 world title points every year up to and including 1973, long after the Japanese two-stroke invasion had spread to the bigger classes.

A total of six 500 cc Patons were made, and all are accounted for today. Pattoni still has his last 4-valve bike, there are two in private hands in Italy—neither has run for some years—one in France, and two are in Britain: one is dismantled (Billie Nelson's later bike), and our test bike is the second. Previously owned by Guernseyman Maurice Ogier I now own and run it myself

The dohc unit employs a central pinion driving the camshafts, and separate barrels (Author)

in classic events, it's the ex-Fred Stevens machine on which he won the North West 200 and reaped so much success in 1967. It is however fitted with the later frame, introduced the winter that Fred retired, bearing no. GPP 500-1, and fitted with engine no. C (Pattoni lettered his engines rather than numbered them: the 250 was A and the 350 B). It's thus the first 500 Paton made, also the most successful: when the later frame was fitted, Pattoni kept the original number to avoid confusion—and to save getting new customs carnets issued! ('I've never liked messing with paperwork. . . .') The updating extends to the engine, which though still only a 2-valver does have the enclosed hairpin valve springs which until 1968 were naked: capacity is now 488 cc.

When Maurice originally offered the bike to me, it was for a racer test at a Classic Mallory meeting in one of the parades; the bike hadn't run for eight years when Maurice acquired it in 1980, and had a broken second gear from its last outing at an Oulton Park meeting, Bill Smith aboard. Giuseppe Pattoni was delighted to supply his last remaining spare gear so that one of his bikes could be used again in anger, and at the same time Ogier checked over the engine, which seemed otherwise in fine fettle. Unfortunately, the Mallory meeting was a near-washout, with constant rain and a flooded track, but I had enough acquaintance with the Paton to realize that not only was it a superb piece of machinery, but also a bike that suited me down to the ground: in short, I have to admit I fell in love with it!

Trouble was, that Mallory meeting looked like being the two-wheeled equivalent of the night you meet the girl of your dreams only to discover she's leaving on the morning plane to darkest Africa, never to return. That is, until Maurice Ogier came up with a remarkable and generous offer: I could continue the Paton racer test in the Isle of Man in the Classic Cavalcade on Friday afternoon of TT race week, if I'd lend him my Aermacchi for the event. I was so surprised, I actually did need asking twice! In fact, it was quite apt that I should evaluate the Paton over the Mountain Circuit, for in its heyday the bike never contested the British short circuits, concentrating exclusively on the GPs and longer non-championship events such as the North West. It's a pity really, for the Paton's success in the Italian championship events shows it would have been at home in Scratcher's Paradise as well. Indeed, at first glance the bike looks designed for Brands or Snetterton: the chunky, stubby machine looks packed with power, yet has a quick-steering wheelbase of only 50 in.—

incredibly short for a 500. Compare it to the 53 in. of a 350 Aermacchi, for example—hardly the rangiest of bikes itself either. The situation is compounded by the present position of the fork yolks, which have been dropped $1\frac{1}{2}$ in. down the Ceriani forks to bring about this short wheelbase: otherwise the length would be 54 in. on this later frame, which itself featured a 2 in. longer oval-section swinging arm than its predecessor used in the 1967 season.

Early Paton engine cases were cast in electron, but sandcast alloy cases are fitted to this motor. The generously finned barrels are separate, with the camshafts driven by a large central pinion directly off the crank. The latter runs in four ball bearings, and is a 180 degree unit, replacing the original 360 degree configuration in an effort to cure vibration; split at the centre, the two halves are joined by a toothed sleeve which in turn drives a countershaft powering the timing gears, oil pump, contact breakers and primary drive. The 6-speed gearbox runs in unit, with a beautiful handmade dry clutch which has a very light but positive action. Two crankcase breather tubes ventilate the rear of the engine, leading to a handbeaten alloy collecting box under the rear of the tank, in turn breathing through two plastic tubes running out through the back of the seat, well away from the rear wheel. Paton did have trouble with oiling and crankcase pressurization to begin with, and though the problem was eventually cured, this layout on the earliest 500 is a reminder of it. A 12V battery, well protected behind the engine, powers twin coils located under the seat, each firing a single plug positioned somewhat awkwardly in an offset position on each side of the head. The cylinder head is a work of art, and took almost as much time to build as the rest of the bike put together (just like a double-knocker Manx!). In common with the Norton, it also cost a great deal: Ian Mackay recalls Hannah sending him over to Pattoni to buy a new head. 'He gave us a cheque in a thin sealed envelope without saying how much it was for; when you held it to the light, you could see that a Paton cylinder head cost the equivalent of £480, when the complete bike sold for about £1400! It was worth the money though—the tolerances were incredible, and we never had any trouble with the top end.' In common with standard Italian practice, the camshaft oil feed is by external flexible piping, while oblique finning cools the generous expanse between the rocker covers; the engine sits bolt upright in the frame, by the way. A long, thin sump carries the oil, filled from the front and finned longitudinally.

Twin 35 mm Dell'Ortos provide the carburation, fed by a single round float chamber set between them. Pattoni would have liked to try fuel injection, but as always, lack of money prevented it. The fuel tank fitted to the bike is the large five gallon GP version, which adds to the chunky appearance; fuel consumption was 24–26 mpg in a race—only the TT needed a fuel stop, even in those days of longer races.

When I first saw the Paton at Mallory I immediately recalled Mike Hailwood's comment about the 125 he rode: the 500 looked so compact I felt sure I wouldn't fit comfortably on it. I couldn't have been more wrong: the footrests and levers are perfectly positioned even for my six-foot frame, and the bulky fuel tank fits snugly between the knees. For sure, there's little room to spare, but the back of the suede-covered seat just holds you in position nicely. The fairing wraps closely round the engine, but there's enough room to tuck your head behind the screen even with a full-face helmet.

The 1981 TT Cavalcade was a real cracker, with a superb turnout of historic racing machinery that both looked and sounded great. It was also a day blessed with hot sunshine, but fortunately no melting tar, that former bugbear of the IoM. Twenty minutes to go, and we wheeled the bikes out on to the Glencrutchery Road: Maurice and I had agreed to warm up each other's bike, as being the one we were most used to, but I did notice how easily the Paton started

from cold, before settling down to a steady throb as the oil was carefully warmed at around 4000 rpm. After a certain amount of fiddling to change the long-reach plugs with the fairing on (you have to use a socket and extension), I was all set to go, starting at no. 42 beside a very pretty 7R. With a choice of clutch or push start I opted for the latter; the Paton cooperated with an instant start after just a few steps, and after a certain amount of fiddling around while I discovered just where in its travel the clutch began to bite, I was off and away down Bray Hill for two of the most enjoyable laps I've ever had round the Mountain Circuit. Taking it easy as far as Crosby to let the engine settle down and reveal any major problems—it hadn't been used in anger since 1973, remember—showed everything to be in order: the 6-speed box was a delight to use in either direction, the changes as smooth as butter and the ratios perfectly matched. The top three in particular were so

*Above* **AC sweeps into the Bungalow on the TT Course during the Isle of Man test of the Paton 500 twin** (*Classic Bike*)

*Left* **Giuseppe Pattoni—dedicated enthusiast and miracle worker, but always short of money to go racing with** (Author)

close together that at least one seemed superfluous at first, until I came to Greeba: I can honestly say that without at all trying hard, I'd never swept through the section from there to Ballacraine so fast before. The reason is that the Paton comes on song at around 5000 rpm, with quite good torque steadily increasing to around 8500, when it really begins to fly. Maximum revs are 10,400 with the 2-valve engine (11,200 on the 4-valver), so you have quite a narrow optimum power band to play with at the top end, though this isn't a problem on slow or medium speed corners because of all the torque low down. Hence the need for three close ratios at the top end, to keep it on the boil—which is exactly what

I was able to do through the swervery of Appledene and the like: great! The quick but precise handling fully played its part, and on the fast approach to Ballacraine the effectiveness of the Fontana stoppers asserted itself. Climbing through the Glen Helen section and later on up the Mountain showed where I feel the Paton scored most over its British single-cylinder rivals: not only was it much faster in a straight line— over 150 mph as compared to 130 or so by a good G50—but the acceleration out of slow and medium speed corners, especially up hill, was vastly superior. I had proof of this on the second lap, when after following a sportingly-ridden G50 up from Ramsey, I left him for dead going away from the Gooseneck: the Paton just leapt up the hill with no hint of megaphonitis, while the Matchless was struggling to get on the megga again.

By now you must surely be asking 'Wasn't there *anything* wrong with it?'! Well, of course no bike is perfect, and my two laps in the TT cavalcade showed up problems that would never have manifested themselves on a GP or short circuit. Firstly, that's the last time I ever ride a bike round the Island without footrest rubbers! By the end of the first lap my feet were throbbing, not only from standing on them to ride out the bumps along the Sulby Straight and the like, but also from the fair degree of engine vibration that transmits itself through the rests. Next, no front mudguard was fitted to the Patons when they were raced, and I wouldn't care to ride in a wet event without one. Also, Maurice had been told that the bike had North West 200 gearing on when he bought it, but that turned out not to be the case, and it was quite a bit undergeared, meaning I had to feather the throttle on all the fast straight bits like the Highlander, away from the Creg, and so on. He didn't get any spare sprockets with it anyway, so it was unavoidable! Lastly, although the Ceriani forks and Girling rear units soaked up many of the bumps, with such a short wheelbase at least one wheel was in the air quite often, whereas a rangier bike would have ridden over them. This was the penalty for having such a quick steering machine, and I think on the whole it was an acceptable tradeoff since for example in the Glen Helen section, and at places like Kerrowmoar, I was able to aim straight at the Joe Thornton yellow peel-off markers before flicking it away at the perfect moment: there aren't many bikes you can do that with.

There was one other tiny problem: the whole left side of the fairing tore itself off on the first lap before Barregaroo! What happened was that the fibreglass had become brittle and cracked around the single side mounting, working itself loose. I confess I didn't realize what had happened for a while, because a problem that dogged Pattoni for some years had asserted itself the day before when both exhausts cracked round the base of the megaphone while testing at Jurby. A bodge-up job only was possible, and I thought this had failed: in fact, it was something else, but at least the spectators on the outside of the course had a nice view of the handsome dohc engine. . . .

Though today Guiseppe Pattoni has achieved a measure of security, with a small Honda agency in his 'Paton Racing Motors' workshop in Milan (he remains an ardent Anglophile), Pep still hankers after the days when he worked till all hours and drove thousands of kilometres round Europe racing his beloved twins. 'Why did I do it? I've always loved making things myself, and going to races: you put the two together, and basically you can say I did what most people would give anything to do: I made my hobbies my life. Of course, I've often wished I had had more money to spend—I actually drew up the plans for a four-cylinder bike to take on the MV and Benelli, but I could never afford to build it. But more money might had led to less happiness; I'm content with the way things turned out.'

| Model | | 500 Paton |
|---|---|---|
| Engine | | Dohc twin cylinder 4-stroke |
| Bore × stroke | | 73·5 × 59·5 mm |
| Capacity | | 488 cc |
| Power output | | 64 bhp at 10,200 rpm |
| Compresion ratio | | 10·8 to 1 |
| Carburation | | 2 × 35 mm Dell'Orto |
| Ignition | | 12V battery/twin coils/single plug |
| Clutch | | Dry multi-plate |
| Gearbox | | 6-speed Paton |
| Frame | | Duplex cradle |
| Suspension: | front | 35 mm Ceriani |
| | rear | Girling |
| Brakes: | front | 210 mm 4LS Fontana drum |
| | rear | 210 mm 2LS Fontana drum |
| Tyres: | front | 3·00 × 18 |
| | rear | 3·00/3·25 × 18 |
| Weight | | 308 lb |
| Top speed | | 152 mph |
| Year of manufacture | | 1966 (updated to 1968 spec.) |
| Owner | | Alan Cathcart, London |

# 1 | Two from *Ducati*— the dohc single and desmo twin

# 2 125 Grand Prix development

I have to own up to suffering from an incurable disease called Ducatitis. Highly contagious once the subject is exposed to a certain Italian four-stroke, there is no certain remedy and only a continued exposure to the cause of infection offers any relief from the disease. Even certain enemas such as continued contact with the machine's electrical system, or on road versions with areas of questionable finish such as flaking chrome or instant-fade paint generally fail to bring about a permanent cure, though moments of complete freedom from the disease may be experienced especially during the course of the electrical treatment referred to above. In short, once you're hooked, you stay hooked!

I first contracted Ducatitis back in the mid-1970s, when like so many other people I started road racing on a 250 single in club events. Progressing thence to a 750SS Desmo production racer, in spite of various flirtations over the years with other marques, I've never really succeeded in shaking off that first respect for and commitment to the products of the wonderfully enthusiastic band of people at the Borgo Panigale factory on the outskirts of Bologna. Few other companies have such an ingrained love for bikes as Ducati, and this enthusiasm is amply reflected by its customers, who must surely be the most loyal bunch of brand supporters in the motorcycling world today.

Ducati designer Ing. Fabio Taglioni has always adhered to one basic development principle:

*Left Déjà vue*—**25 years before our test comparison, a 125 Ducati single and twin take to the streets of Onchan during the 1959 TT. Bruno Spaggiari on a works desmo single (no. 35) leads Mike Hailwood on the 125 desmo twin during practice (Nicholls)**

*Right* **The chunky twin-cylinder engine fills the Ducati chassis, otherwise very similar to its single-cylinder sister (Author)**

if it works on the race track, it'll work on the road. Every single one of his basic designs has been track tested, raced and developed in the white heat of competition before being repackaged for the road and put on sale to the public. This in turn has resulted in two benefits to the customer: a race-bred heritage ensuring good performance and excellent handling, and the ready ability to tune the bike up for competition, often with only the most basic of modifications.

Nowhere was this more true than in the case of his very first Ducati design: the single-cylinder ohc Gran Sport, introduced in 1955 and affectionately christened the Marianna by its loving owners. This little 98 cc machine formed the basis of the whole range of Ducati singles between 1955 and 1976, as a glance at its crankcase would show. Essentially the same bottom end was used on all Ducatis up to 200 cc, and the later 250/350/450 singles are based on a scaled-up version.

But the Marianna was also an ultra-successful road racing machine, dominating Italian racing in the mid-1950s not only in its own class, but frequently beating machines of up to twice its

own capacity. A specially-streamlined version captured 44 world records on the banked Monza track in 1956, from 50 km up to 1000 km, averaging over 100 mph for the shorter distances. The Marianna ultimately had the same effect as its bigger British cousin, the BSA Gold Star, becoming so successful in its class that the category was eventually scrapped.

Inevitably Taglioni and his colleagues at Ducati wanted to go Grand Prix racing, instead of concentrating on the Italian events for sports machines which were the Marianna's province: GP success was judged vital to the company's image in the racing-mad Italian market, and would make their name better known abroad. Accordingly, on 25 February, 1956, a twin overhead camshaft 125 cc version of the Gran Sport engine was unveiled to the public, and no less than a 14 rider team announced to contest everything from the GPs to the Italian Junior Championship.

Sharing the same basic specification as the Marianna, with ten degrees forward inclination of the cylinder, vertical shaft and bevel drive to the camshafts (though in this case with the shaft not

recessed into the barrel), wet-sump lubrication, unit gearbox with gear primary, an oil-bath clutch and battery ignition, this first 125 Grand Prix Ducati was not an immediate success. Development, hampered by a long and harsh winter which permitted little track testing, showed up problems with the valve gear which Taglioni believed could only be overcome by one means: positive control of the opening and closing of the valves, otherwise known as desmodromics.

Time was slipping by, so working swiftly Taglioni—a long time enthusiast of desmodromic valve gear which was at that time being employed with great success by Mercedes-Benz and Osca in some of their racing cars—redesigned the top end to accommodate a triple camshaft set-up, with the two outer shafts carrying the opening cams, and both closing ones mounted on the single central shaft, all operating the valves via forked rockers. News of the modification was not leaked to the press, and indeed the factory deliberately chose the remote non-championship Swedish GP at Hedemora, in the middle of July, for a trial run away from what

they thought would be the glare of publicity, preparatory to making a big splash at the Italian GP at Monza a couple of months later.

In fact, it worked out the other way round: works rider Gianni degli Antoni won the Swedish race with embarrassing ease, lapping every other rider in the field, to give Ducati and desmodromics a memorable Grand Prix debut. Tragically, it was to be his very last race, for he was killed three weeks later in a Monza test session, and his untimely death had much to do with the subsequent surprising failure of the factory to build on that initial success.

Deprived of his principal development rider, it took Taglioni another year and a half to make the desmo 125 competitive. There were problems too with the ultra-high tolerances required to make the design work to advantage, as well as with bottom-end life which became markedly reduced when exposed to the then-astronomical revs, especially on the overrun, permitted by positive valve control. But in 1958, Ducati's efforts were rewarded by a chain of successes both in the classic GPs and elsewhere, culminating with a dramatic scoop of the first five places in the all-important Italian GP. This complete rout of the previously all-conquering MV Agustas was insufficient to win Ducati the World Championship, which they lost out on narrowly thanks to untimely injuries to their star riders Bruno Spaggiari and Alberto Gandossi, but the point was proved: desmodromics worked, and Ducati's GP reputation had been made.

At the end of 1958 the Bologna factory withdrew from racing officially, to concentrate of reaping the engineering benefits of their efforts in developing their road bike range. The squad of works desmo singles were either, in some cases, passed on to team riders for them to continue to race privately (such as Mike Hailwood, Luigi Taverni, Franco Villa etc.) or else had their complicated desmo heads removed and were fitted with double-knocker valve-spring heads to be sold as over-the-counter Grand Prix production racers. The factory were anxious to avoid being pestered with requests for spares and technical assistance from privateers unable to maintain the awkward desmos on their own. Instead, they were quite happy to sell them a near-replica, the dohc Grand Prix, which had been on offer since the beginning of 1957, and was easily the most potent 125 machine readily available to private owners, who had much success with the model both in Italy and abroad.

A few 125 GPs found their way to Britain, and were imported by a keen enthusiast for the marque, Fron Purslow, who himself was allocated one of the scarce desmo-headed machines. He didn't import the road bikes, though, so there was quite an opportunity for an enterprising wheeler-dealer to effect a tie-up between the sale of Ducati's bread and butter products and a supply of the latest in race hardware from the Bologna factory. Stan Hailwood, proprietor of one of the largest dealer chains in the country, Kings of Oxford, was the man.

Stan's son Mike had proved himself to be a more than useful prospect for the future during the 1958 season, making his TT debut after a string of short-circuit successes. However, it wasn't till the end of June that he took part in his first Continental GP, the Dutch TT at Assen: on what was also his debut ride on a Ducati—a make with which he was to be successfully associated for the next 20 years on and off—Mike finished 10th in the 125 race.

Stan Hailwood realized that in spite of his most un-Italian stature, a Ducati would give his son an edge over the competition especially at home. Accordingly, for the 1959 season Mike was equipped with a pair of now-reliable desmo singles for GP races, and Kings of Oxford started advertising and selling Ducatis in a big way. To further strengthen his hand, Stan Hailwood acquired two out of the three desmo 125 twins made, as well as the lion's share of the spares for this exotic toolroom special.

The 125 twin was based on an earlier 175 cc valve-spring machine which appeared with little success in the 1957 Giro d'Italia before eventually finding its way into the hands of the Villa brothers, who converted it into a 250. The 125 desmo version appeared completely unheralded at the 1958 Italian GP, when it was ridden into 3rd place by Franco Villa in the midst of the Ducati 1–5 sweep, thus ensuring another successful debut for one of Taglioni's designs. At this distance in time it's hard to know why he felt it necessary to produce it, since plans were already laid for the factory's withdrawal from racing after that race: probably the machine had been designed some time before, and its Monza outing was just a means of displaying the company's (and Dr T's) technical virtuosity.

Developing 22·5 bhp at 14,000 rpm, the twin was more powerful than the desmo single's 19·5 bhp at 13,000 rpm, with resultant increased top speed of 118 mph over the 112 mph of the single, both with dolphin fairing. But Mike found the bike much more difficult to ride, and though he persevered with it for half a season, ended up concentrating on the single, scoring his first GP win on one at the Ulster in 1959. The twins

Three views of the 125 Grand Prix single—thought to be an ex-works machine converted to valve spring dohc operation before being sold off by the factory. Amadoro brakes looked good and worked well (Author)

were put to one side, then later sold off; ironically, though, the design was later scaled up by Taglioni at the Hailwoods' request to produce a 250 and later 350 version which were scarcely more successful.

My particular case of Ducatitis was still in the embryo stage in the autumn of 1974 when I came across the dohc Grand Prix 125 single featured in this test. As is so often the case I discovered it entirely by accident, having gone to the dealer's shop in Blackpool where it lay on the hunt for something else. The 250 Aermacchi racer I had intended to buy turned out to be a converted road bike, but the Ducati was on offer for very little more: the moment I parted with the cash to acquire it may probably be identified as the instant the disease struck home!

There was no information of any sort with the bike, nor any spares. Acquiring the remains of Mick Walker's 125 cc Ducati stock—he was then Britain's largest Ducati spares dealer—solved the latter problem, but to this day I have no idea whatsoever of the bike's history. It had been rebuilt after a fashion, but to his credit the dealer I bought it from advised me not to run it without having a look inside. That look took seven years to make, as one commitment after another made it impossible to get round to putting it in a fit state to be run, but in 1981 it was completely rebuilt from top to bottom and readied for the track. Unfortunately, an initial outing at a damp Classic Mallory that summer proved that all was far from well in the engine department. Solution? Call in the No. 1 classic racing bike engine man in the business, that doctor of dodgy dinosaurs, Ron Lewis.

Dr Lewis was already engaged in another even more complicated rebuild, for at the end of 1979 I'd heard rumours about an alleged ex-works Ducati 125 desmo that was supposed to be for sale somewhere in the USA. Some weeks of detective work later, I'd discovered the story to be true—except that amazingly what I'd been expecting to be a desmo single turned out to be

Full-width rear stopper is really unecessary on a bike weighing only 177 lb (Author)

that rarest of all racing Ducatis (well, apart from the 125 & 250 fours), a desmo TWIN!

Once I'd got it back into Britain, the bike turned out to be one of the two Hailwood machines which in mid-1960 had been sold to leading British sponsor (and ex-Norton works rider) Syd Lawton. Syd—later to win fame as the Aermacchi importer for the UK—bought it for his son Barry to race in his first season of competition in 1961. Barry's notebook of the era shows that he found the bike a real handful to begin with, thanks to its narrow power band and tricky handling around the tight British short circuits. But once he mastered its performance and idiosyncracies, he won several races with the twin, which before the arrival of the Bultacos and the start of the two-stroke invasion was the fastest 125 in the UK. Lawton even lent it back to the factory for Spaggiari to ride in an early-season Italian meeting at Modena in 1964—unsuccessfully, as he fell off and dinged the engine finning: the resultant dent in the fins is still there today, identifying the bike as the Lawton machine.

Barry Lawton moved on to bigger and faster bikes, and the little desmo twin lay around for a couple of years with a 'For Sale' sign in the Lawton shop in Southampton. Incredibly, nobody bought it until one day Dennis Trollope—later to win acclaim as the man behind Jock Taylor's sidecar world title—snapped it up, fitted a set of flat-slide Gardiner carbs to replace the special Dell'Ortos, and raced it with some success, culminating in a Finishers' Award in the 1970 125 TT. At that race, the bike was bought out of the finishers' paddock by an American enthusiast, who already had the other Hailwood bike. Shipping his new acquisition back to the USA, he did

nothing but look at it for ten years—not even draining the engine oil—till I tracked it down and brought it back to the UK.

When I got the twin it was in very much 'as used' condition, and certainly needed a complete strip and rebuild. Once again, though, there were no details of any kind with the bike, and though Syd Lawton was helpful with some hints he recalled from the days he worked on the bike, his notebook of timing and other info had been long since mislaid. Worse still, even Taglioni himself was unable to help, since details of the bike had been lost in one of the periodic upheavals at the Ducati factory which have resulted in the incredible situation that there are no factory records, even for the road machines, predating 1968.

Only one thing for it—call in Ron Lewis, and hope that the bike finished the TT back in 1970 with the settings unaltered. Stripping the engine carefully and measuring and recording as he went, Ron was able to determine all the necessary

**Tucking the lanky Cathcart limbs away on the 125 single Ducati proved difficult** (*Classic Bike*)

information. Several special tools were required, all of which he made up, including no less than three of the little cog wheels with which to undo the differentially-threaded Hirth couplings comprising the joint of the built-up crankshaft, in order to inspect the big ends: he broke the first two such tools, so tightly clamped together were the radially serrated faces of the couplings.

Just as he was about to start putting the engine together, a stroke of luck occurred when I managed to track down the owner of the other desmo twin which had found its way to America. Ian Gunn had also been fortunate enough to acquire the large box of spares, and from it he produced a pair of very special 23 mm Dell'Orto carbs with integrally-cast oblong float chambers which Trollope had replaced with the Gardiners. 'Take these, they belong to you,' was his only comment, and he would accept nothing in exchange for them. Moreover, he also had the priceless setting details scribbled on a piece of Ecurie Sportive paper: checking them over with Ron Lewis' calculations, we discovered he'd been only one degree out on the ignition timing, and

had correctly estimated the valve timings and clearances!

The setback with the 125 GP single interrupted the Lewis workflow, but the target date for both bikes to be back together and running was none the less met: the Mike Hailwood Day at Donington in July 1982. Finishing the desmo off the night before in his South London workshop, the moment of truth for Lewis had arrived: would she start? Spinning the rear wheel over with the bike on its stand—now that's what I call confidence!—produced the glorious, throaty roar we'd been hoping for from the two open meggas as the engine caught instantly: into the van and off to Donington.

While the single performed superbly well in the Hailwood Day parades in the hands of former 1960s GP rider Giuseppe Consalvi, who raced a semi-works example at one time, the desmo was unfortunately way over-jetted, leaving Barry Lawton, to whom I'd promised a ride, still itching to get back on the bike he had so much success with 20 years ago. A month later, with the right jets now installed, we came to Brands Hatch for the photo session for this test, and I got the

chance to try the bikes for the first time myself.

The single is fitted with twin-plug ignition, a factory mod which saw a 10 mm secondary plug tucked away on the right side of the little engine. Though there's also a bracket on one of the front downtubes for a second coil, in the interests of lack of complication I decided to use just the single 14 mm plug for ignition. The little bike isn't too keen to start on a racing plug from cold, so the approved technique is to turn the engine over by hand with the plug out to get the oil circulating, then warm it up carefully on a soft plug. With all external oilways to the head it's easy to tell when the oil is nicely hot: change to a racing short-reach plug, and you're in business. On a cold day, it's best to warm the oil up on a stove before starting the engine. The GP single has a long, tapering exhaust which reaches out to the edge of the rear wheel, the maximum length permitted under FIM regs. There's consequently quite considerable megaphonitis, and the engine will hardly pull at all under 6000 rpm. Once you reach that figure though—achieved with a heavy rider such as myself, in comparison to the midgets employed by Ducati to ride the

bike in its heyday, only with the help of some fairly hefty clutch slipping—the little engine starts to come alive, and from 7500 rpm up it's a real little cracker. Peak revs are 11,500, which give a useful revband and provided you play the right tunes on the 5-speed gearbox, it's possible to keep the engine on the boil. Early examples had only a 4-speed box, which must have made life very difficult, though by 1958 it was possible to fit 4, 5 or 6 speed clusters depending on the circuit. Using the same bottom end as the 4-speed Marianna, this meant that the two (or one) top gears had to be fitted outside the crankcase wall, behind the clutch. In the interests of originality, I've retained the heel-and-toe Italian rocking pedal gearchange, which actually comes in useful when you're leant over to the right, since the riding position is so cramped that it's almost impossible to hook your toe under the front lever for the next downward change: much easier to use the heel, since in any case it has to rest on the back lever, so short is the gap between the two!

To say the riding position is cramped must be the understatement of the year. How Mike the

*Left* **A real toolroom special. Note the external oil pipes to the triple camshaft desmo head (Author)**

*Right* **Special Dell'Orto carbs and float chambers were obtained as a gift from the American owner of the sister machine (Author)**

Bike, who was only a couple of inches shorter than me, ever rode one for the length of a GP or TT, only increases respect for him. Knees up under your armpits and chin on the steering damper, it seems that the slightest movement of your body will cause the bike to change direction instantly, so short is the wheelbase and light the weight. Sneeze once inside your helmet, as I did at Brands, and you'll find yourself six feet off line and heading for the outside of Paddock Bend!

Fortunately, the powerful brakes and surprising amount of retardation provided by the engine's compression were up to the job: both bikes are fitted with those beautiful Amadoro brakes specially designed for Ducati and cast in light alloy with more than a hint of magnesium. They're very light and highly effective, especially with such a little, light bike as the single and practically the same body weight of rider to haul down. A slightly increased diameter coped more than adequately with the heavier twin.

But using the brakes on bikes like these is to be avoided if at all possible. Like today's 80 cc racers, the idea is to maintain your laboriously-won momentum at all costs, nurturing each valuable mile per hour and 100 rpm which once lost, take for ever to regain. Riding these little bikes is an art every bit as difficult and dangerous as getting the most out of a 500 cc machine, only calling for quite a different set of skills. Keep the bike as upright as possible to minimize tyre scrub and reduce rolling resistance, mould yourself to the machine with knees, toes, elbows and above all head tucked as close in as possible, and then you might, just might start to get the best out of the tiny bike. Riding the 125 Ducatis certainly increased my appreciation for people like Spaggiari and Gandossi who were able to wring that extra little ounce of performance that gave them the racer's edge over the competition.

The desmo twin was a different kettle of fish altogether. Not all that much heavier, it still seems a much chunkier machine than the almost flimsy, toy-like single thanks to its bulky power unit which appears to fill every inch of the frame. Everything is squeezed to fit just so, the double-loop chassis having been precisely calculated to accommodate everything in the smallest possible space. Due to lack of space, single 10 mm plugs are used which are, however, conveniently placed to be changed. A central train of gears drives the triple-camshaft layout, with a duplicated version of the single's oil system, entailing separate external oil feed to each camshaft roller bearing, with return being made through the central row of pinions back to the wet sump.

Even with the proper jets fitted starting is a cinch: you can paddle-start it in two steps, or run it up on the back wheel. But to warm it up you must blip the throttle at around 8000 rpm, else you'll foul a plug very easily. For this reason it's best to use soft plugs from cold, though it

will start and run on racing ones. R20 oil is used, which again should be warmed up first on a cold day.

Astute students of the photographs will note that there's no rev counter cable shown: Auto Tempo were still making one up when the Brands test session took place. For this reason I wasn't able to run the twin too hard, but a week later at Zolder in Belgium for the annual European Ducati get-together the bike was the focus of attraction, and now sported the correct cable. A 20 minute demonstration session had the trackside fences lined with fellow Ducatitis sufferers: 'I never even knew they made a 125 desmo twin,' seemed to be the most common reaction. Seeing is believing!

To get the twin off the mark you have to wind up the engine to around 10,000 rpm, then feed in the clutch gently: too fiercely, and you'll stall the engine. First gear is quite long, but the next two cogs give good acceleration, before you reach the 9·5:1 fourth. With fifth a 9:1 and sixth an 8·5:1 gear, there's only 400 rpm or so's difference between each of the top three gears, which at first made me think the gearchange was balking. The reason for these ultra-close top ratios is in the powerband of the bike on the one hand—power really only comes in at 10,500 on an effective basis—and the riding style necessary to get the best out of these little bikes on the other. No wonder Mike Hailwood found the little twin tricky to ride, especially in the hurly-burly of UK short circuit scrapping.

The advantage of the desmo valve system showed itself on a couple of occasions when I

*Above left* **Midgets only need apply. Getting the most out of the 125 twin required very special riding talents** (*Classic Bike*)

*Left* **In spite of the bulky engine, the desmo twin is remarkably slim** (**Author**)

*Far left* **Looks more like a 250 than a 125! The integral sump is finned for cooling** (**Author**)

missed a gear due to the still rather stiff gear-change: the rev counter sailed round to its 15,000 rpm limit without any dire results, and the engine was actually safe to 17,000 in its heyday. But peak power comes at 13,800, and I was otherwise observing a 13,000 rev limit while bedding the engine in. With a two inch longer wheelbase than the single, the Ducati 125 twin was more comfortable to ride and, thanks to its greater weight, felt much more solid. Specially-fabricated boxed fork yokes give greater front end rigidity, and whereas on the single at Brands I'd felt that the bike was almost too frail, even on its skinny Dunlop triangulars, the twin — with the same size tyres — felt much safer. It also changed direction more slowly, which in fact means that it handled like a normal bike instead of being so susceptible to the slightest movement on my part. The quick left/right flick of the chicane behind the pits at Zolder was a delight to take, even if the front wheel then started waving in the air as I crested the rise immediately afterwards having built up speed through the chicane. No steering damper is fitted to the bike, contrasting with the friction-type one on the single.

The Ducati 125 desmo twin lives today to show the world the bike that Fabio Taglioni would almost certainly have designed in the first place to wrest tiddler supremacy from the MV and Mondial singles, had he not been obliged to work within the constraints of the production bottom end. With the same amount of development lavished on it as the desmo singles received, there's little doubt that the twin would have ended up dominating its class of GP racing for quite some time. As it was, though, Ducati had to wait another 20 years before the very same Mike the Bike brought them their first World Championship on a quite different sort of twin. Ducatitis sufferers everywhere will be sorry that he didn't get the opportunity sooner.

| Model | | Ducati 125 dohc GP | Ducati 125 Desmo twin |
|---|---|---|---|
| Engine | | Dohc single-cylinder 4-stroke | Triple ohc twin-cylinder 4-stroke |
| Bore × stroke | | 55·3 × 52 mm | 42·5 × 45 mm |
| Capacity | | 125 cc | 125 cc |
| Power output | | 16 bhp at 11,500 rpm | 22·5 bhp at 13,800 rpm |
| Compression ratio | | 9·5 to 1 | 10·2 to 1 |
| Carburation | | 27 mm Dell'Orto | 2 × 23 mm Dell'Orto |
| Ignition | | 6V battery/coil: twin plug head | 6V battery/coils: single plug head |
| Clutch | | | |
| Gearbox | | 5-speed | 6-speed |
| Frame | | Duplex cradle | Duplex cradle |
| Suspension: | front | 30 mm Ceriani | 30 mm Ducati |
| | rear | Ceriani | Girling |
| Brakes: | front | 180 mm Amadoro 2LS | 190 mm Amadoro 2LS |
| | rear | 170 mm Amadoro SLS | 180 mm Amadoro SLS |
| Tyres: | front | 2·50 × 18 | 2·50 × 18 |
| | rear | 2·75 × 18 | 2·75 × 18 |
| Weight (unfaired) | | 177 lb | 218 lb |
| Top speed (faired) | | 105 mph | 118 mph |
| Year of manufacture | | 1957 | 1958 |
| Owner | | Paolo Mazzetti, Bologna, Italy | Maurice Ogier, Guernsey, CI |

# 2 | One from East Germany—the *MZ RE125*

'Now let's see—which gear shall I try here?' The author wrestles with an 8-speed gearbox and razor-thin powerband on the way into Paddock Bend during the Brands Hatch test ride (Barnwell)

It's become a truism to say that modern-day Grand Prix racing is dominated by two-strokes. With the exceptions of the remarkable V3 reed-valve 500 Honda and the evergreen piston-port Yamaha TZ, all current GP machines are rotary (or disc) valve strokers whose ascendancy over the previously dominant four-stroke machines is now absolute. There are many reasons for this, not least the FIM's refusal to allow the four-strokes to compete on equal terms by restricting the number of permitted cylinders and imposing noise regulations that would be laughed out of court by the F1 car teams. It's even been argued that any two-stroke is effectively a crankcase supercharging device, and that blowers were banned back in 1946 by the FIM!

Be that as it may, 'two-strokes rule OK' is the theme of current GP motorcycle racing, a fact which 30 years ago when this type of engine design was considered to be suitable only for humble and uncomplicated runabouts of low specific power output would have seemed literally incredible. Yet the man largely responsible for this remarkable transformation in the fortunes of the two-cycle engine is not as one might expect one of the hundreds of Yamaha and Suzuki technicians whose products have become standard wear for the modern crop of GP riders, but the chief engineer of the East German VEB Motorradwerk Zschopau (MZ) concern, Walter Kaaden.

MZ was created in 1946 out of the ashes of

the pre-war DKW firm, whose factory at Zschopau found itself east of the Iron Curtain after the Russian occupation at the end of World War 2. Yet the first MZ racer, when it appeared in 1950, could not have been more different from the pre-war blown split-single 'Deeks' of prodigious thirst and noise, and consummate performance. A humble 3-speed piston-port 125 single, it nevertheless provided the basis for the racing two-stroke's evolution into its present-day position of supremacy, though not—strangely enough—in the hands initially of the MZ factory.

For the inventor of the crankshaft-driven rotary disc valve was a private German tuner named Daniel Zimmermann, who modified his

*Above* **The ample radiator ensured even cooling of the cylinder. Note the location of the carburettor float chamber (Author)**

*Above left* **MZ front brakes worked so well, Kaaden was able to swap one for a pair of Norton Roadholder forks with the late Francis Beart (Author)**

*Above right* **Vestigial finning disguises the fact that the engine is entirely water-cooled. The large-capacity fuel tank denotes the MZ's considerable thirst (Author)**

early MZ production racer by fitting a carburettor to the side of the crankcase, supplying mixture directly into it by means of a disc valve set into the crankcase wall; a modified cylinder with rear-facing exhaust port was also fitted, and Zimmermann also altered the engine's dimensions

specials, all with two-stroke engines. He immediately realized the potential of Zimmermann's design, and to him must go the full credit for developing it into a race winner. His achievement lay in recognizing the importance of a highly resonant exhaust system, combined with the extended port timing made possible by a disc-valve induction coupled with multiple transfer ports and a squish-type combustion chamber.

Kaaden's first disc-valve MZ appeared in 1953; a 125, it produced 9 bhp at 7800 rpm—a scanty 72 bhp/litre in specific power terms. Eight years later, a series of painstaking, lengthy and innovative experiments, carried out on the most slender of resources and with a desperate shortage of suitable materials, had seen him become the first designer ever in the motorcycle field to break the 200 bhp/litre barrier with an engine that produced 25 bhp at 10,800 rpm.

The path to this success was a long and arduous one, not helped by the fact that Kaaden was not only starved of important resources in the sense of the latest in metallurgy and other vital engineering areas, but in addition MZ were desperately short of hard foreign exchange currency. In those days East Germany was an effective outcast of the international community, its passports unrecognized in the West, its currency unchangeable and therefore worthless, and internal restrictions on its citizens' movements greatly hampering. How the small MZ team ever got to compete abroad at all would represent a handbook in how to circumvent red tape and the dead hand of bureaucracy, but Kaaden was less successful at being able to liberate precious funds to purchase badly-needed Western components which might improve his machines' performance. An example of this is the Case of the Norton forks: early MZs were notoriously bad steerers, thanks largely to their ineffectual East German-made Earles-type forks. Kaaden would have given anything to be able to buy a set of AMC Roadholders, as then fitted to the best-

from the standard MZ ones of 52 × 58 mm to the now commonplace 'square' ones of 54 × 54 mm: all future 125 MZ racing singles adopted this cylinder size.

Even without the benefits of a resonant exhaust system—long tapering megaphones were used—Zimmermann's modifications made his bike into a winner in German races of the era. Fortunately, he had taken the pains to patent his invention, so when MZ themselves decided to adopt the disc-valve design, they had to acquire Zimmermann's patents—whether by paying for them or not is unclear.

In 1952 Walter Kaaden joined MZ as development engineer; a former racer of note himself; he had also constructed his own line of racing

handling machine of its era, the Manx Norton, but lack of foreign currency made this impossible. It wasn't until the famous tuner Francis Beart, browsing around Kaaden's bikes at the TT in 1959, happened to mention how much he admired the highly effective front brake of the East German machine (without engine braking of any kind, MZs were amongst the pioneers of modern-type 2LS stoppers) that Kaaden saw his chance. With dozens of sets of Norton forks back in his Guildford workshop off complete machines whose engines he'd robbed to fit into F3 cars, Beart was more than amenable to a swap, and MZs henceforth wore original Norton forks or close copies thereof!

Kaaden's experiments concentrated on exhaust pipe (aka expansion chamber or 'box') design which eventually resulted in a divergent/convergent type that not only sucked out the burned gases when the exhaust port(s) were uncovered, but also sent a powerful pressure pulse back up the pipe to prevent any of the incoming charge escaping out of the open port and indeed to compress it—hence the four-stroke diehard's accusation of supercharging, by the way. Combined with the extended inlet port openings permitted by use of a disc valve induction system—as much as 200 degrees or even more without significant blowback through the carburettor—these developments dramatically increased engine power, but only at the expense of reliability in a number of vital areas. Chief amongst these was the risk of piston seizure, caused by a variety of reasons. Kaaden opted early on for a rear-facing exhaust port, primarily to achieve better crankcase sealing with the exhaust port on the forward rotational engine which manifested itself in improved torque and acceleration. However this did not as many thought lead *per se* to a hot-spot around the exhaust port on the air-cooled cylinder; indeed the reverse was the case, thus providing a valuable spinoff from the rear exhaust placement (which also resulted in a straighter pipe). With

a front exhaust port, all the air's coolness is immediately expended since it meets the hottest part of the engine first, whereas with a rear exhaust a more even cooling of the cylinder is permitted, with the cold reaching round to the back via the extensive finning.

In spite of this however Kaaden's air-cooled cylinders still distorted: first because of the imbalance between hot exhaust gases on one side and cool incoming charge from the transfers elsewhere, and secondly due to minimal lubrication. In order to increase performance and prevent plug fouling 40:1 petroil mixture is common amongst today's crop of GP racers, and 20:1 was Kaaden's starting point. Moreover, today's synthetic oils were unavailable in the 1950s, when the demands of a small, specialist two-stroke manufacturer dabbling in ultra-high performance racing two-strokes did not rate high on the list of priorities of the major oil companies: ten years later, it was a different story.

Cylinder distortion gave Kaaden two headaches: at the worst the engine would seize, sometimes too fast for the rider to grab the clutch, since with a single-cylinder engine there's little of the warning that a multi-cylinder design can give as the free cylinder(s) try to drag the seized one around. Engines are expendable, but riders aren't. Secondly, even if the distortion was insufficiently great to cause the engine to seize, it did preclude the use of close piston clearances which were a pre-requisite of competitive two-stroke power. The only solution open to Kaaden was water-cooling—at first of the cylinder only, then later of the head as well. Resources dictated the use of a thermosyphon system rather than a lighter impeller as the Japanese employed, and full water-cooling was resisted as long as possible not only for the weight penalty entailed: apart from being able to lift the head more easily to check the mixture and combustion process, an air-cooled head provides more power because it runs hotter and aids combustion. Unfortunately, no spark plug in the world will stand up to that sort of temperature, especially as revs increased and cooling-off time between ignition strokes diminished. Hence the adoption by Kaaden of full water-cooling in 1963.

Another major problem as development of the MZ racers proceeded was seizure of the small end bearings, especially once Kaaden lowered the ratio of oil to fuel in the mixture; at the same time, then-astronomical revs especially on the overrun under braking into a corner put extreme pressure on the conrod and big-end bearings. There was no outright cure for either problem, but the use of needle roller bearings at either end of the beefed-up, I-section, forged nickel–chrome rod did much to improve things. Caged on the big-end, the needle rollers on the small end were simply of the crowded type: as anyone who's ever tried to assemble one will attest, these

are tricky to put together but are more able to carry heavier loads without failing than the caged type. Oiling slots in the big-end eye helped extend bottom-end life.

A perennial difficulty in the early years was the unreliability of the East German-made IKA magnetos with which Kaaden was originally obliged to work. Battery ignition was tried for a while but then discarded as offering no real improvement at the expense of increased weight. Ignition timing is critical on a two-stroke, with burnt piston crowns the least painful result of even a slight variation of as little as five degrees. Eventually in the mid to late 1960s Kaaden was able to acquire a supply of Lucas electronic units which proved mostly satisfactory on the 125 single, but on the 250 twin (always essentially a doubled-up version of the smaller bike) backlash in the coupling splines on the crank provided an inbuilt timing variance which was never completely solved till the introduction of a one-piece crank.

**Left side of the bike shows long tank and high exhaust. Excellent restoration makes this bike a prize (Author)**

There were many other problems, both with engine and cycle parts, encountered along the way to that 200 bhp/litre target (and beyond): the book on MZ racing history has—surprisingly, in view of its significance in modern-day terms—yet to be written, and a full development history would easily fill it. Suffice it to say that Kaaden's breakthrough came in 1959 with the adoption of a third transfer port, bridged like its two companions and the exhaust opposite which was thus located in order to prevent the single piston ring snagging on them. An important side benefit to the improved cylinder filling and extra power thereby achieved with the third port was better lubrication of the small end rollers, and MZ reliability, hitherto suspect at competitive speeds, improved dramatically thereafter. Further painstaking works on expansion box design was all that was needed to make the MZ 125 and 250 the bikes to beat.

Unfortunately, the lack of hard currency meant that MZ were never able to match the terms offered to star riders of the day by their Western rivals. Several times the team stood on the edge of World Championship success, only to lose out at the crucial last hurdle. Horst Fugner won the make's first GP in Sweden in 1958, on the 250, and beat the great Carlo Ubbiali for second place in the world series that year, while in 1959 Gary Hocking scored two GP wins on the 250 to again score runner-up place in the championship; the following year MV stepped in with an offer Hocking couldn't refuse and MZ couldn't match, and the team's chance of 250 honours disappeared.

In the 125 class the adoption of the third transfer port catapulted the MZ into contention in 1959, culminating in Kaaden's chief development rider and trusted collaborator Ernst Degner scoring a dramatic victory by half a length over Ubbiali's MV in Count Agusta's home GP at Monza. Degner repeated the success two years later during the marque's most successful season; he won three GPs in all and would certainly have taken the World Championship had he not taken that moment, just before the final crucial race in Argentina, to defect to the East via the West, so to speak. For Degner's ultimate destination once he found himself on the other side of the Iron Curtain from East Germany was the Suzuki race shop in Hammamatsu, Japan, and through him most of Kaaden's brilliant work on the development of the racing two-stroke became known and exploited in first the Orient, then Europe.

Degner's defection revolutionized Suzuki's previously miserable GP record, and within a year he had gained them their first world title in the 50 cc class. In Britain though, even before this development, Kaaden's technology had begun to filter through: Joe Ehrlich's EMC was in many ways a close relation of the MZ, and proved a strong contender in the 1961/62 GPs in the hands of Mike Hailwood and others. As the Japanese invasion force advanced in subsequent years, fuelled by Kaaden's ideas and the sort of development budget he could only have considered having in his wildest dreams, the EMC's fortune faded while at the same time MZ stood firm, so that by the middle of the decade the East German company stood alone as a potential European race-winner against the might of the Orient in the lightweight classes. The riders who carried MZ's hopes were Degner's replacement Heinz Rosner and two Britons from Lancashire, Alan Shepherd and Derek Woodman, but appearances outside the Eastern bloc countries were severely restricted after Degner's defection: even so, the East German two-stroke many times proved to have the beating of its Japanese descendants in the relatively few classic races it contested.

Genuine MZs are few and far between in Britain: I once had a bike with water-cooled barrel and air-cooled head which certainly incorporated many MZ parts, but seemed more likely to be either an EMC or an East German special than the real McCoy. An interesting feature of

**Alan Shepherd samples the Midland Motor Museum's test bike during the Mike Hailwood Day at Donington Park in 1982 (Author)**

the pile of bits I acquired with it was the presence of no less than 52 spare pistons—of which over half were seized! Much more certainly authentic is the machine in the Midland Motor Museum at Bridgnorth; bearing engine no. 6/65, it's unquestionably a works bike of that year, but its history before becoming part of the museum's excellent bike collection is shrouded in mystery. Alan Shepherd rode it in the Hailwood Day parades at Donington in 1982 and didn't recognize it as one of his, but it could indeed be the bike he later sold to Peter Inchley which featured in British national events around 1970.

Whatever the case, the chance to try such an original example of one of the most influential bikes in racing motorcycle history was too good to pass up, however strong my reservations about mid-1960s strokers and their propensity for nipping up. The bike's presence at Brands Hatch for the Derek Minter Day provided the opportunity, with the reassurance of full medical facilities on hand as compared to a normal practice day should the worst come to the worst. You think I'm joking? Ask Frank Perris how many times he got thrown off the works Suzukis of the

same era when they seized on him.

My peace of mind was further improved by the irony of having ex-World Champion (on Suzuki's MZ copy) Hugh Anderson try the bike before me to make sure all was in order. 'Leave the air control where it is, keep your fingers on the clutch lever and don't rev it over 11,000—otherwise it's fine,' was Hugh's advice to me, and needless to say I tried hard to follow it. It had been particularly interesting for him to have his first ride on an MZ, having as likely as not raced against this very bike in the year it was built, 1965, when he scored his second 125 cc world title for Suzuki—with Derek Woodman third for MZ. Too many years had gone by to make a direct comparison with the Suzuki, but Hugh was none the less able to confirm the potency of the little green and silver machine.

Shoehorning myself on board—the MZ is built to scale with its cubic capacity—I paddle-started

Derek Woodman rounds Sulby Bridge en route to 4th place in the 1965 125 cc TT. Though fitted with a different fairing, this may be the test bike, but if not, one identical to it in other respects (Nicholls)

the little bike easily enough, then screwed the engine up to around 8000 rpm before trying to feed in the clutch slowly. I almost stalled it a couple of times before finally gaining enough forward motion to put my feet on the high-set rests: with the sort of abuse necessary to get away from corners like Ramsey Hairpin or Spa's La Source the 12-plate clutch (6 steel/6 friction) is exposed for cooling, but once on the move you shouldn't use it at all for upward changes. There's so little momentum from the bevelled flywheels that the engine will lose revs instantly unless you swap cogs quicker than a flash, and with the ultra-narrow powerband you can't afford the luxury of a leisurely change. The engine starts to come alive at around 8000 revs, but real power doesn't come in until over 9500. In its first flush of youth this 1965 model would produce 29 bhp at 11,600 rpm and was supposedly safe to 12,000 or so, but don't bet on the bottom half putting up with that sort of abuse for very long. With my self-appointed 11,000 rpm maximum, I didn't have much of a power band to play with.

Fortunately Kaaden had thought of that and provided an 8-speed gearbox with which to row the little single along. Playing musical tunes on the gearlever—once I'd persuaded my size nine

boot to find it—was the only means of maintaining satisfactory forward motion. Forget conventional notions of gear changing and keep one eye glued to the little mechanical Smiths revcounter. On my MZ bitza some kind chap had painted a yellow line on each side of the revband, but no such help was at hand here. You have to imagine that line at the 9500 rpm mark: when the needle falls below it, pull up with your boot on the gear lever. When it reaches the invisible line at 11,000, press down with the same foot. What gear did I take Paddock in? Who knows! How many cogs did I notch it back for Druids? As many as it needed—though here you have to be more careful because coming up to a slowish corner you have to change down through the box all at once till you're in the gear you want to be in. There I did use the clutch, blipping the throttle slightly with each change and trying to avoid any engine braking—not that there would have been much to speak of anyway—to avoid imposing unnecessary loads on the conrod and its bearings. I think I took Druids in second—or was it third?

Though most of the gears were perfectly matched there was a curious gap between sixth and seventh when the engine would fall out of the powerband even if I changed up right on the limit. Taking the unit to 11,500 might just have made the difference but it was a strange choice of gearing which Hugh Anderson also noticed and couldn't explain. Thinking of all those seized pistons back home in my garage I was doubly glad he'd ridden the bike before me, especially as he'd left the air lever on a slightly rich setting: just the way I wanted it! Back then, the air lever was at least as important a control for the MZ (and other two-stroke) riders as the throttle. It would be used to richen the mixture for long flat-out straights or climbing hills under load so as to prevent seizure, while for slow corners it would be worked the other way to prevent the plug fouling, as well as to provide snappier performance out of the corner. 'At least part of every practice session would be devoted to learning just how best to work the air lever', said Hugh as we chatted afterwards. 'It was a vital part of a two-stroke rider's skills in our day, together with such other critical skills as deciding whether to come down a size on the main jet if the weather changed slightly, or to maybe come down a quarter of a tooth on the back wheel if the wind changed slightly along the main straight in the hour before the race. I remember sometimes sitting on my own for a couple of hours before a race wondering whether to lower the needle a notch or raise the float level an eighth of an inch. Getting the best out of these bikes was that critical—a wrong decision either way could be the difference between winning the race or landing yourself in hospital.'

Fortunately I had no such choices to make, but I did get the little MZ running fast enough to find out that the handling and braking were absolutely superb—'just about the best in the class at the time,' said Anderson. The large double-sided front brake was smooth and effective, though at under 200 lb ready to race there's relatively little weight to stop, while the steering of the duplex frame and its Roadholder-pattern MZ forks was above reproach. My only difficulty under braking was changing gear downwards

fast enough while at the same time coping with the braking, but if I had more practice on a stroker I doubt if I'd have found it as awkward. The gearchange is very sweet.

The Midland Motor Museum deserve a pat on the back for keeping a display bike in such obviously good mechanical order, and I'm grateful to them for allowing me to experience such a rare and original example of 1960s two-stroke state-of-the-art technology. It seems unjust that Walter Kaaden was never rewarded with that elusive world title for all his shoestring efforts, but he came mighty close and on many occasions must have caused the mighty Japanese legions deep despair and frustration by achieving so much with so little. His reward is to be known everywhere amongst knowledgeable racing enthusiasts for what he is: the father of the modern racing two-stroke.

| Model | | MZ RE125 |
|---|---|---|
| Engine | | Single-cylinder disc valve water-cooled 2-stroke |
| Bore × stroke | | 54 × 54 mm |
| Capacity | | 124 cc |
| Power output | | 29 bhp at 11,400 rpm |
| Compression ratio | | 15 to 1 |
| Carburation | | 32 mm East German Amal copy |
| Ignition | | IKA magneto |
| Clutch | | 12-plate dry |
| Gearbox | | 8-speed MZ |
| Frame | | Duplex cradle |
| Suspension: | front | MZ |
| | rear | MZ |
| Brakes: | front | 200 mm 2LS MZ drum |
| | rear | 180 mm SLS MZ drum |
| Tyres: | front | 2·50 × 18 |
| | rear | 2·75 × 18 |
| Weight | | 186 lb |
| Top Speed | | 117 mph |
| Year of manufacture | | 1965 |
| Owner | | Midland Motor Museum, Bridgnorth, England |

# 3 | Back from Barcelona—
## *Derbi 125 and 250*

*Above* **Angel Nieto at Montjuich Park in October 1972, en route to 3rd place in the Spanish 125 cc GP on the Derbi twin, and another World Championship for both himself and the Barcelona firm** (*Motociclismo*)

*Right* **A fine period detail shot of the 125 Derbi, taken at the 1972 West German GP. Note the supplementary fuel tank in the seat, later outlawed by the FIM** (*Woollett*)

1984 saw the official return to Grand Prix racing of one of the great names in the recent history of international road racing: Derbi. Since 1975, having won four constructors' World Championships and five riders' titles, the bright red machines from Barcelona had been absent from the race tracks of the world, while the parent company developed a successful record in off-road competition, and consolidated its position as Spain's most successful motorcycle manufacturer. To good effect, since the family-owned concern now makes over 50,000 two-wheelers each year—and sells every one: instead of the gloomy industrial picture painted by other famous names in the Spanish industry, the Rabasa family's business has a different kind of problem—how to increase production capacity and so satisfy the demand for their products.

But again this background of commercial success, the firm headed by Andreu Rabasa—son of founder Don Simeon Rabasa Singla, who began business in 1922 as a bicycle manufacturer, moving on to motorcycles in 1950, hence the legend 'Derivado de Bicicleta', or Derbi for short—decided to return to the tarmac GPs in the new and highly competitive 80 cc class, with a strong team of riders led by former World Champion Ricardo Tormo, and star of the future Jorge Martinez, known as 'Aspar'. There seemed a strong probability too that the company would field a 125 cc entry in 1985, thus returning to the class in which they won two of their world titles—perhaps even with the man who was responsible for those won to date, Angel Nieto.

Against this background of Derbi's return to GP competition, the chance to ride and assess two of the bikes that earned the firm its considerable reputation at the highest level of road-racing was particularly timely. It might have been three, except that cranking the Cathcart legs up close enough to my chin to squeeze on to Nieto's title-winning 50 cc tiddler would have been near enough impossible to make an effective test ride out of the question. So on a dry but overcast January day at Jarama, with a chill wind blowing down from the snow-capped peaks of the nearby Sierra Guadarama, the bikes that Juan Pares, himself a former Derbi road racer of no little renown who now works for the factory's competition department, had brought for me to try were an updated version of the 125 twin

which was gradually developed throughout the 1970s after winning its first world title in 1971, and its sole surviving 250 cc bigger brother. On hand as well were Aspar and Tormo, the latter about to have his first ride on a works Derbi—but of rather different vintage than the new 80 he would debut at Misano in the April 1984 Italian GP!

While the two Derbi stars stayed warm in the Tormobus, I found myself pressed into the role of hack rider as Pares sent me out for a couple of slow laps on each bike to warm them up before a photo session with the two factory teamsters aboard. The 125 was first, just as it was in the development sense, inasmuch as the 250 was a direct product of the smaller Derbi twin, with which it shares the same basic engine design. However, it was not the factory's first entry in the quarter-litre class, which actually

came in 1966 with a narrow-angle air-cooled V-twin. With twin rotary valves on the left of the separate crankshafts, geared together to transmit the 32 bhp ultimately obtained at 14,000 rpm through an 8-speed gearbox, the first 125 Derbi represented something of an engineering tour de force, but neither it nor more importantly the Spanish factory's racing budget were a match for the might of Yamaha and Suzuki in the GPs. However, the machine was developed gradually to a sufficiently high degree, in spite of the factory's greater commitment to the 50 cc class, to be able to win the 1969 Spanish title in Nieto's hands, before being rendered obsolete by the FIM's ban on more than six gears at the end of that season.

So for 1970 the Derbi engineers started with a clean sheet, and in doing so designed an engine that by any standards is both modern and compact in design. A water-cooled disc-valve parallel twin, its siamezed cylinders nevertheless pointed horizontally forwards, unlike the norm established by its later Morbidelli rival which now sees all 125 GP machines with inclined cylinders: presumably Derbi adopted this format in the interests of lowering the centre of gravity, though they later followed the trend in designing the 250, whose principal difference from its smaller relative in the engine department is that its cylinders are inclined only 30 degrees or so from the vertical. In all other respects the engines of the two bikes are similar.

Both are the product of a team of engineers in the Derbi competition department, though leader Francisco Tombas was principally responsible for the engine design. This features progressively developed barrels with six transfer ports and a single exhaust, with a built-up crankshaft running in ball bearings with fibre inserts. The conrods run in roller bearing big ends with needle rollers for the gudgeon pin, and like the crankshaft components were entirely made in the Derbi factory: no subcontracting of the manufacture of such key components to outsiders such as Hoeckle or Mahle as was and is the norm for the Spanish company's Italian competitors. Initially, the engine yielded 34 bhp at 13,000 rpm, but work on the porting and exhaust pipes, and particularly with new pistons, soon raised this to 37 bhp and eventually to just over

41 bhp by the end of the decade. A 6-speed gear-box is driven through a large, multi-plate dry clutch on the right side of the crankcases, with a spur gear running off the clutch pinion which drives the Motoplat ignition mounted above the gearbox on the left, and on the right the water pump. A large-capacity alloy radiator is carried in front of the cylinders. Two 30 mm Dell'Orto carburettors are fitted, and the compactness of the unit as a whole may be gauged by the fact that the 125 Derbi measures only 15½ in. across at its widest point.

The engine is fitted in a tubular twin-loop frame that is essentially the same as the one with which Nieto won Derbi's first 125 world title in 1971, but with the benefit of modern adjustable Marzocchi suspension front and rear. The original twin-shock swinging arm is still employed, however, though modern mag alloy wheels and floating front discs are a recent touch. The bike I was to ride at Jarama was in fact mechanically similar to the 1971/72 title-winning machine, but had received the later modifications while being ridden by Benjamin Grau in the Spanish championship and occasional GP during the 1970s. Its

last outing was however in the hands of the great Nieto himself at Sevilla in 1980, when the Derbi won by two seconds from Tormo's Bultaco, and was pronounced to be going 'very well indeed' by the master.

I was soon to find out how well, for in spite of the fact that it was still on Sevilla gearing and therefore slightly undergeared for Jarama's longer straight with its fast downhill entry, I found the 125 Derbi surprised me. Though the engine characteristics in some ways betray its age, the overall impression from riding it is of a bike ten years younger which would be fully competitive with the best of the current breed of production MBAs which now dominate 125 cc grids, and in turn this shows not only how advanced the bike was for its day, but also how continuous updating has enabled it to keep pace with with more recent designs. It must be accounted a surprising error of judgement by the Derbi management not to have commercialized the machine as an 125 cc Angel Nieto Replica after their first retirement from racing at the end of 1972, just as they had previously done with their 50 cc bike: that there was a ready market for such a production

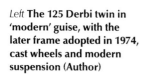

*Left* The 125 Derbi twin in 'modern' guise, with the later frame adopted in 1974, cast wheels and modern suspension (Author)

*Right* Given that it was executed some years before the later Italian disc-valve twins, the Derbi may be regarded as a trendsetting design by any standards (Author)

*Above* **The 125 Derbi felt suprisingly easy to ride hard (Herrero)**

*Left* **While Juan Pares shivers in the chill of a Spanish winter astride the 250 Derbi, the author demonstrates the compact stature of the 125 twin** (Boet)

*Above right* **Spanish street circuits make the IoM TT course a model of safety! Here's Nieto en route to another victory in 1974 aboard the 250 Derbi twin** (*Motociclismo*)

racer was proved by the commercial success of the MBA (née Morbidelli), yet the Derbi would have offered superior initial performance three years earlier, and could well have scooped the pool. Wonder why they didn't do it?

Why so positive about the bike? Well, in spite of its dimunitive 51·5 in. wheelbase and compact build I found the Derbi surprisingly easy to wrap my lanky frame around, and incredibly confidence-inspiring to ride. Even on a cold day and with treaded Michelin tyres fitted, I soon found I could throw it around at will without provoking the slightest misbehaviour. Starting off is a bit of an acquired art, because while pulling in the clutch with your left hand you must also keep the index finger on the air lever even after you've let the clutch out, till the engine's picked

up: once the temperature gauge has reached the 60 degrees mark (70 degrees is normal) you can then open the engine up, and in doing so I found firstly that the clutch action is very light and progressive, but secondly that in what is apparently normal Derbi racing style, all the engine's power is at the top end of the rev band. Power only starts to come in at around 10,000 rpm, but even then there's no real poke until the Krober's needle hits 12,200 or so—then, whoosh! There's good strong horsepower up to 14,500 revs, though in deference to the bike's age Pares had asked me to keep it down to 14,000, which exacerbated the narrowness of the powerband. Fortunately, the 6-speed gearbox (with right foot, one up change just like on all 'proper' British or Italian bikes: well, if you've been riding as many

years as Angel Nieto, that was the way you learnt when you were a kid!) allows sweet, clutchless upwards changes to enable you to keep the engine on the boil: bottom gear was rather too low, though. But the power characteristics are definitely a throwback to the bad old days of razor-edged MZs or Japanese bikes, rather than comparable with the powerful bikes of today with their much wider rev bands: even the Garelli Nieto has won the last two world titles on gives him 3500 rpm to play with, while yielding 46 bhp.

Having said that, the Derbi's engine does feel very smooth, strong and otherwise modern, with a good pull up the hill on the Rampa Pegaso, followed by superb braking from high speed for Ascari and Portago. The non-adjustable steering damper was rather ineffective, and I had a good fright on two occasions when I ran over the piece of concrete or whatever it is jutting out into the apex of the Virage del Tunel and had the front wheel flap from side to side like a flag, sending the Derbi into a tank-slapper that resolved itself by the simple expedient of keeping the power wound on. The frame is good enough to put up with this kind of abuse without landing you on your ear.

If the 125 Derbi was surprisingly modern and

a delight to ride, the same sadly could not be said about its 250 counterpart. Though the bike had an unprecedented run of success in scoring ten Spanish championship wins in a row between 1971 and 1980 in the hands of Grau and Nieto, it must be said that with the difficulties of importing TZ Yamahas into Spain the opposition was not considerable, and on the few occasions it was pitted agianst GP-calibre opposition, it did not shine. Perhaps because they were able to win so easily in Spain, or maybe because they preferred to concentrate on winning world titles with the 125, Derbi never really seemed to make the effort needed to develop a promising design properly, and indeed only two bikes were ever constructed, of which the one I rode at Jarama, bearing engine no. 101, is the sole survivor.

Yet it could all have been so different, because right from its debut at the start of the 1971 season the 250 Derbi seemed to have a bright future. Apart from the MZ twin it was the only disc-valve, water-cooled machine to appear on the 250 GP scene at that time, and when Britain's star of the future Barry Sheene found himself duelling for the lead in what was only his second-ever GP at Austria in 1971, on a bike that had only been completed a week before the race,

Derbi might have been forgiven for thinking they had a winner on their hands. Sheene wound up retiring from 2nd place with a misfire that day, did the same thing a week later in Germany with fuel starvation while 3rd, and had a nasty turn when the right-hand suspension unit broke off on the first lap of the Dutch GP at Assen. Since Barry was proving to be the only real threat to Nieto's (and Derbi's) first 125 championship on his elderly ex-works Suzuki twin, it was deemed prudent not to extend his three-race contract, but Swedish rider Borge Jansson gave the bike its only GP victory at the 1972 Austrian classic before it was retired to the less strenuous confines of Spanish national racing. In due course it too received updated suspension, brakes and wheels, though engine development was hardly pursued after the initial improvement from 56 bhp at 12,000 rpm up to 63 bhp at the same engine speed achieved by similar means to the

*Above* **The 250 Derbi's bulk is well demonstrated by this shot of Nieto at Sevilla in 1974** (*Motociclismo*)

*Above right* **The 125's slim tank and tight-fitting fairing result in a wind-cheating riding position** (*Author*)

*Below right* **Little and large: the 250 Derbi towers over its smaller sister, while the 1984 Derbi team discuss plans for the new 80 cc Grand Prix bike. Riders Jorge Martinez ('Aspar') and Ricardo Tormo are on the far left and right respectively, with the chief mechanic Juan Pares in the woolly hat** (*Author*)

125. Most major change was the adoption of cantilever rear suspension in 1978 which Grau requested after seeing the latest production Yamahas: in the event, a similar design using a Yamaha suspension unit was employed.

Standing the 250 next to its much smaller 125 cc relative gives an unfair impression of bulk, but setting the bike on its own confirms the initial view that it's awfully tall and bulky for a 250, especially in modern terms. Though only 17¼ in.

wide—not too bad for a disc-valve design with those carbs poking out on either side—it measures 44 in. high at the screen; wheelbase is 53 in. The fairing design doesn't help, being rather slab-sided at the front, but the overall impression is of a bike that's only a little smaller than the current breed of GP 500s, and at a dry weight of 110 kg it's 20 kg over the 250 class minimum weight and a good 10 kg heavier than, for example, Carlos Cardus's 1983 Eurotitle-winning Kobas-Rotax.

But all of this could have been eliminated by some determined development, of the type that turned the 125 Derbi into such a successful machine. The rewards were there, for the 250 cc production racer market could have provided Derbi with some healthy pickings at home and abroad, but no doubt for their own perfectly good commercial reasons they declined to take this opportunity either. Instead, the 250 twin was attended to just enough to assure the factory a valuable stream of local victories, yielding useful publicity benefits at home.

The 250 Derbi engine is an enlarged version of the 125 twin, but housed in a much taller frame. Monoshock rear suspension was a 1978 modification (Author)

Getting on the bike immediately after riding the 125 made it seem even bigger than it is, but with a high seat you do feel quite a way off the ground at the best of times. Starting requires the same juggling with the air lever but as soon as it fires up you know you're on a different generation of racing motorcycle. Not only is there an old-fashioned rasp from the unsilenced exhausts, but a considerable degree of vibration throughout the rev range which becomes positively toe-tingling once you start to explore the upper reaches of the rev counter. And once again, like the 125, all the power is right at the top end, with nothing much below 9500 rpm up to 12,000 rpm maximum. Even compared to a non-power valve TZ250 that doesn't give you much to play with, and compared to the 4000 rpm of the Kobas' Rotax it shows how far disc-valve technology has progressed in the last few years.

Handling was not particularly confidence-inspiring (though the brakes again worked superbly), with a curious feeling of top-heaviness which was probably just that. The power comes in with a bang, and climbing the Rampa Pegaso cranked over before the bridge caused the front wheel to start pawing the air like a circus horse while the totally ineffectual steering damper allowed it to flap from side to side: exciting! I didn't dare explore the concrete patch at Tunel on this bike, and anyway there wasn't much point since it was so grossly overgeared I was getting top before the start line and having to feather the throttle down the rest of the straight. Then after five laps or so the engine slowed just crossing the line and after a push back to the pits, my fears that a piston had gone were confirmed: the chill wind had doubtless made jetting difficult. I can't say I was too disappointed: my brief acquaintance with the bike had only increased my respect for Grau and Nieto for having achieved so much success with what was basically an underdeveloped motorcycle that can't have been much fun to ride hard.

When and if Derbi do indeed return to the

125 cc GP class, it'll be interesting to see how closely their chosen design resembles the title-winning bike I rode at Jarama. Having sampled both the Garelli and an MBA I can honestly say that the Derbi gave remarkably little away to either in spite of its age by the standards of latter-day GP racing. Too bad they never made a customer version: would have helped Spain's balance of payments!

**Racer testing isn't always a bed of roses: here's the author on the vibrationary 250 Derbi just before it seized! (Herrero)**

| Model | | Derbi 125 | Derbi 250 |
|---|---|---|---|
| Engine | | Twin-cylinder disc valve water-cooled 2-stroke | Twin-cylinder disc valve water-cooled 2-stroke |
| Bore × stroke | | 43·5 × 42 mm | 57·5 × 48 mm |
| Capacity | | 124 cc | 249 cc |
| Power output | | 41·5 bhp at 14,400 rpm | 63 bhp at 12,000 rpm |
| Compression ratio | | 14 to 1 | 14 to 1 |
| Carburation | | 2 × 30 mm Dell'Orto | 2 × 36 mm Dell'Orto |
| Ignition | | Motoplat electronic | Motoplat electronic |
| Clutch | | Multi-plate dry | Multi-plate dry |
| Gearbox | | 6-speed | 6-speed |
| Frame | | Full twin-loop tubular | Full twin-loop tubular |
| Suspension: | front | 32 mm Marzocchi | 35 mm Marzocchi |
| | rear | Marzocchi | Monoshock cantilever with Yamaha suspension unit |
| Brakes: | front | 2 × 200 mm floating alloy discs | 2 × 270 mm floating steel discs |
| | rear | 1 × 200 mm fixed steel disc | 1 × 250 mm fixed alloy disc |
| Tyres: | front | 2·75 × 18 | 3·25 × 18 |
| | rear | 3·00 × 18 | 13/66 × 18 |
| Weight | | 185 lb | 242 lb |
| Top speed (estimated) | | 130 mph | 145 mph |
| Year of manufacture | | 1970 (updated to 1979 spec.) | 1971 (updated to 1978 spec.) |
| Owner | | Derbi Nacional Motor SA, Barcelona, Spain | Derbi Nacional Motor SA, Barcelona, Spain |

# 4 | Most powerful—the *Garelli 125*

*Above* **Past master of the tiddler classes, Angel Nieto streaks round Silverstone in the 1982 British GP on the 125 Garelli, en route to yet another World Championship (Morley)**

*Right* **Daniele Agrati, boss of the Garelli concern, in the GP team's workshop with the 125 twin soon after it adopted its red and black livery for the 1982 season: bike was formerly a Minarelli (Author)**

Ask most road racing enthusiasts which they consider to be the most successful Grand Prix bike of recent years, and they'll probably plump for the RG500 Suzuki, which in various guises had reaped four world 500 titles. Other contenders might also be Spencers NS500 Honda, the 250/350 tandem twin Kawasaki which dominated the intermediate classes for the best part of five years, or even the amazing TZ250/350 Yamaha—that Manx Norton of the 1970s which even in the 1980s is capable of defeating the best of the disc valve designs.

Yet it's perhaps a reflection of the lack of appreciation of the smaller GP classes outside the Latin countries that the bike which stands more clearly head and shoulders above its rivals should be practically unheralded amongst racing fans the world over. In the 500 arena a machine which won a world title for its class in both the riders' and constructors' categories by scoring eight wins out of the 11 Grands Prix contested by the works teams, and provided the runner-up in the riders' table to boot, would be rightly acclaimed as the bike of the season—the champion of champions. But because the disc-valve Garelli twin is but a humble 125 semi-tiddler, its achievement in scoring such overwhelming success, against far from negligible opposition, has gone largely unsung outside Italy—its home—and Spain, home of unarguably the greatest lightweight rider of modern times, 11 times world champion, Angel Nieto.

Nieto strolled the 1982 championship, winning the first five GPs he contested on the trot, before slackening off a bit to allow teammate Eugenio Lazzarini to catch up closer in the points table: he repeated the act in 1983. But even more significant was the Garellis' amazing reliability record; out of 21 GP starts in 1982 there were only two retirements for mechanical reasons—one a failed ignition system. Given the pace of the titanic struggle for supremacy between the MBA, Sanveneto and Garelli squads, such a record was simply remarkable.

It's even more remarkable given the power produced by the tiny $44 \times 41$ mm cylinders. An output of 46·8 bhp makes the 125 Garelli today's most powerful GP bike in specific terms, at just under 375 bhp/litre. Compare that to the 40 bhp or so churned out by the V4 Yamaha of the Read and Ivy era to gauge the full measure of the

Garelli's worth: a lighter, less complicated design with half the number of cylinders (thanks to FIM rules), offering a broader power band to cope with the maximum allowable six speeds in the gearbox, yet producing 15 per cent more power than the bike most people would nominate as the most exotic 125 road racer yet built. Indeed, the Garelli is almost certainly the most powerful bike of any capacity ever raced in specific terms, rivalled only by the VanVeen Kreidler with its 20 bhp claim from a single eggcup-sized cylinder.

Under these circumstances when the chance came to test ride Nieto's title-winning bike at Monza in the close season, I needed little prompting. 'Only one problem,' worried Roberto Patrignani, the affable Garelli PR head who rode in the IoM TT back in the 1950s on a little Ducati. 'I hope you can manage to fit on the bike: Nieto must be a good nine inches shorter than you,

and it really is very small.' Mentally pondering the possibilities of a bionic cut-and-shut job on my legs, I rode up to Monza on a gloriously sunny winter morning to find the entire Garelli racing team, plus ex-world champion Eugenio Lazzarini, awaiting my pleasure. Confidence turned to curiosity, then consternation, as I realized this entire session was being laid on just for my benefit, as the only non-Italian journalist to ride this world-beating machine.

The Garelli's engine was designed in 1977 by Jorg Möller, the journeyman two-stroke wizard from Germany who's made a career and name for himself working in Italy. Möller originally designed the unit for Minarelli, the huge proprietary engine concern under whose name it first appeared in public, winning its debut race in Venezuela in 1978 clad in a tubular frame and ridden by then champion Pierpaulo Bianchi.

*Above* **Continued development by Dutch engineer Jan Thiel brought the Garelli 125 cc disc-valve unit's output up to a remarkable 46·8 bhp (Author)**

*Right* **Mechanical anti-dive was first employed on a BMW Superbike in the USA in the mid-1970s, then by Kawasaki on the unsuccessful 500 cc GP bike. Garelli were the first to win a world title with it (Author)**

Nieto joined the team during the course of that season, but too late to win the title. The following year he made amends, scoring eight GP victories and winning every race he finished in en route to the championship. Bianchi only managed 10th in the table and departed the team at season's end, along with Möller whose contract had expired and, more importantly, had achieved its purpose.

To replace him the other two freelance two-stroke wizards were hired away from Bultaco, where they'd been working with Nieto for several

and small-capacity bikes. Agrati bought up the entire team lock, stock and barrel—except for Mijwaart who'd returned to Holland—repainted the bikes in red and black Garelli livery, and the rest is history. After a gap of 50 years' absence from racing Garelli—one of the world's oldest-established bike manufacturers who beat the likes of Guzzi and Gilera to Grand Prix success with a then-unfashionable split-single 350 two-stroke in the early 1920s—won their first world title at the initial attempt.

Just what is it about the Garelli's specification that makes it stand out in a hotly-contested class whose regulations appear to impose a uniform design of parallel twin-cylinder disc-valve engines with 6-speed gearboxes and water-cooling? To a certain extent the answer lies with Möller's original design, which produced a remarkably compact engine unit that measured only 15 in. across with the 29 mm electron Dell'Orto carbs removed. Thiel's reduced this even further to just under 14 in. across, and combined with the very low monocoque frame and highly efficient streamlining, developed in the Fiat car firm's wind tunnel, this very small frontal area and the engine's amazing power result in a top speed of just on 145 mph—from 125 cc!

But this low aspect calls for specially-tailored riders—star midgets able to mould themselves to the tiny machine, heads under the screen, elbows and knees tucked inside the fairing, cheating the wind of every last ounce of drag. As Patrignani had noted, I'm no Nieto, and jacking my knees up high enough to fit them on to the footrests was a major project; keeping my legs tucked behind the fairing was no problem since it's quite wide thanks to the crankcase-mounted carbs, but I was unable to get my head inside the screen with a helmet on, and it took quite some time to figure out how to change gear with my size nine left. Nieto has somewhat smaller tootsies!

The overwhelming impression when you first see or sit on the Garelli is how slim it is. Three

seasons: Dutchmen Jan Thiel the engine man, and chassis designer Martin Mijwaart. A year after joining the team the pair guided the green and yellow Minarelli-mounted Angel Nieto to yet another world title in 1981, after narrowly missing the boat the previous year.

An internal shake-up at Minarelli at the end of 1981 spelled the end of the Grand Prix effort. At one stage the team seemed sure to be broken up—but then in stepped Daniele Agrati, boss of the old-established Garelli factory who are Europe's third-largest manufacturer of mopeds

*Above* **Monocoque chassis has twin fuel taps, offering direct feed to the twin magnesium Dell'Orto carbs (Author)**

*Left* **Bulky seat was wind-tunnel designed to improve top speed (Author)**

*Right* **The author samples the Prince of Tiddlers round the Monza Parabolica in December 1982 (Crose)**

years after Mijwaart designed the first steel monocoque to replace the less rigid tubular frame, the Garelli and the 500 cc Kawasaki and Morbidelli were still the only GP bikes outside the tiddler 50 cc class to employ this type of chassis—if one excepts the NR500 Honda of sporadic appearance. The monocoque of the bike I rode was made of dural, weighs a scant 6 kg and contains 15 litres of 50:1 mixture in the baffled fuel cell. It's also extremely rigid, and the wonder is more race bike designers haven't opted for this design. Jan Thiel thinks he knows why: 'It really only works with a twin-cylinder engine because of space limitations and you have to design a bit of extra strength into the engine cases too. It's difficult with four cylinders to squeeze the exhausts in, which is why I admire the Kawasaki so much—they did it really well.'

Admiration extends to outright copying of the KR500's mechanical anti-dive front suspension, itself borrowed from the Udo Geitl BMW Superbike ridden by John Long in the mid-1970s in America, and here mated to 32 mm Marzocchi forks. The effect is stupefying: rush up to a tight corner at top speed, leave your braking impossibly late, grab the front brake as hard as you like in the dry, zip down through the box and while you're doing it a great big hand has reached out and halted your progress: no diving forks, no chattering rear wheel, no transfer of weight on to the wrists—the Garelli just stops, in a perfectly level plane, the system of rods transferring the braking forces from the caliper to the steering

head in a simple but effective manner. Every bike should have one!

Of course, there's not much to haul down, relatively speaking, though at 78 kg dry the Garelli is still some 3 kg above the 125 class weight limit. Thiel had plans to narrow this gap, with Kevlar streamlining scheduled to replace the present seat and fairing, and Brembo working on carbon fibre disc brakes (a spin-off from the Ferrari F1 car project) instead of the already very light plasma-sprayed alloy Zanzanis then fitted. A carbon-fibre monocoque would lose the lot in one go, but Thiel smiles ruefully at the thought. 'We had a budget of 500,000 dollars to go racing with in 1982,' he says, 'which must be the biggest in the smaller classes, but even we couldn't afford that sort of technology. Only car teams can!' So instead he concentrates on the art of the possible, wringing increasing fractions of a horsepower from that amazing engine. The separate cylinders are made by Hoeckle in Germany, as is the pressed-up crank which runs in four ball bearings, with needle roller big and little ends. Great care is taken not to leave any cylinders lying around within reach of prying eyes, but there are 7 ports in the Gilnisil bores (6 transfer, 1 exhaust), in which run Mahle pistons each with a single chromed L-ring. The rotary valves are steel and feed the 50:1 mixture at the rate of 28 mpg. Krober ignition is fitted, and a hefty water pump sits atop the engine on the right, driven off the gearbox whose six speeds have three alternative sets of ratios which cannot however be changed without splitting the engine horizontally. The same exhaust design is used for all circuits, and total dry weight of the engine less carbs is just 23 kg. A 14-plate dry clutch has 7 sintered alloy plates, and 7 friction ones.

I'd expected the engine to have an ultra-narrow powerband, necessitating much abuse of the clutch to keep it on song yet produce the horsepower to win championships. I couldn't have been more wrong. Admittedly nothing much happens below 9000 rpm, except a lot of noise and fumes but nil forward motion. Then the power starts to pick up till at 10,500 rpm it comes in with a bang—and you better be ready when it does, for much to my surprise this little 78 kg racer actually pulled a wheelie on its similar-weight rider. I was so surprised I almost fell off—you don't expect a 125 to start pawing the air like a circus horse—but coming out on to the straight leading down to the Parabolica it would lift the front wheel every lap as I accelerated hard while still leaned over. No wonder a small steering damper is fitted to the left stanchion. Once the Garelli's in the powerband the perfectly-matched gear ratios come into their own, zipping you up to the 14,500 rpm maximum before the next sweet upward change: I used the clutch for downward changes only, but still managed to miss a couple of cogs coming out of the Parabolica when my oversize foot failed to function as it ought. Maximum torque occurs at 13,800, so with so much pulling power and such a wide powerband it's little wonder that the Garelli has the legs of the opposition. It may be fast, it may be powerful, but its very easy to ride. . . .

During 1982 Jan Thiel concentrated on making the bikes reliable with a new crankshaft, improving air penetration, and increasing low end torque matched to new gear ratios. The chassis received little attention apart from the addition of anti-dive, so it's a tribute to Mijwaart that it handles as superbly well as it did. Once again my expectations were false; I'd been anticipating a nervous, twitchy little bike which my every breath would send skittering in a different direction. After a handful of laps I had as much confidence on the Garelli as if I was on one of my own racers, thanks to the combination of the stiff chassis and sticky, skinny Michelin slicks. Surprisingly, the bike was still fitted with old-style rear suspension, featuring twin Bitubo gas units suspending a fabricated alloy swingarm with eccentric adjusters. Even on Monza's bumps the ride seemed adequate, without being exceptional, and when I mentioned it to Jan Thiel on my return he nodded his head. 'Monoshock rear suspension isn't really necessary yet with a lighter bike like a 125,' he averred, 'Though we might try it soon and if we do it won't be a cantilever like the MBA and Sanvenero: that's all wrong. But what we'd really like to experiment with are some 16 in. wheels—we've been asking the tyre companies for them since 1976, but still no sign of them in our sizes! That would help us reduce the frontal area still more.'

| Model | | Garelli 125 |
|---|---|---|
| Engine | | Twin-cylinder disc valve water-cooled 2-stroke |
| Bore × stroke | | 44 × 41 mm |
| Capacity | | 125 cc |
| Power output | | 46·8 bhp at 14,600 rpm |
| Compression ratio | | 14 to 1 |
| Carburation | | 2 × 29 mm Dell'Orto PHSA magnesium |
| Ignition | | Krober electronic |
| Clutch | | 14-plate dry (7 steel/7 friction) |
| Gearbox | | 6-speed CIMA |
| Frame | | Dural monocoque incorporating fuel cell |
| Suspension: | front | Marzocchi 32 mm with mechanical anti-dive |
| | rear | Bitubo |
| Brakes: | front | 2 × 20 mm discs (floating) |
| | rear | 1 × 210 mm disc (floating) |
| Tyres: | front | 2·50 × 18 |
| | rear | 2·75 × 18 |
| Weight | | 172 lb |
| Top speed | | 145 mph |
| Year of manufacture | | 1982 |
| Owner | | Agrati–Garelli SpA, Monticello, Italy |

# 3 250 Grand Prix development

## Four of the best—
### *Benelli 250 Four* **of 1966**

Asked to name the company who first explored the realms of small-capacity, four-cylinder racing engine technology, most followers of road racing history would quite reasonably think immediately of Honda. But while it's true that the Japanese giant did produce a series of technically brilliant 125 and 250 fours (as well as five- and six-cylinder designs) in the course of their titanic struggle for domination of the Grand Prix scene in the 1960s, not only were they not the only company to manufacture four-strokes of this type then, but when their first 250 cc four appeared in 1960, it did so 20 years after the first such machines in its field.

Instead, the mantle of originators in this area falls jointly on the Italian Benelli and Gilera firms, each of whom produced supercharged 250 cc fours in 1940, both of which appeared too late to race in public before the outbreak of hostilities, and were then obsolete after World War 2 by the FIM's ban on supercharging in 1946. Though Gilera managed to make their blown 500 four reasonably competitive bereft of its supercharger, their 250 was too heavy to make a similar exercise worthwhile, and in the case of the Benelli this was compounded by the fact that, unlike its rival, it was water-cooled. But new ground had been broken, and though Gilera's retirement from racing at the end of 1957 meant they never again trod the path of small-capacity multis, the 1960s decade saw the little Benelli factory at Pesaro, on Italy's Adriatic coast, field a

You can almost hear the scream of the four-cylinder Benelli engine as Tarquinio Provini hustles through Whitegates in the 1964 IoM 250 cc TT. He retired on the last lap (Nicholls)

range of four-cylinder machines in the 250, 350 and 500 classes which seriously threatened the domination of Honda and Yamaha in the smaller classes, and their compatriots MV Agusta in the larger.

I'm not alone in believing that Benelli have never really had the recognition they deserve for their racing efforts in the 1960s: they've always been regarded as the makers of the 'other' Italian four, much as Alfa Romeo have played second fiddle to Ferrari in the car world during the past 20 years. Yet given that their GP involvement was bankrolled exclusively by the ultimately failing profits from their manufacture of road machines, rather than from the considerable resources of one of Europe's leading aeronautical concerns, as was the case with MV, the fact that they succeeded not only in producing a series of technical tours de force culminating in a 250 cc V8 but also had their efforts rewarded with a World Championship crown in 1969 thanks to Aussie Kel Carruthers, merits considerable applause.

And to carry the MV analogy further, the reason that their feats have gone largely unrecognized is mainly due to the low key, unostentatious atmosphere which pervaded their racing team: instead of a bombastic, larger than life personality like Count Domenico Agusta, the retiring Benelli family ran a close-knit squad of designers, mechanics and usually just one or two riders at a time: headed by a Benelli cousin, Count Nardi Dei, the Pesaro-based team none the less achieved considerable success on the track, with riders of the calibre of Provini, Pasolini, Read, Hailwood and Saarinen happy to ride for them even though the straitened finances of the little factory meant they were unable to pay them the sort of fees available from the likes of MV and Honda. And when the racing department was closed down in the wake of the company's takeover by de Tomaso in 1971, Benelli's legacy to the racing world was already manifest, with ex-mechanic Eugenio Lazzarini a future world champion and staff from the old team behind the successes gained by Morbidelli, MBA, Sanvenero, Bimota, Ringhini, Piovaticci and all the other Pesaro-based companies whose existence in this hotbed of European road racing derived directly or . indirectly from Benelli's efforts.

Benelli is actually one of the oldest surviving motorcycle manufacturers, dating from 1911 when the six Benelli brothers were set up in business to repair mechanical objects of any nature by their despairing, but wealthy mother. In 1921 they manufactured their first complete motorcycle, and as the company prospered expanded into competition, spurred on by the youngest brother Tonino, who was a useful rider. In the 1930s they began the series of bitter struggles in the 250 class with rivals Moto Guzzi, which would lead after World War 2 to a World Championship for the Pesaro firm in 1950, thanks to rider Dario Ambrosini. The machine employed was a development of their prewar dohc single, but after Ambrosini was tragically killed the following year in France, it was a mark of the close relationship between the Benelli family and their riders that they lost interest in racing for many years, returning only at the end of the decade with a modernized version of the single-cylinder bike which scored some successes, notably in the hands of Geoff Duke at the Locarno GP in 1959.

That same year the first 250 cc four from a major manufacturer to appear in competition had made a dramatic appearance in the Asami Volcano races in Japan, clinching five out of the first six places on its debut: the bevel-driven dohc Honda. But that machine, essentially a doubled-up version of the 125 twins with which Honda had made a steady if unremarkable entry on the European scene at the 1959 TT, was scrapped in favour of an entirely new design, with gear-driven dohc valve-gear, with which the Japanese firm contested their first full season of Grands Prix in 1960. Though they ended the season only as runners-up to the MV twins,

Honda did enough to scare MV out of trying to defend their title the following year, leaving the field clear for the Japanese firm to win the first of a hat trick of 250 titles in 1960.

Thus it was left not to the MV team, who concentrated henceforth on the 350 and 500 classes, to produce the European answer to the Honda four, but to a then completely unexpected source: Benelli. In the summer of 1960 they astonished the racing world by unveiling the prototype of the magnificent range of in-line 250 cc four-cylinder machines which would be an integral part of the Grand Prix scene for the next decade. The machine had been designed jointly by No. 2 brother Giovanni Benelli and the firm's racing technician Ing. Savelli, and owed nothing at all to the pre-war blown engine, being a small-scale version of what had come to be a typically Italian multi-cylinder unit. Fitted transversely in the frame, the engine measured $44 \times 40.6$ mm for a capacity of 246·8 cc, dimensions which were to be retained up to and including Carruthers' world title-winner, with vertically positioned cylinders and twin overhead camshafts actuating the two valves per cylinder. The engine was dry-sumped, with a rather bulky oil tank under the seat, but the chassis sat ill at ease with this thoroughly modern engine, begin rather heavy-looking and over-engineered in true 1950s style. Wheel rims on the other hand were skinny, a 2·50 × 18 front tyre matching a 2·75 section rear, and a dry weight of only 122 kg was claimed, though in retrospect it seems certain that it was considerably more, in spite of much expensive use of electron in the engine castings. Forty bhp was claimed at 13,000 rpm, which compared well with the 42–43 bhp quoted for the contemporary Honda, but with work having only been started on the machine at the end of the previous year, it was almost completely untried and works rider Silvio Grassetti was forced to rely on an updated version of the dohc single until the opening of the 1962 season.

Two years of development had evidently been well spent, for the speed of the Benelli four startled observers when it made its racing debut at Imola in April 1962 in Grassetti's hands. A missed gearchange and pinged valves robbed him of victory first time out, leaving Tarquinio Provini on the remarkable Morini single to romp home in the lead, but at the next race at Cesenatico it was Grassetti all the way, and Benelli's 250 four won a race at only its second attempt.

Many changes had been implemented on the machine since its first appearance, the most critical being the removal of the oil tank under the seat in favour of a large-capacity bolt-on sump with two-way oil pump mounted above it, and running off the camshaft drive pinion which was placed between the middle two cylinders. Similarly, ignition had on the prototype been by battery and four coils mounted under the fuel tank, with the points driven off the left end of the inlet camshaft. For its Cesenatico success this was replaced by a Lucas magneto mounted on the right front side of the crankcase, bevel-driven off the camshaft pinion again, for it had been found that the four-lobe contact-breakers' points floated open at high revs, acting effectively as a rev limiter! The use of the British magneto also had the desirable side effect of reducing weight, with the elimination of the battery and coils.

The chassis also had been somewhat redesigned, and though handling was by no means perfect, the result looked considerably more workmanlike: slightly wider section tyres were now fitted. But Grassetti, for all his skill as a brave and aggressive racer, was no development rider, and for the rest of that season and throughout 1963 the Benelli four's development was stymied because of this, in spite of successful development of the engine on the Pesaro test-bed, to the point that it was now giving 45 bhp at 14,000 rpm.

By 1963 Honda had advanced to the top of the Grand Prix tree, so that yesterday's

**The Benelli frame is liberally braced around the steering head (Author)**

neophytes had become today's team to beat. And beaten they almost were that year, by what they must surely have regarded as the most unlikely possible threat to their multi-cylinder domination, in the shape of Tarquinio Provini and that incredible Morini single: 'Old Elbows' and his supposedly obsolete 12,000 rpm thumper came within a whisker of rubbing

**One-piece crankcase required the engine to be assembled via holes in the sides and front (Author)**

services of one of the greatest and most experienced riders Italy has ever produced, and twice a world champion to prove it.

Under Provini's influence the Benelli four was completely redeveloped: a smaller, lighter frame featuring a long, thin, carefully-shaped fuel tank to enable the rider to squeeze low under the screen took shape, while careful attention to weight-saving brought the scales down to 112 kg dry—this time without a thumb on them. Revised camshafts narrowed the powerband but raised the rev limit, so that 48 bhp was now available at 14,500 rpm, still with 2-valve combustion chambers and single-plug ignition; however with Provini aboard the deficiencies of the gearbox became apparent and this was redesigned, with a seventh speed added (to supplement the six used from the beginning) to compensate for the narrower rev range. The separate pairs of 20 mm Dell'Orto carbs each shared a flat-sided float bowl positioned between them. The Benelli four had now assumed the basic format which would eventually result in Carruthers' world title, but first it was Provini who was to reap the benefits of his own development talents by easily winning the 1964 Italian 250 title, after being victorious in every race. More to the point though was his magnificent defeat of the Honda, Suzuki and Yamaha works teams in the opening European GP of the season round the tight and twisty Montjuich Park circuit in Barcelona, and though a 4th and two 5th places was the best he could manage during the rest of the season, Benelli were now at last on the move.

For the 1965 season more modifications were made, with the inlet and exhaust ports modified for better breathing, and new camshafts fitted offering greater lift and dwell, but still with two valves per cylinder. Usable power came in at 8500 rpm up to 14,500 revs, at which point power output was now up to 52 bhp, with the engine safe to 15,000 rpm on the overrun. Combustion chambers and piston crowns had been modified to give more squish, and larger 24 mm

Honda's nose in the dust, only losing out on the world title to Redman's four in the last round in Japan, after each had won four GPs. Morini were a tiny company whose resources were even smaller than Benelli's, and Provini knew that 1963 had been their best shot. Accordingly, he changed camps for the 1964 season, and Benelli suddenly found themselves endowed with the

carburettors were now fitted, with specially-tuned intake stubs which were found to produce nearly 2 bhp difference on their own. But most important mechanical development of all was the substitution of the Lucas magneto by one off a Mercury four-cylinder two-stroke outboard engine, modified for four-stroke use: the Lucas, designed originally for the lower-revving Gilera and MV 350 and 500 fours of the 1950s, proved unreliable at engine speeds over 12,000 rpm, but the new US-made unit completely cured the problem and was retained to the end of the model's development in spite of some experiments with an early form of electronic ignition.

The chassis was also modified for 1965, being lowered and shortened even more, and equipped for the start of the season with American-made Airheart disc brakes: Benelli were amongst the first teams to employ this now commonplace feature on their bikes, and possibly were the first to do so on the Grand Prix scene. However, two small 7 in. discs originally designed for go-kart use proved insufficient to stop a 112 kg motorcycle travelling at the 143 mph of which the Benelli was now capable, and a problem of lack of pad choice was also a factor in these early days. By season's end the team had reverted to drum brakes all round, particularly after wet braking problems experienced during that year's Italian GP at Monza, run in driving rain and won so convincingly by Provini and the Pesaro four that he ended up lapping every other finisher! Another Italian championship was also attained, compensating for a disappointing year in the GPs, apart from the Monza victory, and a 4th place in the 250 TT. More power was needed for a serious chance of success on the Grand Prix scene, especially with the bitter struggle being waged between Honda and Yamaha in the 250 class, which had the effect of accelerating development. The Honda six was now producing nearly 60 bhp while weighing only eight kg or so more than the Benelli, and in 1966 Mike Hail-

wood's talents would see the bike at last begin to handle properly. Something had to be done if Benelli were not to be also-rans on the world stage.

The answer was twofold: first the 250 four was scaled up into a 322 cc version measuring 50 × 40·6 mm, yielding eventually 53 bhp at 14,700 rpm, still with seven speeds and a two-valve head. Provini splashed his way to third place in the 350 event at Monza on the bike's debut in 1965 in the Italian GP, and bettered this by coming second to Hailwood's 297 cc six in the 1966 season opener in Germany. Encouraged by this, Benelli bored the engine out to the maximum permissible oversize of 52 mm, for 345 cc, in which form it eventually produced 64 bhp at 14,500 rpm, with four valves per cylinder, and finished runner-up to Ago's MV in the 1968 World Championship in the hands of Renzo Pasolini.

Benelli's attentions in the winter of 1965/66 were however more closely directed to the 250, and an interim version was constructed with three valves per cylinder, two inlet and one exhaust. This had the desirable effect of increasing bottom end torque, but not absolute power, so finally Savesi took a leaf out of Honda's book and produced the first 4-valve Benelli engine in the spring of 1966. This increased safe revs to 16,000, and bumped the power up to 55 bhp, still with an acceptable though inevitably narrower power band. On this machine, now painted a dull slate grey in place of the colourful Benelli green and white livery which would be revived in time for Carruthers' world title, Provini won his third Italian title in a row for the Pesaro company, but failed to make any impression on the Japanese bikes in the Grands Prix. Then sadly he was seriously injured in late August when blinded by sun while practising for the Isle of Man TT (the races were held later that year because of a seamen's strike) and suffered such back injuries that he was never able to race again.

Such a vital loss was a tragic blow to Benelli,

but they decided to continue, and enlisted the services of Aermacchi rider Renzo Pasolini to replace Provini for the 1967 season, and also produced a new 500 cc four, a 491 cc machine based on the 350 (and thus on the 250) which produced 75 bhp at 12,800 rpm and won first time out at Vallelunga in late 1966. But Paso took longer to find his feet on the little multi, especially after the quite different experience of a pushrod single, and it was not till 1968 that he began to shine on it, winning both 250 and 350 Italian titles (beating the MVs in the process in the latter class), and finishing second in the IoM TT in both classes. The long years of painstaking development by the small Benelli racing department was now beginning to bear fruit, and though their

task had been somewhat eased by Honda's retirement at the end of 1967 (and would be further by Yamaha's at the end of 1968), there's no doubt that the 'other' Italian fours were now highly competitive.

Pasolini proved as much at the start of 1969, winning all seven races in the keenly-contested Italian season openers on tracks such as Imola, Riccione, Rimini and the like, and defeating Agostini's MV comprehensively on six out of seven occasions in the 350 class to boot. Both rider and team were in seventh heaven, riding on the crest of a wave of success that seemed to repay all their long years of labour. Sadly for Pasolini, by general consent an odds-on certainty for that year's 250 world championship, he fell off in practice for the first GP at Hockenheim, and was sufficiently badly injured to miss the first three GPs, the third of which was the crucial IoM TT. With Santiago Herrero's amazing Ossa single

**Elderly tyres and the presence of a large Italian crowd restricted the author's cornering exuberance on the Benelli four. The front end dipped noticeably under heavy braking (Zagari)**

well in the lead of the championship, Benelli team manager Nardi Dei had to act decisively. He drafted in reigning world champion Phil Read to the team, backed up by Aussie privateer Kel Carruthers: Read retired in the TT race, but Carruthers repaid the confidence shown in him magnificently by sweeping home to victory over three minutes ahead of Perris' Suzuki twin. He was rewarded with a regular place in the team for the rest of the season even after Pasolini returned to win the next GP in Holland, and as Herrero's challenge faded it was left to the two Benelli riders to battle out the title. Sadly, though, the little bespectacled Italian's exuberance got the better of him once more and he hurt himself falling off again in Finland, putting himself on the sidelines for the rest of the season. Benelli then moved Carruthers up to team leader, gave him an 8-speed 4-valve engine (whereas he'd been using the less powerful two-valvers up till then), and kept their fingers crossed: the Aussie won two out of the last three GPs and finished second in the other, to clinch his first world title and Benelli's second. Pasolini was fourth in the world championship, but easily won both Italian 250 and 350 crowns.

Sadly, that was to prove the Benelli 250 four's swansong, and indeed it had won the world title at its last chance: for the following season the pernicious FIM rule limiting 250 cc machines to a maximum of two cylinders and six gears was introduced, denying the 250 V8 Benelli that had been built in the summer of 1968 the chance to appear in public, as well as strangling future small-capacity four-stroke engine development on the race track. After 1969, it was many years before a 250 Benelli four appeared on a circuit again, though there are various machines in differing states of completion dotted all round the world, none of which appear to be runners. Similarly, 'Old Elbows' Provini had absented himself from the growing historic racing scene, in spite of earnest entreaties by various organizers to one of the best-loved and admired riders of

Pure sixties—drum brakes and four open meggas (Lewis)

the classic era to turn out in such events, preferring to concentrate on building up his successful Protar plastic scale model business, as well as supporting his two sons' motocross efforts.

But at the Italian historic meeting at Misano in 1983, only a stone's throw from the Benelli factory, the long-awaited reappearance of man and machine took place in front of an ecstatic and adoring crowd. Mounted on a 1966 Benelli four-cylinder 250 owned by the factory and specially prepared for the meeting, Provini showed that in spite of a somewhat more ample waistline than in his heyday he had lost none of his old verve and skill. Scorning the opportunity to simply complete a handful of parade laps, he actually took part in the 350 cc race on the 250 multi, and in spite of a handful of slides occasioned by the elderly Dunlop triangular tyres fitted to the bike, held a magnificent fourth place behind a pair of fleet 350 Aermacchis and Franta Stastny, another old adversary from the past on his 350 Jawa twin. The wonderful, musical exhaust note of the four-cylinder bike as it tore round the Adriatic track, had spectators entranced, and Provini himself was visibly moved by his reception. 'If I'd known these old-bike events were so much fun I'd have started doing them years ago,' he confided to me afterwards. 'Must try and lose some weight for the next meeting so I can go a bit faster!' That's the last thing his rivals want to hear. . . .

The opportunity to ride the first Benelli 250 four to appear on the tracks for well-nigh a decade was too enticing to pass up, but fortunately word of my Honda six test appeared to have reached Italy, and after a quick phone call to the factory to secure permission, Provini was eager for me to try the bike. First though, he and mechanic Sergio Censi, a faithful colleague who was Provini's right-hand man throughout his racing career, following him from Mondial to MV and thence to Morini and Benelli, told me some of the technical secrets of the bike I was about to ride.

After a certain amount of discussion as to whether it was the 3-valve interim model or the 4-valve prototype, Provini and Censi settled on the latter. The bike dates from 1966, and like all the small Benelli fours has the crankcase and gearbox casing cast in one large but very light piece of electron magnesium, with holes on either side through which the engine internals were slotted. This naturally results in a very strong bottom end that was also notably free from oil leaks, though the external oil lines were prone to coming adrift or splitting. A large rectangular front crankcase cover, coupled with four round side covers, two of which locate the ends of the six-bearing crankshaft in large ball bearings, enables the engine to be quickly rebuilt with the minimum of inconvenience. Drive to the double overhead camshafts is by a train of three gears up the centre of the engine, and the cylinder head is split into two parts, divided at this point. Both the heads and four separate finned barrels, the latter with austenitic liners, are made in light alloy, as is the long rectangular oil sump, holding only two litres of Castrol R, bolted to the underside of the engine. As with all Benelli fours, the primary drive is taken off a large pinion between the first and second crankshaft journals on the left: the forged conrods run in caged roller bearings, with plain bearing little ends in spite of the high revs, and full-circle flywheels pressed on to the built-up crank. A 7-speed gearbox was fitted to this particular bike, with multi-plate air-cooled dry clutch on the left, quite large in diameter compared for example to similar Honda units. Gearbox tooth contour and width was modified for the 1965 season to reduce friction.

The bike which appeared at Misano was also fitted with the Mercury outboard magneto, bevel-driven off the central camshaft drive via a spur gear. Four rubber-mounted 24 mm Dell'Orto carburettors were fitted, with rod linkage and each pair sharing a single flat-sided float chamber. Compression ratio was between 10·5 to 1 and

The Benelli fuel tank was specially shaped to permit Provini to tuck as low as possible under the screen (Lewis)

11 to 1—'Feels like the lower end of the scale!' said Censi as he turned the back wheel over with the bike in gear.

The chassis is the one which Provini himself had a hand in developing, and he pointed out to me the various bracing struts around the steering head which he had added in the course of sorting out the handling. It's a full-cradle duplex tubular chassis, with a long, slim light alloy fuel tank carrying 22 litres of petrol and shaped in such a way as to allow the rider to get right under the screen. After the unsuccessful disc brake experiment, this bike has a 4LS Ceriani drum brake at the front, mounted on 35 mm forks from the same manufacturer, with an alloy splash guard underneath the head stock which also served to duct cool air to the cylinder heads. In spite of the upright cylinder configuration, in marked contrast to the Hondas' forward inclination, even cooling of the heads was not apparently ever a problem, even with the four valves per cylinder layout.

Provini obviously recalls his days at Benelli with a mixture of pleasure and regret: 'It was a very happy team, and because it was so small but yet was a part of quite a big factory, we were able to get things done very quickly. By the time I'd finished with the frame the bike handled really well—I think the Japanese were surprised just how well, especially at Montjuich in 1964. Honda were always photographing it, so they must have thought we knew something they didn't! But power was always my problem: the Honda fours were just that bit quicker, and the Yamahas about five mph faster, which was quite a bit. Strangely, even though it was less powerful the Morini was in many ways a more competitive bike at the time, because it had a lot of power low down and consequently you could ride it harder everywhere becuse of its good torque. But the Benelli was eventually the best Italian quarter-litre four-stroke ever made, and I'm only sorry that the way things worked out I wasn't able to win the world championship on it that they eventually deservedly got.'

Given the choice between stepping down into a snake pit and riding a literally priceless piece of Italian motorcycle racing folklore in front of a crowd of fervent, avidly envious Italian fans, I'd probably decide I had a deep but undiscovered interest in reptiles and try for a starring role in the remake of 'Raiders of the Lost Ark'. But the chance to try out one of the rarest of all works machines of the postwar era was not to be turned down, so with the kind agreement of the organizing Club Il Velocifero and the Race Director Sig. Rubini, it was agreed that I could take the Benelli for a run after the last event of the day at the Misano meeting was concluded. Coincidentally, this was the 500 cc race, and when I walked in from the countryside after my G50 Matchless' crankpin had snapped clean in half while I was in third place behind the great Walter Zeller and John Surtees, I might have forgiven Provini and Censi for concluding that here was a bike breaker they'd be better off not entrusting their fragile jewel to! Instead, they helped compensate for the disappointment by letting me do twice as many laps as we'd agreed. . . .

So just as the last Manx Norton thumped its way in off the track, Censi pushed me off on the little Benelli for a quarter hour of rapturous delight. Having notched first gear—one up on the 7-speed box—I dropped the clutch after a couple of steps and as the engine fired instantly clutched it again while the revs picked up. Blipping the throttle at around 5000 rpm, I cautiously moved out on to the circuit, focus of a thousand jealous pairs of eyes whose owners each doubtless wanted to know why this foreigner was being allowed to ride their country's pride and joy, rather than them! Feeding the clutch out gently so as not to stall it, I noticed that in spite of the small diameter flywheels the engine picked up cleanly from around 4000 rpm, up to my Censi-appointed limit of 13,000 revs. Provini had told me beforehand that he used to take the engine regularly to 16,000 in top (while using 14–15,000 in the gears), and on the last lap had even on occasion gone to 18,000 without mishap. But he'd been using a 14,000 rpm ceiling earlier that day in his race, in deference to the bike's age, though it was evident from the superb response of all the controls, and the perfect note of the engine that it had been very well prepared in the Pesaro factory for the Misano meeting.

Sitting on the bike was surprisingly easy in spite of my long legs, though I had trouble with my right foot since the footrests are mounted just above the gracefully upswept exhausts, resulting in my heel resting on the top of the pipe and slipping off it when I came to change gear. It is indeed a small machine, with a 50·5 in. wheelbase rendered possible by the upright cylinders, but the very narrow clipons, which practically meet each other round the front of the steering head are mounted so far forward that a stretched-out but comfortable riding position results. The long fuel tank sat snugly into my lower body and allowed me to get right down under the screen on the straights, but its shape meant that it was impossible to grip it with my knees when I hit one of Misano's few bumps, instead being forced to rely on a combination of squeezing the sides of the tank with my elbows—is that how Provini got his nickname?— and the upper frame rails with the insides of my knees: they're even padded for this purpose. It's a bike built for getting down to it on: Provini's style was always to ride flat out under the screen, even round relatively slow corners, and this bike shows it.

All the controls are incredibly light, especially the clutch which you can work with a single finger. The bars are bound with red bandage rather than more conventional rubbers, but the complete lack of vibration from the beautifully-balanced engine makes any kind of cushioning for the hands unnecessary. The front brake lever has a light pull to it but the brake takes a bit of getting used to if only because it's perfectly set up: it works lightly but only partially for the first half of its pull, then very strongly and suddenly, giving the rider the option of a slight touch on the stoppers if he overcooks a corner slightly, as I did once going into the fast sweeper leading away from the pits, or strong, safe braking at the end of the main straight. Using only 13,000 revs—well OK, maybe a bit more after a couple of laps!—on Misano gearing meant that

I suppose I was doing about 120–125 mph at the end of the long straight, yet once I got to feel at home on the bike I could regularly brake well within the 200 metre board at the end of it—and that's without any real engine braking effect thanks to the small flywheels.

Mind you, whatever the flywheel diameter on the Benelli is, it must be more than on the Honda six I had previously ridden in Canada, for the Italian bike had none of the Honda's propensity to kill the engine stone dead below 9000 revs or so. Changing gear was easy, thanks to the short but precise lever action, and though I started out using the clutch in both directions, soon began making clutchless upward changes except for just one place: in front of the pits, where the assembled gallery were doubtless hoping fervently I'd miss at least one cog so they could turn to their neighbours with a knowing look: 'I told you so—why did they let HIM out on it!?' But the Benelli didn't let me down, though I was interested to note the choice of ratios: bottom is very low, for ease of starting and getting round tight hairpins, but the next four gears are all very

close together before a quite noticeable gap between fifth and sixth, which has seventh (and top) gear very close to it. When I mentioned this to him afterwards, Provini nodded: 'Sometimes on very fast circuits we used to run with very tall gearing—like at Monza, for instance: having the top two gears close together was like having a kind of overdrive which could be invaluable if you came upon a slower rider in a fast corner, for example. Then the four middle gears are close together to keep the engine on the boil at tight circuits like Montjuich: I would only get top gear there once a lap, but the way the internal ratios were usually arranged (and incidentally it was possible to remove the gearbox to change ratios without disturbing the rest of the engine) I would have a gear for every corner.'

Provini had told me that the Benelli had little torque, but determined to discover how little I instead got a pleasant surprise. Coming on to the main straight one lap about three gears too high, I cracked the throttle open wide at around 5000 rpm and was astonished to find the Benelli responding by pulling effortlessly and cleanly up

*Right* **Relatively compact in spite of its in-line four-cylinder design, the Benelli had a 7-speed gearbox driven by countershaft off the crank (Author)**

*Left* **The four-cylinder engine packs the twin-loop frame of the 1965 Benelli. Front forks are 35 mm Cerianis (Lewis)**

through the rev range. Noticeable urge began to be apparent at around 7000 rpm, but then at 8500 revs the power came in very strongly: nevertheless, for a four-cylinder racing machine of the classic era this was an impressive display of flexibility, which must have made the Benelli much easier to ride round a circuit like Montjuich than the low-torque Honda four-strokes and Yamaha and MZ two-strokes with their razor-thin power bands. If it hadn't been for the restriction on the number of cylinders, the Benelli could certainly have lived with the FIM's short-sighted limit on the number of gears, the more so since the bike I was riding was the supposedly less flexible 16-valve unit.

Provini had obviously done his homework in the chassis department too, for the Benelli proved to be a fabulous steerer, in spite of the weight and bulk of the engine sitting relatively high up in the frame. Misano has several long, sweeping corners where a bike that isn't perfectly set up will start to understeer outwards or else fall into the corner in a way that makes you reluctant to commit yourself to a fast line. The Benelli had perfectly neutral handling characteristics, practically finding its own way round the turns, though here I must admit to having chickened out of exploring the cornering power at true racing speeds: 15-year-old T-compound triangular tyres, fitted to an Italian heirloom, don't inspire the sort of confidence one requires to do so, and after the back end stepped out twice on one of the long left handers I decided I didn't want to live on a diet of pasta and water in some Latin lockup for the rest of my days, and cooled my impetuosity.

Instead, I concentrated on playing beautiful music on the four-cylinder organ: each lap as

I passed the pits I'd see out of the corner of my eye the crowded grandstands filled with people turning to each other wreathed in smiles and shaking their hands in that peculiarly Italian gesture of appreciation: '*Che bella macchina, che bello rumor!*' Indeed it is a lovely bike, and though by the time Censi waved me in after 20 minutes or so I was beginning to wish I'd worn a set of earplugs, I have to say that the Benelli's engine note must be one of the sweetest sounding four-cylinder trademarks ever heard. 'You sounded as if you had it running really well,' said an appreciative Provini as I lifted myself off the seat while Censi took the bike from me. 'What did you think of it?'

What indeed? Well firstly the bike was in a really excellent condition, and a lesson to other Italian manufacturers that there's no real excuse for either not preparing their similarly exotic machines properly for such outings or leaving them in a state of neglected disrepair in the factory museum. Full marks to Benelli, and here's hoping the bike will reappear in the future to remind other enthusiasts who weren't there at Misano to see 'Old Elbows' do his thing just what a great racing history Benelli has—and one which ultimately resulted not only in the 750 and 900 six-cylinder road bikes, but also in the oddly-styled but nicely engineered four-cylinder 250 cc road bike: why Benelli didn't try to identify that machine more closely with the racer is a mystery.

But besides all that I found the 250 Benelli four to be a surprise—perhaps revelation is not too strong a word for it. It's far easier to ride than a Honda six and surely also than a Yamaha or MZ, if not quite as powerful in the '66 form in which I rode it. I can't imagine how the handling could be faulted, so the reason that the bike took so long to win its justly deserved world title must be a combination of money—Benelli's racing budget was always a fraction of the Japanese teams'—and power: it just never quite had that little edge of performance necessary to win consistently. Though never confirmed, Carruthers'

16-valve engine was rumoured to be producing close on 60 bhp in 1969, and had that sort of output been available earlier in the decade, Benelli might have had more than one world title in the 1960s. Reliability must have been a factor as well, certainly early on. But ultimately, as with the Honda six, the Benelli 250 four is a monument to the golden age of technical development on the Grand Prix scene, one which is unlikely to be equalled or surpassed until the FIM abandon their restrictive constraints on designers and engineers. Indeed, even more than the Honda, the Benelli may claim to be the perfect epitome of 1960s GP development—a living, musical monument to the Classic Era. For its development lasted the whole decade: conceived in 1960, it finally reached fruition in 1969, just in time to be banned for being interesting, complicated and evolutionary. Sad, isn't it?

| Model | Benelli 250 Four |
|---|---|
| Engine | Dohc 4-cylinder 4-stroke |
| Bore × stroke | 44 × 40·6 mm |
| Capacity | 246·8 cc |
| Power output | 55 bhp at 15,000 rpm |
| Compression ratio | 10·5 to 1 |
| Carburation | 4 × 24 mm Dell'Orto |
| Ignition | Mercury magneto |
| Clutch | Dry multi-plate |
| Gearbox | 7-speed |
| Frame | Duplex cradle |
| Suspension: front | 35 mm Ceriani |
| rear | Ceriani |
| Brakes: front | 210 mm 4LS Ceriani drum |
| rear | 190 mm Fontana drum |
| Tyres: front | 3·00 × 18 |
| rear | 3·00/3·25 × 18 |
| Weight | 255 lb |
| Top Speed | 146 mph |
| Year of manufacture | 1966 |
| Owner | Benelli SpA, Pesaro, Italy |

# 2 | Six of the best—
## *Honda's 250 RC166* of 1967

**The greatest combination of man and machine in the history of motorcycling? Mike Hailwood screams the 250 cc Honda six to yet another victory at Oulton Park in 1967 (Nicholls)**

Of all the bikes associated with the late, great and sadly missed Mike Hailwood, the 250 and 297 cc six-cylinder Hondas are the most fondly remembered by a generation of racing enthusiasts the world over. Not only did Mike himself regard the six as well-nigh the ideal racing motorcycle, but a combination of the amazing exhaust note, the exotic appeal of the multi-cylinder engine incorporating the ultimate in engineering miniaturization, and the emotive feeling that here at last was a high-tech four-stroke capable of stemming the inexorable advance of the raucous two-strokes, combined to make the Honda six more different people's favourite racing motorcycle than any other. Even diehard opponents of Japanese motorcycles and all they stand for will grudgingly concede they might make an exception in this one case. As for enthusiasts of Oriental technology—well, it's the *ne plus ultra*, the absolute greatest, simply . . . the *best*.

For it was those very two-strokes which were directly responsible for the creation of the RC164 250 cc Honda six, and its ultimate development the RC166. By the summer of 1964 the quarter-litre class had become the most intensely competitive category in Grand Prix racing, with no less than 11 works teams contesting the honours. Admittedly, some of these like Bultaco, Aermacchi or CZ could never hope for outright victory save in the unlikely event of a 100 per cent attrition rate amongst the faster, mostly Oriental,

mostly two-stroke machines. That unlikely event did come very close to occurring a couple of times, for the ferocity of battle between the four leading teams was literally incredible. The East German MZ and its near-carbon copy Japanese counterpart, the RD56 Yamaha had now achieved sufficient measure of reliability to win races and present a real threat to Honda's mastery of the class, and though the RZ63 square-four Suzuki's terrifying handling and propensity for seizure—thus aptly earning for itself the nickname of the 'Whispering Death'—were to prevent it ever becoming a GP winner, there's no doubt that Honda technicians were shaken by its phenomenal straight-line speed.

Honda had dominated the 250 class for the previous three seasons, Mike Hailwood handing them their first world championship in 1961 before moving to MV, with the dependable Jim Redman following up with two more titles in the succeeding years on the four-cylinder RC163. But all the time the two-stroke challenge, and especially Yamaha, were creeping closer; Ernst

Degner's defection from behind the Iron Curtain at the end of 1962 released a wave of rotary-valve technological information which was eagerly snapped up by Oriental engineers, and while his Suzuki employers channelled his knowledge into achieving success in the 50 and 125 cc classes, their Yamaha rivals set sights on the 250 crown. With better materials and infinitely greater budgets at their disposal than MZ's Walter Kaaden could have ever dreamed of having, it took only a short time for the Japanese to get on terms with the East Germans (though Kaaden still had a few tricks up his sleeve!), then start gunning for Honda.

In spite of a near-disaster the previous year when Provini's incredible Morini single came within an ace of robbing Redman of the 250 crown, Honda entered the 1964 season confident that they could keep one jump ahead of the two-stroke opposition by updating their existing 250–4. Such belief was rudely shattered, for Yamaha had now added rider strength to match the undoubted power, adequate handling and

*Above* **Canadian GP scrutineering sticker from 1967 carries Tom Faulds' handwriting to denote this was one of the two Hailwood bikes at that race (Author)**

*Left* **The six-cylinder engine forms a semi-stressed member of the Honda frame (Author)**

located plug which in turn reduced the length of the flame path and provided a hotter spark. Squish bands to the front and rear compressed the combustion chamber to provide a fiercer explosion of the mixture, and forward-inclined cylinders allowed necessary cooling air to the hot-spots between the valves.

This basic specification, allied to oversquare cylinders, unit-construction gearboxes with gear primary, gear-driven double overhead camshafts and—by the standards of the day—astronomical revs of 14,000 rpm and more, brought Honda great success in GP racing in the early sixties, and at the same time set the company on the path to its present pre-eminence in the sales field also. For winning at racing wasn't just a question of self-esteem for Honda; it was a vitally-important ingredient in the company's plans to achieve a dominant position in the commercial sector, through shrewd exploitation of a carefully-nurtured sporting track record. Instant heritage it may have been, but it also meant that their principal manufacturing rivals in Japan, Yamaha and Suzuki, were forced to join in competition with Honda on the race track as well as in the showroom. What happened as a result stamped the 1960s as one of the golden ages of motorcycle road-racing.

These factors explain Honda's immediate response—almost without consideration for any budgetary aspects—to the slightest threat to their hard-won road-racing supremacy in the early 1960s. Having fought so hard to achieve success, they HAD to keep winning, and when first Suzuki, then Yamaha produced motorcycles that outperformed the equivalent capacity Honda, then it was immediately back to the drawing board for Mr Irimajiri and his colleagues, to come up with the answer. This traditionally came to mean more, smaller cylinders, higher revs and increased power, sometimes however at the expense of reliability. Limited by materials than available, the maximum piston speed the Honda engineers could hope to aim for and still

new-found reliability of their air-cooled twin, Phil Read and Mike Duff dominated the class, with Read scoring five GP wins and the Canadian one to hand Yamaha their first world title. The writing had been on the wall since Fumio Ito's win in the Belgian GP the year before, and when Read won the 2nd GP of the 1964 European season over the twisty and demanding French Clermont–Ferrand circuit, Honda recognized that action was required if they were to save their and Redman's crown.

The Honda engineers—led by 24-year-old Soichiro Irimajiri, later to achieve further renown as the designer of the six-cylinder CBX road bike—depended on a combination of adherence to basic engineering principles, coupled to high-precision technology that was just then becoming available, to achieve their success. The use of four valves per cylinder, previously discarded by European engineers, reduced reciprocating weight in turn permitting higher revs, offered improved breathing due to greater valve area, and better combustion thanks to a centrally-

produce a bike capable of lasting out the minimum one-hour long GPs of the day was 4000 rpm. With the four-cylinder 250, the 44 × 41 mm RC163—already nearing that figure and still getting beaten by the Yamahas, a shorter stroke and higher revs were out of the question. There was only one thing for it: a six-cylinder 250.

Beginning work in June, Irimajiri and his team had the first RC164 prototype running by August: two months from zero to reality was an incredible achievement even by the remarkable standards Honda had set themselves. Redman—lying second to Read in the championship and desperate for something with which to counter the now superior Yamaha—interrupted the GP season to fly to Japan to test the bike. Reporting plenty of power in the cool Oriental springtime but at best questionable handling, he nevertheless decided to ride the six in September's Italian GP at Monza. He *had* to win both the last two GPs in Italy and Japan to retain his title, and the four was obviously inadequate.

Twenty years down the road, it's difficult to imagine the stir that the appearance of the Honda six caused at Monza when it made its debut there in 1964. Nowadays, three different manufacturers offer six-cylinder road bikes, and anything other than a four seems unconventional. Mind you, a six-pot 250 would be pretty heady medicine even today, but when Honda unveiled the RC164 at Monza on the first day of practice it literally stupefied observers. They'd brought it there in great secrecy, even removing one megaphone on each side to make it appear that beneath the dust-cover that perpetually covered it from its arrival at the circuit lurked nothing more exotic than an updated 250–4. It was one of the best-kept secrets in GP history, for the first the rival teams knew of the bike's existence was when Redman hopped on board to go out for practice.

Though the new machine was unquestionably fast, a fairy-tale debut was not to be. Redman set Honda hearts a-fluttering by leading the first lap going away from Read, but then a combination of the baking hot Italian sun and insufficient time for development began to tell. As the engine overheated and flagged, first Read then Mike Duff slipped past on the Yamahas, and Redman trailed in 3rd on the six, almost caught on the line by newcomer Giacomo Agostini on the Morini single.

If the Honda six had disappointed in its first race, it did everything expected of it in its next, as Redman won the Japanese GP on home ground—but not before Mike Hailwood, riding a solitary MZ twin had led the race before stopping for a plug change. Ironically, Honda had signed the MZ's usual rider Alan Shepherd only a few weeks beforehand, in order to ride the new six the following season, leaving Redman to concentrate on the 350 class and, so it was said, to drive the new Honda Formula 1 racing car. But tragically Shepherd was never to race the six, for he crashed in practice on a 350–4 for the Japanese GP and was seriously injured, resulting in his retirement from racing.

These events are not as peripheral to the main story as they might first seem, for the future development of the RC164 was shaped by them. Redman stayed in the 250 class for 1965 after all, but met little success with the six, in spite of a winter's development resulting in the updated RC165 version. Honda's GP car project was in full swing by now, and its demands on the company's racing department seriously affected their motorcycle effort: poor preparation and loss of reliability ensued. Instead of Redman sweeping to victory after victory on the invincible new six-cylinder machine, it was Read's Yamaha that scooped the pool, winning seven of the 13 GPs to Redman's three. But then Jim only came to the startline six times, as Honda morale plummeted: even such a giant organization as the Honda racing department could be over-extended. In site of this Honda had reached the decision to move up to the 500 class;

Redman had retained his 350 title, and wanted to concentrate on the bigger bikes (he never did get to race the F1 car, though another former World Motorcycle Champion did—John Surtees). This meant Honda really did have to engage a top-notch rider for the 250 and 350 categories (though in the event he was to out-shine Redman in the 500 class as well). Thinking back to the previous year's Japanese GP, Honda chiefs remembered how with little practice on a strange circuit, a lone MZ rider had led the might of Japanese technology till he struck trouble. He also happened to have won the 500 cc world title for the previous four years in a row on the MV Agustas. His name: Mike Hailwood.

Honda didn't sign Mike up straight away, though, but instead offered him first a one-off ride at the end-of-season 1965 Japanese GP on a 250–6. In pre-race testing Hailwood experienced for himself the principal reason for the six's inability to match Read's Yamaha twin: the handling was atrocious. But how to get this across to the assembled crowd of engineers and company dignitaries? A now-famous story tells that Mike got off the bike and took one look at

the Japanese rear suspension units. Asking the mechanics to remove them so he could examine them, Hailwood then strode purposefully to the adjacent lake and threw them in! Returning to his kitbag, he produced a pair of Girlings and asked for them to be fitted. The incident made headlines in the local papers, and caused deep embarrassment to the Honda management, unused to such direct and public criticism of any aspect of their engineering. But Mike wanted to make it clear that unless they would listen to him, there was little point in Honda availing them-selves of his services. In spite of the dramatic incident, he raced the six in the GP a few days later and comprehensively trounced a field which included two of the new water-cooled V4 Yamahas. It was the start of a beautiful friendship.

A winter's work saw rider and technicians pro-duce a bike for the 1966 season that differed greatly from the previous year's model. A much stiffer chassis, improved brakes and suspension and a now-reliable engine allowed Hailwood to register the incredible record of winning all ten Grands Prix he entered, breezing the World title with Read and Yamaha unable to touch him.

Oil coolers are fixed to the fairing, hence feed pipe unions must be unbolted to permit removal (Author)

They came closer the following year, as Mike came in danger of spreading himself too thin, eventually becoming the first rider to win 250, 350 and 500 world titles in the same season—the 350 crown achieved with the bored-out 297 cc version of the smaller six which was to become his favourite racing bike. Read actually scored more 250 cc points than Hailwood in winning four GPs to Mike's five, but once they'd both dropped their lowest scores, the resultant dead-heat on points was decided in the Honda rider's favour by his one extra win.

That extra victory was registered at the Canadian GP at Mosport, just outside Toronto, penultimate GP of the 1967 season. Hailwood and teammate Ralph Bryans arrived with three bikes between them, an RC165 for the Irishman and two of the latest-type RC166s for Mike the Bike: main difference was in the carburettors, which permitted peak revs of 18,000 rpm on the later bike as opposed to 17,000 on the older one. One of the scrutineers that day was expatriate Scot Tom Faulds, himself a former racer of note on Manx Nortons and the like, and today Service Vice-President of Honda Canada. He actually passed the two Hailwood bikes for the race, and takes up the story of what happened next.

'Mike won the race from Read's V4 Yam, and as it turned out that win gave him the championship. That year was our Centennial, and one of the big events was the opening of the Ontario Science Centre, which was to act as a showpiece for the latest in science and technology in a wide variety of fields. They wanted to include a motorcycle exhibit, so contacted Honda and asked them if they would loan a bike for display which represented the last word in two-wheel engineering. Back came the reply that they'd be happy to lend one of their six-cylinder GP bikes, but only after they'd finished using it at the end of the season!'

The unlikely decision had come about because, unbeknownst to the outside world, Honda chiefs had already decided to withdraw

from GP racing at the end of the 1967 season, so had no further use for their bikes. The machines returned to Japan from Canada, and one of the Hailwood bikes was converted to left-foot gearchange for use by a Japanese rider in the local GP. Ralph Bryans won that race on his older six, Hailwood became world champion thanks to his Mosport victory, and Honda shocked the sporting world by retiring from racing. Faithful to their promise, a refurbished RC166 duly arrived in Canada for display in the Science Centre. Bearing Tom Faulds' writing on the scrutineering sticker still carried on the fairing, it was one of Hailwood's two bikes used at the Canadian GP, but to this day nobody knows if it was the one he won on, or his practice spare.

The 250–6 became one of the prize exhibits in the Science Centre, and in time part of Canadian motorcycling heritage. It was after all the only 250–6 on public view anywhere in the world, since in common with its Japanese rivals Honda sadly has scant regard for its obsolete racers, tucking those fortunate enough to escape the crusher or the electric knife out of sight in some distant corner of their R&D department. Two cultures, two attitudes to the past.

In 1976 the phone rang one day at Honda Canada; it was the Ontario Science Centre on the line. 'Excuse me,' went the jist of the conversation, 'but please could you come and take away your old bike. We're not a museum, you know, and what we really want to get hold of if you can help is something more up to date that represents modern-day motorcycling, not the past.' Curious but true, and fortunately Tom Faulds happened to be in the office that day; which is how the ex-Hailwood 250–6 came to be traded for an early Honda Gold Wing prototype, and came back into circulation.

On receipt of the bike from the Centre, Faulds' first thought was to get it to run—but would it be complete, rather than a bare set of cases without internals? Amazingly, it was: Honda Japan appeared to have completely refurbished

the bike after its last race, the only problem being that the carbs had got gummed up. After stripping and cleaning them out, and with a fresh set of the special 8 mm plugs provided by NGK, Faulds was ready for a historic moment; would the bike start?

'We've got a big warehouse,' said Tom with a smile, 'so I thought I'd try to fire it up inside in case it needed some fiddling with to get it to go. I took a couple of steps and dropped the clutch—when it fired first time after ten years of disuse I almost fell off in surprise! I quickly realized the exhaust note would bring the roof down, so we shut it off and took it outside. The entire building must have emptied to come and look and listen to the machine. It was a great moment.'

A new set of Michelins to replace the now board-hard Dunlop triangulars, and the Honda six was ready for the track, naturally with Tom himself aboard. In the past couple of years since getting the bike running again he's demonstrated it by request at a couple of meetings, and even brought it over to Britain in July 1982 to thrill enthusiasts on this side of the Atlantic with the six's 'barking dog' exhaust note at the Donington

*Above left* **Exotic, horribly complicated yet compact: carburettors are 17 mm flat-slide Keihins with no less than five jets (Author)**

*Above right* **Front 220 mm 4LS drum brake was necessarily effective, with minimal engine braking available (Author)**

Hailwood Day meeting. Ralph Bryans rode it in one of the parades, and Tom in the other; perhaps the most incredible thing was the way the six's exhaust completely drowned out an entire grid of other Honda works bikes, two MVs, and a bunch of British singles, and the like: they might as well not have been there!

RC166-F-102 is that rare thing: a works racer that's completely unchanged from the day it left the factory. Not restored, not hacked about, it's been caught in a time warp that enables us all to appreciate its engineering to the fullest. Engine no. RC174-E-302 is the ultimate version of the 250 cc six, with 7-speed gearbox, 39 × 34·5 mm cylinders, gear-driven dohc one-piece head with four valves per cylinder, and one-piece barrels inclined forward by around 30 degrees to duct much-needed cooling air to the centre and rear of the engine. A built-up crank which scorned the use of counterweights gave two-stroke like revving characteristics, running to 18,000 rpm with the help of peakier cams than on the RC164, made in two pieces joined at the gear wheel and operating the paired valves via cylindrical cam followers. The same central gear pinion driving the camshafts also works the hefty Kokusan magneto perched atop the gearbox beneath and behind the bank of six 17 mm flat-side Keihin carbs. There are three sets of points, and three condensers rubber-mounted to the frame to the rear of the cast-in catch-tank for the engine breather. Three sets of coils live under the tank, firing the single 8 mm plug per cylinder.

The wet-sump oil system employs a narrow deeply finned sump which projects down past the belly-pan of the fairing, into the cooling air-stream under the bike. Twin oil coolers mounted in the leading edges of the fairing, one each side, further help the hard-pressed castor-based lubricant remain at a lower effective operating temperature. By 1966 the overheating problems of the early six were a thing of the past. A 16-plate (8 fibre/8 steel) dry clutch pokes out to the right side of the engine to transmit the 60-odd bhp to the rear wheel. No wonder Hailwood regarded the six so fondly, and reaped so much success with it in British and Italian non-championship events even after the factory had withdrawn from the GPs. In an open race such as the Hutch or Race of the Year, even in 250 cc form the bike had the beating of the Manx Nortons and Seeley G50s that made up the bulk of British fields. 60 bhp from a dry weight of 250 lb was better than the best of the 500 singles could offer, before taking into account nippier handling and the like. And when in 297 cc form the six churned out over 65 bhp without any increase in weight, it was a match even for Ago's 500 MV.

Yet the remarkable thing is that all this was achieved with impressive reliability after the end of 1965, and with an engine that managed to pack six tiny cylinders into the space of the previous four: the 250–6 engine measured just 14 in.

across, and viewed externally the bike as a whole was no wider than the Yamaha twin. The resultant straight-line speed was exceptional— around 153 mph in 250 form—and was the machine's strong point from the very beginning. It was only after Mike the Bike had got to work on it that its handling and roadholding matched that speed, enabling him to win on any type of circuit. And in doing so—had he not been one of nature's genuinely modest men—he could have given the lie to those detractors who dubbed him a mechanical dunce. Certainly, he couldn't and wouldn't want to build an engine— but Mike Hailwood had few equals in the art of tuning a bike's chassis to perfection, getting the handling and steering and chuckability of the bike just so. That he succeeded better than anyone could with the Honda six is borne out by comparing the machine's track record before and after he began to ride it. More than any other machine, the RC166 Honda is an enduring testament to the skill of the greatest rider that ever raced.

I've always worked on the principle that if you don't ask, you don't get. So when I went to see the ex-Hailwood Honda six back in the depths of the Canadian winter, it was just a matter of how long it would take me to summon up the nerve to ask for a ride on this historic and priceless machine. 'Sure,' said Tom Faulds, 'when do you want to do it?' Resisting the urge to ask him to fit snow tyres to the bike and let me do it right then and there before he changed his mind, we eventually settled on a date. The place picked itself: what better than Mosport, scene of Mike Hailwood's last classic victory on the 250–6?

I later discovered how honoured I was by being allowed to ride the bike; Tom had resolutely declined all other requests, howsoever couched, for assorted journalists, enthusiasts and golden oldies to ride the bike. Alas, Mosport suddenly became unavailable for the week I planned to be in Canada due to a car race, and with travel plans already firmed up there was nothing for it but to switch the venue to the little Shannonville track, a sort of backwoods Brands Hatch 120 miles from Toronto. The 1·2 miles long twisty track wouldn't really allow me to get the Honda flying in top gear, but thanks to Tom Faulds, who had a specially large rear sprocket made for the outing, I'd still be able to sample the delights of life at 17,000 rpm on the ultimate in motorcycling exotica.

I'd be lying through my teeth if I said I wasn't petrified as I approached the little (it's only a 250, remember) Honda at Shannonville. Fall off a works Ducati? They can repair it from off the shelf. Unload from someone's pristine Manx Norton or 7R Ajay? Might have to hunt around a bit for the parts, but it's repairable. Rubbish the Honda six? They tell me hara-kiri is still practised in certain strata of Japanese society. . . .

First though I had to find which way Shannonville went; Tom Faulds had even thought of that too, bringing along one of the 4-valve Honda Ascot 500 singles for me to course-learn on, while he warmed up the six and took it out for a few laps to check everything was OK. At last the time had come, and with trembling knees I approached bike-racing's Holy Grail, listened carefully to Tom's instructions, and set off for the Racer Test of a lifetime.

That first lap was a DISASTER, and if I'd been Tom Faulds I'd have hung out the 'Come In no. 18, Your Time Is Up' sign before I could have embarked on a possibly even more catastrophic second. Riding a bike—any bike—for the first time is like a first date. You allow plenty of time to get to know each other before coming on strong, and try to discover her strong and weak points for future reference. Since each bike has its own little quirks, racer testing involves finding these out before they cause you personal and lasting damage, and usually entails trickling round gently for a couple of laps just off the power band while you get to know each other and decide if you're going to fall in love.

It would be fair to say my relationship with the Honda six could not have got off to a worse start. Getting under way was easy enough: starting from cold you can use the same plugs as for racing—NGKs traditionally have a much wider heat range than the competition's products—but must tickle all six carbs which have their own integral float bowls. Tom warms it up at between 10–12,000 rpm, while the engine emits those distinctive whoops which have bike enthusiasts of whatever persuasion covering their ears and smiling with delight. Out of the dozen people attending our test, three had tape recorders!

Once warmed up, the bike starts instantly from still: simply sit astride it if you have quite long legs as I do, take a couple of paddling steps, drop the clutch and immediately pull it in again as the engine fires, winding it up to 14,000 or so before feeding it out. The clutch action is beautifully silky and controlled, so what sounds like a fairly tricky operation is actually quite straightforward.

But then almost at once comes the time to change into 2nd, and that's when your troubles begin. Tom had asked me to keep the revs down to 16,000 at best (!), so once the needle on the Smiths revcounter started hovering around 15 grand I tried to change gear. Two things happened: I missed the gear anyway, and the engine cut out. Fortunately I had enough forward motion to bump start OK, but when it came to change gear while I did manage to notch the cog this time, the engine died away again. I'd heard of lack of flywheel effect, but this was ludicrous! Aware that three different tape recorders were making a permanent record of my every cock-up, I tried again, and this time managed to persuade myself that changing gear without closing the throttle while the engine beneath me was turning at over twice the revs of a G50 Matchless was the Hot Tip: it was! Mind you, I still missed two more gears that first lap before trundling forelornly into the pits to have a talk with Tom Faulds and myself.

'No problem,' said Tom breezily: 'You're just doing exactly what I did the first time I rode it as well.' I could have kissed him, handlebar moustache and all. What apparently may have happened is that in cleaning out the carbs after the bike's ten-year layoff, some of the jets may have inadvertently been switched around. That was Ralph Bryans' theory after riding the six at Donington, since normally it should run happily as low as 5000 rpm in spite of the minimal flywheels and no counterweights: as it is, the engine stops so suddenly when you come to change gear that if you're not prepared for it the noise seems to go backwards. Hailwood's 297 cc bike would run cleanly from 4000 rpm up, and this abetted by the instant starts he was able to make on the bike made it such a fearsome short circuit special as well as superb GP bike.

The flat-slide ('trap-door') Keihins are in many ways the heart of the engine. According to Ralph Bryans there are no less than five jets per carburettor, none of which is a needle jet—there aren't any. Instead, the five work in relays with a single main jet, intermediate air and petrol jets, and ditto slow-running jets. Moreover, there were three different lengths of induction rubbers on which the banks of carbs were flexibly mounted to prevent fuel frothing. The shorter the rubber, the greater the power but the narrower the power band: such a set-up would be used for a track like Hockenheim, with its two ultra-fast straights. Medium length rubbers were used for most circuits, while the long ones would only be used for tight, twisty courses like Montjuich Park where bottom-end power was all important. Ralph believes this bike has the medium length ones fitted, and indeed once I got the engine wound up to 10,500 rpm it completely smoothed out and started pulling, with a real surge of power from 12,000 up.

After altering the gearlever to a more comfortable position, I was ready to try again. This time the Honda and I got off on a better footing, and I was able to revel in the smooth, powerful acceleration and perfectly matched gears, enabling you to keep the engine well on the boil above the 12,000 rpm mark. Doubtless Mike would have only used the clutch for downward changes, but mindful of the lack of spare parts for the machine I used it both ways, thus losing precious fractions of a second on upwards changes that on such a quick-revving engine added to the lap times as a result. And once I got the knack of not closing the throttle while changing gear, the engine stopped cutting out—but it demanded a whole new riding technique and a stern mental approach to remember what I was riding.

The wheelbase of the 250–6 isn't as long as it looks in the photos, and the riding position is quite cramped as a result. Principal reason is that Hailwood changed the weight bias when he started developing the bike, moving the rider forward to get more weight over the front wheel to permit a better drive out of corners while still cranked over, so my knees stuck up and/or out quite readily. 25 laps or so round Shannonville was one thing, but an hour-long GP would have been another, especially having to make a conscious effort to tuck knees and elbows inside the incredibly slim streamlining, a mere 16 in. wide at its broadest point beside the cylinders. And the noise! Standing trackside and listening to someone else riding it is one thing, and I can't deny the thrill of giving a concert performance myself. But you'd have had to wear earplugs to ride the bike in GPs, and whatever you do don't ever offer to help pushstart it in a fit of misplaced enthusiasm without wearing ear protectors. When I did that to Tom Faulds the resultant 15,000 rpm blast left my ears ringing for the rest of the day. A watching Mike Duff recalled how he'd gone partially deaf following Redman round Spa for the length of a GP, and how the Dunlop technicians on the Isle of Man refused to check the Honda six's tyres with the engine running!

Curiously, I was surprised at the Honda's handling round the bumps and twists of Shan-

*Above* **The ride of a lifetime: author at work on Honda six (Petro)**

*Right* **Opposition's view of the Honda six: Mike Duff recalls being literally deafened by following the bike round for the length of a GP (Petro)**

nonville. I suppose that I was sub-consciously expecting a junior version of the 500 cc camel that not even Mile Hailwood could tame, rather than the well-mannered, responsive six. For that I should really thank Mike the Bike, for the RC165 was every bit as unmanageable till he got to work on it. The result is there to see: a box-section swinging-arm with sheet steel stiffeners welded inside for extra bracing; extra tubes grafted into the open-cradle chassis which follows Honda racing tradition in using the engine as a fully-stressed member; gussets at every joint; and a heavily-braced steering head at which point the main frame tubes running under the light alloy tank swell to 35 mm diameter for extra rigidity. That tank's a work of art, and with its lightweight plastic cap and the carbon-fibre fairing shows Honda—and Hailwood—believed in saving weight, but only where it didn't matter.

Front suspension by 35 mm telescopic forks offered excellent damping over the ripples leading into the one fast sweeper on the little track, but dived noticeably under heavy braking for the next sharp right-hander. The front brake's a classic, providing instant retardation with finger-tip control, while if I used the back as well to the full under engine braking the rear wheel hopped up and down. Mentioning this to Ralph Bryans

he too said he almost always experienced the same thing when he was racing the bike, so much so that he rarely used the back stopper much at all—the bike's basically overbraked, though I expect after several hard stops in succession at racing speeds at Montjuich, for example, you were glad of it. Bryans also used Showa rear units as fitted to this bike, instead of the Girlings the heavier Hailwood and Redman preferred. I wasn't about to start trying hard enough to really test them, but they seemed OK.

After adjusting the lever position the gear-change was superb, with very closely spaced ratios that hardly altered the engine note if you could change fast enough. Having been last ridden by an Oriental rider it has a left foot change, though the boss for Hailwood's right foot shift is still there. I could use fifth gear out of the seven comfortably, but the track was too short for maximum use of the available cogs. Changing from second to bottom was the only difficult change, a notchy, awkward swap that probably wouldn't have been much used if at all when the bike was raced; on this gearing though, it was the only way round Shannonville's tight Turn 5.

After 15 laps or so on the Honda six I suddenly realized I was feeling much more at home on the bike; I was also subconsciously riding it harder, a fact brought forcefully to my attention when the back end stepped out rounding the tight left hander before the back straight. It's a rotten but demanding corner, and the only way round it is to go for maximum lean—on the Honda around 50–55 degrees before the three tucked-in exhausts, welded-up from steel pressings, on each side start grounding. I never got *that* far over, but I certainly reached the limit of the PZ2 hard-compound Michelins; fortunately I was too panic-stricken at the thought of writing off a Canadian national heirloom to react, which gave the Honda time to do the work for me. A slight shake of the head as if to tell me off and the six righted herself with just a slight rise and fall of the exhaust note to tell me I hadn't imagined it all. No need for hara-kiri just yet.

A few more laps at slightly reduced speed and my ride of a lifetime was over. Had I enjoyed it, I was asked. Well, strangely enough the answer is probably not, for the simple reason that almost all the time you're out there riding the bike you can't forget what it is, represents and would cost to repair—if you could. I cheerfully ride bikes like my G50 or Aermacchi quite hard, on the basis that what man has made, man can make again, but I don't think that precept is valid in the case of the Honda. I did find my ride enormously satisfying—like the man who's just climbed the Eiger or made his first free-fall parachute jump!— and to be able to say to myself that I've experienced the thrill of riding one of the very greatest motorcycles in the history of road racing is something I can never lose.

But I found just being around the Honda while

Tom fiddled with and fettled it a profound and ultimately sad experience. Why so? Because I happen to believe that it represents the apogee of Grand Prix bike racing, before the misguided functionaries of the FIM slapped their artificial, restrictive constraints on the ingenuity of designers like Mr Irimajiri and his ilk. For two years later the Honda became obsolete, when the FIM imposed a maximum of two cylinders and six speeds on the 250 cc class in all ill thought-out, misguided effort to provide cheaper racing— surely a contradiction in terms. Bikes like the Honda and the Benelli V8 that was certainly built, as well as all the fours, disappeared overnight, opening the field to an uninterrupted run of success by TZ Yamahas and other relatively uninspiring two-stroke twins. My ride on the Honda six was a look into the past, but also into how the future could and should have been.

| Model | Honda 250 RC166 | |
|---|---|---|
| Engine | | Dohc 6-cylinder 4-stroke |
| Bore × stroke | | 39 × 34·5 mm |
| Capacity | | 247 cc |
| Power output | | 60 bhp at 18,000 rpm |
| Compression ratio | | Not known |
| Carburation | | 6 × 17 mm flat-slide Keihin carburettors |
| Ignition | | Kokusan low-tension magneto |
| Clutch | | 16-plate dry unit (8 fibre/8 steel) |
| Gearbox | | 7-speed Honda |
| Frame | | Open-cradle tubular using engine as stressed member |
| Suspension: | front | 35 mm Showa |
| | rear | Showa |
| Brakes: | front | 220 mm 4LS drum |
| | rear | 200 mm 2LS drum |
| Tyres: | front | 3·00 × 18 |
| | rear | 3·25 × 18 |
| Weight | | 260 lb |
| Top speed | | 153 mph |
| Year of manufacture | | 1967 |
| Owner | | Honda Canada Inc., Scarborough, Canada |

# 3 | Spanish Rotax winner—*Kobas 250*

**Carlos Cardus en route to the 1983 European 250 cc title on the Spanish-built Kobas-Rotax (Author)**

Since the Austrian tandem-twin Rotax engine first appeared in Grand Prix racing in 1980, it's fair to say that until 1983 it flattered to deceive. Touted as Europe's answer to Japanese domination of the 250 class, the engine certainly enabled many small chassis manufacturers to realise all-European bikes, but without really permitting them to get on terms with the oriental machines, nor with the factory specials such as the MBA and Pernod.

But 1983 was the year that the Rotax finally began to fulfil its promise. Three years of intensive development had eradicated initial design faults that in races resulted in either loss of performance or retirement, and thanks to the careful attention to detail that characterises Teutonic engineering, the engine was now reliable enough to win a Grand Prix. Which is exactly what it finally did in—aptly enough—Austria in May '83, in the hands of German Manfred Herweh whose Spondon-framed Real convincingly defeated the cream of international competition on the Salzburgring. Two weeks later Irishman Con Law won the gruelling Isle of Man TT on the Ehrlich EMC, whose Rotax engine took him round the 37·75 miles course at over 110 mph for the first time ever in the 250 class. And to cap a heartening season for users of the Austrian firm's engines, Spaniard Carlos Cardus was a clear and convincing winner of the European 250 Championship on his Rotax-powered Kobas.

In many ways, Cardus' success was the most

*Above* **Stripped of its bodywork, the Kobas' unusual but effective chassis design can be seen to advantage (Author)**

*Right* **Trademark Kobas rear suspension gives full rising rate and offers compact installation, at the expense of raising the centre of gravity (Author)**

praiseworthy of all, for though sponsored by Barcelona dealer and enthusiast Jacinto Moriana (also known as 'J.J.', and a successful endurance racer in his own right), Carlos did not have the luxury of two identical bikes nor anything like the same sort of budget as his well-heeled German rivals. Yet in spite of the vast distances which the FIM's curious calendar required him to travel, as far afield as Imatra in Finland and Brno in Czechoslovakia, Cardus dazzled onlookers with a year-long display of fast and aggressive riding which literally meant that when he stayed on the bike, he won. Victories at his home round in Jarama, then at Salzburg, Paul Ricard, and Brno gave him an unassailable lead in the series, which he clinched one round from the end by a steady 6th place at Assen after all but writing both himself and the bike off when he fell in practice.

Having already tested Dr Joe Ehrlich's EMC-Rotax, I was particularly glad to have the opportunity to try out Cardus's JJ Kobas-Rotax especially since from the first time I saw the distinctive U-framed Spanish bike in the Dutch GP paddock in 1982 I've been impressed by its design and performance: So it was with some degree of pleasurable anticipation that I awaited Carlos and the team's faithful mechanic Gines Guirado on a beautiful crisp and sunny January morning at Jarama, with the nearby peaks of the Sierra Guadarrama capped with freshly-fallen snow providing a picturesque backdrop for a test of the bike which dominated the 1983 European Championship, and in doing so provided the Rotax engine with its first major international title.

Designer of the bike is 31-year-old Antonio Cobas: 'Why call the bike a Kobas, with a K?' I once asked him. Turns out the guy who designed the tank badge thought it looked better as Kobas rather than Cobas, so it was so: honest! After working for a racing car manufacturer while still at engineering college, and after, Cobas eventually returned to his first love of motorcycles, first as a technical writer for one of Spain's motorcycle magazines, then as a designer and constructor in his own right. His first commercial design was the spaceframe Siroko, of which no less than 54 were made mostly for 250 cc racing and fitted with either Yamaha or Rotax engines. After leaving Siroko he freelanced for a while, designing the unique and successful Tecfar-Ducati with which Carlos Cardus first made his name by defeating the might of the Japanese multis in the Spanish F1 championship in 1982, then built the short run of Kobas GP bikes totalling eight in all (seven with Rotax engines, one with a Yamaha) with one of which Sito Pons entered the GP scene in 1982. Debuting at the French GP at Nogaro that year, the Kobas almost had a fairytale start when Pons lay 2nd at half-distance before crashing out of contention; he did exactly the same in his home GP a week later, again while in 2nd place. So it was not till Cobas was united with Carlos Cardus under the JJ banner that the bike really began to shine, and European and Spanish title crowns in 1983 were the just reward.

One look at the Kobas, and you know it's something out of the ordinary, with its bluff-fronted fairing, semi-monocoque alloy U-frame and far forward riding position, almost like one of the current F1 racing cars. But in a way even more remarkable was the reliability record of the team's Rotax engines during the 1983 season: they covered a total of 12,800 km in testing, practice and races without a single mechanical breakdown, in spite of being taken to 13,500 rpm as a matter of course when Rotax themselves advise a 13,000 red line. Surely, I asked Antonio Cobas when I went to see him in Barcelona a couple of days after the test, they must have made some pretty major internal engine modifications, even perhaps as drastic as Dr Joe Ehrlich had made to the EMC, in order to achieve this remarkable record? 'Not a bit of it,' was Antonio's reply. 'The engines are basically completely standard Rotax units: it takes us only two days' work

*Left* **The extreme forward weight bias can be seen to advantage here, as the author cranks round one of Jarama's several tight left-handers on the JJ-sponsored Kobas 250 (Herrero)**

*Right, above and below* **The Kobas U-frame design proved a landmark in GP motorcycle chassis design: the following season both Yamaha and Gallina-Suzuki produced very similar machines for the 500 class (Author)**

to modify them to our specification, which mostly centres around our own design of combustion chamber, and cleaning everything up. Since they modified the standard primary gears, the only weak point is the clutch, and you must just be careful using it. The secret of our reliability, if there is one, lies in taking meticulous care of the engines, replacing components well before their life is ended and building the engines up very carefully.' But hang on—when I rode the bike I was amazed at the tractability and smooth, wide power band, especially compared to the all-or-nothing characteristics of the EMC, which lit up like a rocket ship at 10,000 rpm and petered out at 13,000. On the Kobas, there was usable power from as low down as 8000 rpm, with good, strong pulling horsepower from 9000 up, with the engine seemingly happy to go on churning it out up to the 13,500 redline—there was no falling off in torque or any increase in vibration above the factory's 13,000 limit, and in fact the Kobas-modified engine even wanted to run on above the team's own redline. A 4500 rpm powerband for a modern, disc-valve 250 is incredible, and

a lot better than the standard Rotax unit: how did they do it? Antonio smiled: 'It's basically all in the exhaust pipes,' he replied. 'The suppleness comes from that, which considering we only have occasional access to a testbed is something I'm quite proud of. I'm glad you liked it!'

If I've seemed to concentrate rather unexpectedly on the bike's engine performance, when after all it's the unusual chassis design which aroused most attention, it's simply because a lot of other Rotax users could take a lesson from the JJ team's approach to engine development and maintenance. But there's no getting away from the fact that the Kobas chassis is the real show-stopper: termed a 'semi-monocoque' by the GP cognoscenti, because although the large U-shaped alloy structure weighing only 3·5 kg which took ten days to make appears to be a modern version of the Ossa or John Player Norton monocoque chassis, in fact the fuel is carried not within the frame structure but in a separate tank perched on top. Why didn't he design a monocoque, given that it couldn't have been much more time-consuming or costly to

ible. The U-frame was the result—once you add the three bracing holes on each side it becomes incredibly stiff, and the layout also permitted me to concentrate as much of the bike's mass as possible close to the centre of gravity, to reduce the polar moment of inertia and make for more stable handling. That's one reason for my rear suspension design—it offers a true rising rate and variable flexibility, while getting the suspension unit close in to the centre of the bike.'

Yes, but the weight distribution is another matter: when most other designers are striving to achieve 50/50 weight distribution, Cobas has gone out on a limb to make a bike that obviously concentrates a larger proportion of the sprung weight on the front wheel: how much, and why? 'I don't believe that 50/50 weight distribution is ideal: that varies from bike to bike, depending on the tyres you can use and the suspension geometry, but on the Kobas it's 51/49 frontwards without the rider, and with someone of Cardus' weight aboard it's 55/45.' In other words the riding position is calculated in such a way as to throw the rider's weight on to the bars even more than on other bikes? 'Correct, because in my opinion the single most important thing about a bike's handling is how it enters a corner: that determines everything else—cornering speed, acceleration, even top end performance. In turn that means that it's vital to keep the front wheel glued to the ground and permit as high an entry speed as possible, so by opting for a forward weight bias I'm forcing the front wheel on to the track and discouraging it from breaking away, under braking or acceleration. And being able to fit a 16 in. front wheel—we were one of the first teams to do so—gives us a wider contact patch as well as lighter steering. The 1984 bike I'm designing right now will have a 55/45 weight bias without the rider—I expect about 57/43 with Carlos sitting on it.'

That new bike would also be a spaceframe, like the Siroko, because though light and rigid the Kobas chassis and its fittings were also easily

build, I asked Antonio, and what were his aims in the design in the first place?

'Monocoques are all very well,' he replied, 'but if you want them to hold fuel then they become not only bulky, but wide—look at the 500 GP Kawasaki for example. Fitting an engine as inherently slim as the Rotax into a chassis like that would have meant throwing away some of its main advantages in terms of making the bike wider than it need be, but that wasn't the real reason I didn't build one. A wide structure is also a flimsy one, and I was concerned to build a chassis that was as stiff and rigid as I could possibly get, while at the same time being as light as poss-

damaged in an accident (as Cardus' efforts at destruction testing showed during the 1983 season!) and weren't really robust enough for GP use. It also was difficult and expensive to make for sale as a production chassis, a point which the commercially-minded JJ was keen to rectify! Interestingly, Gines had brought along the team's backup bike to Jarama, an 1981 Siroko-Rotax which enabled a firsthand comparison to be made of the evolutionary aspect of Cobas' design philosophy, but sadly it holed a piston while Cardus was warming it up, so I never got the chance to ride it.

Instead, I spent 20 laps aboard the European title-winning Kobas, trying out Antonio Cobas' radical engineering ideas for myself, and it would be fair to say that after watching the Kobas from the sidelines for the past couple of years, when the time came finally to try it out, I was not disappointed. It did feel very strange getting on to it for the first time: you sit on rather than in the bike, with your hands seemingly somewhere down around your boots, so accentuatedly far forward is the riding position. Both rider and designer admit that the Kobas is tiring to ride, especially on the shoulders and arms, until you either get used to it, or get fit, or both! Pushing off, I found to my surprise that it started very easily—with both pistons rising and falling together, starting a Rotax-engined bike is something of an acquired art. I spent the first couple of laps trying to find a comfortable compromise in terms of squeezing my 6 ft frame into the space normally occupied by the 5 ft 3 in. Cardus, but having once done so I noticed how slim the Kobas is—only 15 in. wide, in spite of the side-mounted 36 mm magnesium Dell'Orto carbs which had been ported to around 37·5 mm and were partially at any rate responsible for the top end power: Cobas quoted 72 bhp at 13,200 rpm for the best engine they'd put on a brake, which is adequate but not exceptional for the 250 class nowadays. Engine accessibility is outstanding: it can be removed from the chassis in ten minutes.

Making best use of that power is therefore the primary objective, and after a couple of faster laps I discovered what the Kobas is all about. I'm no Cardus, but thanks to the outstanding Brembo discs I found myself braking ever deeper into the corner at the end of the main straight at Jarama, till by the end of my stint I was shutting off from around 220 kph at the 160–170 metre mark, zipping down through the gearbox from sixth to third, notching second just as I heeled over into the first part of this double right-hander, still braking but not so hard. A chat with Carlos after confirmed what I'd found out for myself: the art of riding the Kobas fast requires that you brake hard while in a straight line, then peel off into the corner still braking but gradually easing up on the lever, so that in effect you're completing your residual braking actually on the entry to the corner. Even though standard Yamaha TZ forks are fitted to the bike, without any anti-dive, this wasn't a problem at Jarama where the surface is pretty smooth, but I'm not sure that the Kobas would take kindly to this kind of treatment on a bumpy track like Nogaro, because the effect of all that forward weight transference would surely be to freeze the forks up—unless the fact that the bike is already set up with more weight on the front wheel than normal means that in fact the reverse happens.

Now of course the more weight you have on the front wheel, the less there is on the rear, which must mean that traction out of turns should be a problem: it wasn't, but riding the Kobas hard does require additional alertness on the part of the rider to prevent the back wheel breaking away under acceleration. Most 250 cc bikes have an extra margin of rear end safety which the majority of riders never get close to exploring: all that Cobas has done is to take some of that margin and transfer it to the front. I did ride the bike pretty hard in the end, and only got a trace of a rear wheel slide a couple of times. On the other hand, cresting the Rampa Pegaso under the Michelin bridge, where most bikes paw the air with their front wheels, the Kobas front end just got slightly light even accelerating as hard as I could while still leaned slightly over, and the steering damper took care of any waggles before they happened. Nice.

Really the only problems I encountered with the handling were on downhill, fast sweepers, of which there are two at Jarama. The shake I got on the right hander entering the main straight was simply caused by riding over the bumpy piece of road jutting out into the track: taking a wider line and cranking over further cured that. But on the even faster left-hander sweeping down to the Bugatti Esses, I felt the front wheel pattering when cranked hard over on the limit in fourth gear; short-shifting and taking it one gear higher didn't cure the problem. Asking Carlos about it afterwards, he confirmed he was getting the same symptoms, but not as badly as me because the bike's suspension was set up for his weight: he thought it was a problem with the front suspension, rather than the tyre. But coming out of the Bugatti, exiting sharply uphill, the Kobas would get a lovely early drive on with the back wheel just starting to spin under hard acceleration—very controllable and actually quite satisfying!

Compared with other Rotax-engined bikes I've ridden, the Kobas' engine was a revelation—smooth, supple and easy to ride with that delightful flat, off-beat exhaust note that characterises the 360 degrees tandem-twin. Perfectly geared at the top end for Jarama, my only desire would have been for a slightly higher bottom gear: a low Calafat first gear was fitted, which meant screaming the engine through the tight Le Mans complex when using less revs would have made taking the corners more comfortable and ultimately faster. The Rotax 6-speed gearbox has a choice of alternative ratios for first, second and top gears.

I can pay Antonio Cobas no higher compliment than to say that if I had personally decided to go 250 racing in 1984, I'd have chosen one of his U-frame bikes fitted with his version of the Rotax engine: I'd also probably have wanted him and Gines to look after it for me! The bike was streets easier to ride than the EMC, and though by the end of my 20 laps my shoulders were aching from the pressure of the forward weight distribution, I didn't at all notice it on the bike while I was riding it, and probably wouldn't once I got fit enough for GP racing: my excuse is that January is off-season for road racers! But the combination of that late-breaking, easy-steering, light, slim chassis and the torquey, smooth engine helps explain how Carlos Cardus brought Spain her first European Championship in 1983 on the bike I rode at Jarama: if he'd only restrained his natural exuberance and stayed upright more often, he'd probably have won even more races than he did!

| Model | | Kobas 250 |
|---|---|---|
| Engine | | Twin-cylinder disc-valve 2-stroke |
| Bore × stroke | | 54 × 54 mm |
| Capacity | | 247 cc |
| Power output | | 72 bhp at 13,200 rpm |
| Compression ratio | | Not known |
| Carburation | | 2 × 37·5 mm Dell'Orto |
| Ignition | | Motoplat |
| Clutch | | 14-plate air-cooled dry |
| Gearbox | | 6-speed |
| Frame | | U-frame alloy construction, semi-monocoque |
| Suspension: | front | 35 mm Yamaha |
| | rear | Monoshock swing arm with De Carbon unit |
| Brakes: | front | 2 × 240 mm Brembo floating discs |
| | rear | 1 × 220 mm Brembo fixed disc |
| Tyres: | front | 12/16 × 16 |
| | rear | 14/68 × 18 |
| Weight | | 213 lb with oil/water, no fuel |
| Top speed | | 152 mph |
| Year of manufacture | | 1982/83 |
| Owner | | Jacinto Moriana, Barcelona, Spain |

# 4 Formula 750

**Terrible twins—**
*John Player Norton*

Some moments you just never forget. About the most vivid road racing memory I have from my days as a spectator, before I screwed up enough courage to do the unthinkable and start racing myself, is of the 1974 Race of the Year at Mallory. The advent of the TZ700 Yamaha had sounded the death-knell of the four-strokes in F750, and Peter Williams' terrible accident at Oulton Park a couple of weeks before had knocked the stuffing out of the John Player Norton team, leaving the man who for many was the greatest combination of rider and development engineer ever to cock a leg over a bike with severe injuries that resulted in his losing the use of his left arm.

It seemed pretty hopeless for the banger brigade, then, though Phil Read was there on the 500 MV which was still highly competitive. We were watching from the mudbank at the entrance to Gerards, and as the flag fell a cloud of 'stroker smoke' arose as front wheels of 120 bhp triples and fours pawed the air. Through the murk—it was a pretty miserable day with a slightly greasy track—the expected leaders jostled their way into Gerards: Sheene and Smart on the Suzukis, Kenny Roberts on the Yamaha, and Grant's Kawasaki—Japanese two-stroke multis all. Suddenly, there was a much deeper rumbling exhaust note in evidence—and a flash of white leathers and candy-striped white machine: it was the inimitable Dave Croxford on the air-cooled JPN twin, giving away over 40 bhp to his rivals and now the main hope of the Andover-based equipe afer Williams' accident, determined as ever to wave the four-stroke flag and the Union Jack together.

Crox always rode with an open-face helmet, and even in the gloom you could see the gritted teeth set in determination, his mind intent on reaping the utmost advantage on this long, long corner where the JPN's undoubted handling superiority could pay off. Rushing past gaggles of slower riders on the approach, he lined himself up about 2 in. from the left-hand grass verge, cranked the bike over to an impossible angle, and opened the throttle wide. It was unforgettable. From about 8th into the corner, he started to pass one rider after another on the outside: you could actually see the rear wheel stepping out of line as it scrabbled for the limits of adhesion, but still Crox kept the power screwed hard on. Suddenly the crowd all around us became aware we were watching something we'd never forget: someone took up the chant—and next thing we were all shouting out in unison as the JPN swooped past first one rider, then another: 'Fourth ... third ... second', we shouted in ecstasy—then 'FIRST!' as Dave streaked past a no doubt astonished Barry Sheene on his Suzuki triple to lead the pack down the back straight past the lake. Flat on the tank, rider and machine merged into one white streak, but inexorably the

pack of strokers rushed past again, with Ago on the 700 Yamaha—no doubt wishing he had a combination of his own machine's power and the Norton's handling at his disposal, hitting the front at the end of the first lap.

Croxford finished a superb 5th in that Race of the Year, and had we but known it, we were watching the swansong of the John Player Norton team, which had given British racing fans so much to shout about for the previous three years. At the end of that season, the cigarette company withdrew their support, and the Andover team laboured abortively on the Cosworth-engined Challenge before being dragged under by the financial demise of the parent NVT company. It was a sad ending to the tale of the team whose efforts had deserved so much more—and had successfully taken on the might of the Japanese factories with an obsolescent air-cooled twin-cylinder four-stroke that was however clothed in a series of frames that made maximum use of available technology, within the rigours of a tight financial budget.

*Below left* **Peter Williams hard at work at Mallory Park in the Post-TT International in June 1974, on the spaceframe JPN featured in this test** (Nicholls)

*Below* **Mick Grant rounds Ramsey Hairpin in the 1973 TT, mounted on one of the low-built monocoque JPNs** (Nicholls)

If on that murky day at Mallory back in 1974 you'd have told me that one day I'd get to ride the bike on which Dave Croxford thrilled us all, I'd have said you were mad. But thanks to the generosity of the machine's present owner, Spaniard Joaquin Folch from Barcelona, I was able to do so at the 50th Anniversary meeting at Donington in 1981, when an F750 retrospective parade brought together the cream of the big bikes of the early 1970s and many of their riders for the first time since their heyday. And when as an added bonus Peter Williams was there to drop the flag on the parade, it was a wonderful opportunity to talk to him about the bikes he had so much of a hand in creating, and which carried him to TT and short circuit victories galore. The John Player Norton story harks back to 1971, when Williams, who scored some good wins and places on race-prepared production Commando machines in 1970/71, successfully persuaded the Norton board—headed by ex-GP car racer Dennis Poore—that it would be a worthwhile project to go racing with the existing long-stroke power unit in the new Formula 750 class as a means of stimulating customer interest in the range of Norton big twin road bikes. A new shorter stroke engine was on the way, but not expected before the end of 1972 at the earliest. Perhaps surprisingly, the decision was made to go ahead, and the Norton-Villiers performance shop at Thruxton circuit was given over entirely to the manufacture and development of the new machines, Phil Read and Tony Rutter recruited to join Peter Williams as riders, and ex-Suzuki and AMC works rider Frank Perris signed up as team manager on his retirement from racing. As the final ingredient in what was to prove a fascinating cocktail of talents, Dennis Poore was able to use some of his contacts in the car racing world to attract motor sport's leading sponsors, the Imperial Tobacco Company, to support the team under their John Player brand name, in what was the first example anywhere in the world of a two-wheel team fully supported by an outside sponsor. The framework had been laid.

At the team's launch in November 1971 John Player laid down a tough deadline for the new equipe to beat: two machines were to compete in the Daytona 200 in just three months' time. This power circuit presented a daunting challenge to a team relying on the limited power of a 360 degrees twin-cylinder four-stroke engine whose origins lay in the 1948 Bert Hopwood-designed Dominator motor which had formed the backbone of Norton's production for over 25 years. (By a stroke of irony, Hopwood was now engineering chief at the rival BSA/Triumph factory, whose three-cylinder machines had become the principal rivals of the fledgling Norton team.) Fortunately, though, Peter Williams had access to the MIRA wind-tunnel, which enabled him to demonstrate that with a specially-designed fairing and frame alterations which permitted him to achieve the lowest possible wind resistance, it would be possible to attain a top speed of over 150 mph—'a purely nominal figure,' says Peter, 'but it gave us something to aim for'—with the slightly modified Combat engine. Would reality prove his calculations correct?

When the first JPN machines were uncrated in the garage area at Daytona in March 1972, the assembled onlookers saw for the first time the future hallmarks of the Williams-designed Norton twins, for as well as being a team rider and the development engineer, Peter was also the designer of the cycle parts. Decked out in royal blue livery with white stripes, the bikes looked smaller than many 500s—yet they were full 750 machines, incorporating the lessons learnt in the wind-tunnel.

'We realised we would have our hands full with the Suzuki triples,' recalls Peter Williams, 'since though they had appalling handling (hence their nickname of "the Flexi-flyers") they did produce around 117 bhp and so were very fast on the banking. We could outhandle them—but with only 69 bhp at 7000 rpm, only 14 bhp more than the standard Commando engine—we had

**1974 spaceframe design improved engine accessibility, but only at the expense of increasing frontal area (Author)**

to have a means of increasing our top speed. The other problem was that we had to carry 24 litres of fuel to be able to get away with less fuel stops than the Suzukis and other much thirstier machines—but how to do this without jacking up the centre of gravity and increasing the frontal aspect, as well as having tanks so big that the rider would be unable to tuck himself away behind the fairing?'

How they did it was to fit pannier fuel tanks that partially enveloped the engine, carefully shaped to allow the rider to get down low, and completely filling the otherwise 'dead' space between the fairing and engine. The oil tank was carried under the seat. The conventional tubular chassis, like the tanks, were built at Andover, and though the geometry was not perfect, so that the machines tended to be front-heavy, correspondingly allowing the rear wheel to step out if the power was applied too hard or too soon exiting a corner, the frames did permit the

desired low frontal area to be achieved. Williams' claims were completely vindicated when both he and Read topped the 150 mph mark in qualifying—155·17 mph in Phil's case, and a highly satisfying race debut saw Phil Read finish in 4th place overall after briefly leading at one stage during fuel stops. Particularly satisfying was the fact that this was the first 'real' F750 bike home, behind three 350 Yamahas, and ahead of all the Suzukis, BSA/Triumph triples and the like. As a successful advert in the important American market, it could scarcely have been bettered.

Back home though, the rest of the season proved less satisfactory, as endless gearbox problems manifested themselves (the same difficulty had caused Williams' retirement at Daytona): Peter was lying 2nd in the F750 TT when forced to retire for this reason. But development continued apace on other fronts, and in shorter races where the gearbox problem was not so acute, some good wins came in the second half of the season: Williams won at the 'Hutch', then new team member Mick Grant led a JPN procession to victory on Scarborough's 'mini TT' course, while Read wrapped up the year in fine style with a win at the end-of-season Race of the South at Brands. For a debut year, it had proved reasonably satisfactory in terms of results, and much useful development work had been carried out.

The 1972 JPN frame had in fact been designed by Peter Williams a couple of years before after his experiences with the PR Commandos. Retaining the large-diameter backbone tube of the road bike, as well as its Isolastic engine mounting and swinging arm location on engine plates behind the gearbox, it was greatly reduced in scale for the aforestated reasons of frontal area. Though a mid-season change from a siamezed exhaust to twin pipes caused ground clearance problems which necessitated a switch from 18 in. to 19 in. rims, the bike was still very low—and quite light, at around 345 lb. Norvil front discs (a single one for Williams, twin units for everyone else) proved a modern comparison to the bikes' rear wheels, which contained a link with Norton's glorious racing past—they were Manx Norton units!

From the humble 69 bhp at Daytona, the team progressed through the season to the point that they were able to extract 76 bhp at 7500 rpm from the $73 \times 89$ mm, 745 cc engine. The GP Amals originally used were soon scrapped in favour of Concentrics, and further experimentation with camshaft profiles, port shapes, valve sizes and induction lengths produced the extra horses. But all this additional power only exacerbated the bike's principal weakness—the gearbox.

'Though we learnt a lot that first year,' says Peter Williams, 'it was all really rather problematical, and the results weren't as good as we'd have liked. The gearbox was the main bone of contention: partly it was because of the extra power, and partly also that the Norton primary transmission with triplex chain had never been asked to cope with the speeds involved in 150 mph racing. The chain pull exerted a large leverage on the mainshaft, which bent it, and as per witness marks on the broken gears the teeth were peeled off due to too much unit load being imposed on them as a result of their being out of line with the mating gear on the layshaft. This effect was especially noticeable on the constant mesh pair, and on the first and second gear pairs, which were closest to the main bearings of the shafts. I hasten to say that this was no reflection on Rod Quaife, who built the 5-speed clusters, and tried manfully to help us solve the problem: it was simply an inherent fault of the Norton primary drive.'

During the winter of 1972/73, much hard work was put in at the Thruxton race shop to produce completely new machines for the 1973 season. With a new short stroke ($77 \times 80$ mm) 749 cc production Commando engine with beefier crankcases at their disposal, the team put in a lot of work in redesigning the primary drive to produce a chaincase containing a third bearing, to eliminate the problem of shaft deflection. By using dished sprockets, they were able to place the primary loads directly on to the bearing itself, rather than the shaft. Peter Williams also speeded up the gearbox, so that less torque on unit loads was taken up on the gear teeth themselves, which in addition had a redesigned profile. Finally after experiments with a gearbox-located shock absorber the previous season, this was relocated on to the crankshaft, and together all these modifications worked so well that Williams claims they never had another gearbox failure from then on. A dry clutch was incorporated into the redesigned primary, resulting in narrower, stiffer cases.

But the most dramatic feature of the 1973 bike was the use of a monocoque chassis, of double-skinned mild steel construction which weighed in at 37 lb. This might at first sight seem heavy, but when you realise that the fuel and oil tanks were incorporated into the structure, as well as such fitments as the fairing brackets and so on, its use becomes more rational, especially since by doing so Williams was able to carry the same amount of fuel as on the 1972 bike, but reduce the frontal aspect and centre of gravity still further. A thinner, lighter version in stainless steel came later.

The incredibly low build on the monocoque John Player Norton bears comparison with mid-1950s Guzzis of Giulio Carcano, and Peter Williams is proud to admit that he knelt at the same altar of reduced frontal area and decreased drag as a means of obviating the disadvantages of a modest power output. 'We were able to reduce the drag coefficient to 0·39 Cx at the MIRA wind tunnel,' he says, 'and one of the things we found to be most important in attaining this was to smooth the airflow over the rider's back when lying prone on the tank. I designed a fairing with fully-enclosed handlebars and a screen that was just the correct height in relation to the rider's shoulders when flat on the tank, so that the airflow ran over the screen and down along his back—our leathers contained no lettering on the back which might disturb this. The seat design—or rear fairing, if you like—was just as important too, to smoothe the airflow. I was very proud of that drag figure, and to be honest, I still am!' The overall height of the new bike was $2\frac{1}{2}$ in. less than the 1972 machine, thanks partly to the use of 18 in. five-spoke cast magnesium alloy wheels, whose use was already familiar to Peter Williams' race fans thanks to his exploits on the 'wheelbarrow' Arter Matchless—a fascinating parallel story in itself. Windscreen height was a whopping 5 in. lower on the new bike.

Engine modifications included not only the dimensions and gearbox changes described above, but also a larger inlet valve with modified valve angles, a new camshaft, and steel pushrods for better valve gear control. This seems to fly in the face of accepted wisdom which dictates making the valve gear as light as possible, but the team found that alloy has a much lower Young's modulus—the coefficient of resistance to compression—than steel. This meant that the alloy pushrods compressed about twice as much as the steel ones, building an undesirable degree

of springiness into the valve gear. Similarly, the new Williams-designed camshaft was actually made in cast iron rather than steel: this produced a quite noticeable power increase over the previous steel version, since the more rigid component ran truly concentric with the bearings and was less susceptible to wear: 2 bhp increase to 78 bhp at 7400 rpm wasn't to be sneezed at (PW: 'I never *ever* revved my engines above 7400, and then only if I really had a fight on my hands. It was said that they were safe to 8000, but I *always* changed up at 7000 rpm—and didn't do too badly!').

The 1973 monocoque-chassised JPN brought the team and John Player the success they'd been waiting for. After a very disappointing Daytona debut, which showed that development work was far from complete, the new white-liveried machines with the famous red and blue stripes carried very nearly all before them that year. Williams won three of the six races in the Easter Transatlantic Match Races, ending up highest scorer on the British side and with four fastest laps to his credit. After further success at Cadwell and Brands he went to the TT, and at last earnt the Island victory his application and dedication towards mastering the Mountain circuit merited, when he held off the challenge of Jack Findlay's works Suzuki to score a thoroughly popular win in the F750 race at the record speed at 105·47 mph, lapping at an incredible 107·27 mph to slash Ray Pickrell's lap record by 20 seconds and become the 2nd fastest man ever round the Island—all on a production-based pushrod twin! The success was captured forever in a BBC documentary and surely remains the John Player Norton team's finest hour.

Contributing to the success were new front forks, consisting of the team's own cast sliders and AJS motocross yokes and stanchions. Peter Williams: 'We did a lot of work on front damping, and discovered that with large aspect ratio springs (small diameter/longer length, so greater displacement) it's impossible to design a really effective spring: if we'd kept on with development, I'd have gone eventually to either air forks or an outside spring. Our new sliders featured a leading axle location, because in 1970 I'd learnt that the more weight one can get back to the line of the steering head, thus reducing the polar moment of inertia around the steering head itself, the easier and more positive the steering will be.

'Also in 1972/73 we had moved the engine back in the frame by an inch relative to the wheel centres, as for 1971 we'd placed the motor much further forward than on the production Commandos to prevent the front wheel lifting on accleration thanks to the much more powerful engine. But that year I noticed especially at Silverstone that if you really leant it into a corner the back end would break away very easily, then once you'd got it lined up with the power on for the exit, the front wheel would come up anyway. So for the first JPNs in 1972 I moved the engine $1\frac{1}{2}$ in. back to achieve 50/50 weight bias, then an extra 1 in. more for 1973. That weight distribution, together with the low centre of gravity and rigid frame achieved by the monocoque construction, made the '73 JPN *the* most superb motorcycle it has ever been my privilege to ride. People won't believe me when I say that I could go into a corner, lay it over on its side, get both the rear *and* front wheels sliding, then put the power on and keep it in a two-wheel, controlled drift round any corner faster than Druids at Brands. It was a really wonderful *little* machine—smaller than almost any 500 cc machine, yet quite powerful enough—I bet that surprises you!—and with perfect steering and good acceleration thanks to its light weight and controllable power.'

Why then was this paragon amongst motorcycles dropped for the 1974 season, especially after coming within an ace of scooping the MCN Superbike Championship, when Williams and Barry Sheene tied for points at the end of

the season, the Suzuki rider having unfortunately scored one more victory to take the tie-breaker? The answer lies in the internal team politics, which saw the mechanics at odds with the development engineer over the admittedly poor engine accessibility of the monocoque chassis; it must have been very time-consuming and frustrating to work on, and moreover difficult if not impossible to repair in the event of a crash. The famous (and true) story exists of the team's second rider, Dave Croxford, having the shunt to end all shunts at Woodcote Corner at Silverstone in 1973. Fortunately unscathed (did Dave ever hurt himself all those times he went just a bit too far beyond the limit?), he was presented with the twisted remains of his monocoque chassis, suitably reworked into a coffee table, by the team of mechanics with the inscription 'We make 'em, you break 'em!'

Team manager Frank Perris was swayed by the arguments in favour of a spaceframe chassis, and gave permission for mechanics John McLaren and Robin Clist to evolve their chosen design: it's this bike which Joaquin Folch brought to Donington, and which Peter Williams, on seeing, exclaimed 'Oh, dear—that's the one I don't like ... apart from the fact that it very nearly succeeded in killing me, the spaceframe JPN was very short-sighted. We'd been promised the water-cooled Challenge engine for 1974 (in the event it arrived two years late), and that was specifically built by a racing car engine designer—Keith Duckwork of Cosworth—with a monocoque chassis, using the engine as a stressed member, in mind. There was no way we could adapt any lessons learnt with the spaceframe to the Challenge—it was a blind alley, and never even began to match the attributes of the monocoque bike.'

Daytona 1974 unfortunately appeared to prove Peter Williams' fears were justified: Using the same mechanical package as the previous year, lap times were slower than in 1973, and this unfortunately proved to be the case elsewhere

Oil tank is mounted at the front of the engine, with the filler cap on the left. To increase fuel capacity a secondary tank was added in the tail, which adversely affected handling on the spaceframe JPN . . . (Author)

during the season. Never mind that the opposition was finding more power and better handling—the JPN team couldn't even match their 1973 performances. A good example was their Silverstone lap times: in 1973 Williams had managed to equal Saarinen's outright lap record of 1 min. 38·1 secs on the monocoque bike, only to lose what seemed certain victory when he ran out of fuel on the last lap. In 1974 on the spaceframe machine, he was unable to beat 1 min. 41 secs—a whopping 3 secs a lap slower, while Croxford was a further 2 secs off the pace. A disastrous TT, when both riders retired on the first lap, was only partly compensated for by Williams' win on a streaming track at the Hutch in August: two weeks later he was in hospital fighting for his life, his involvement with the John Player Norton team at an end.

Williams is reluctant even today to elaborate on the internal tensions that struck the team before and during that 1974 season. Whatever, it appears obvious that he and Frank Perris were not getting along well, and the spaceframe bike

may have been a result of that simmering feud. (What poor old happy-go-lucky Dave Croxford must have made of the whole thing would make interesting listening!)

Constructed in 20-gauge Reynolds 531 tubing, the 1974 JPN scaled in at 355 lb, as opposed to the stainless steel monocoque version's 368 lb. Though the nickel-plated frame weighed a mere 16 lb, it should be remembered that the much heavier monocoque did include the tanks, fairing brackets and so forth. But the main difference was in the dimensions: though appreciably easier to work on, the new design stood a full 2 in. higher at the front, with correspondingly higher centre of gravity, not helped by the location of the main fuel tank in the conventional position on top of the engine. Located by twin rubber-mounted anchor points, it was this rather flimsy fibreglass unit which broke loose and caused Williams' accident. To make things worse, though, there was insufficient fuel capacity in the main tank for anything but short circuit races, so the decision was made to install a secondary tank in the back of the seat for longer events. This had the most undesirable effect of increasing the polar moment of inertia of the bike as a whole, exacerbated by the fact that as the tank drained the fuel would slop around as you laid the bike over into the corner: it was in effect a highly unpredictable sliding pendulum!

Though two bikes were retained for use during the 1975 season pending arrival of the Challenge design, the other two machines of the four made were sold to the Spanish Norton importer, Juan Antonio Rodes. Rodes was a Norton fanatic, who had already taken delivery of one of the 1972 pannier-tanked models. He wanted nothing so badly as to win the Spanish Road racing Championship with a Norton, and in 1975 his dream came true when Benjamin Grau scored a series of wins on the Iberian street circuits and tracks to clinch the title ahead of the works Ducatis. A second attempt in 1976 was unsuccessful, and

at the end of that year Senor Rodes' Norton business was wound up, as the parent company itself folded. His second-string rider, Maurizio Aschl, was a friend of Joaquin Folch, already a confirmed Norton addict when not racing a modern two-stroke, thanks to his ownership of a 500 Manx. Rodes offered the whole stable of three bikes and spares to Joaquin, which is how the greatest extant concentration of John Player Norton machinery happens to be in Barcelona!

When the time came to try the bike for myself, my first reaction was how incredibly small it was. Interestingly, I'd literally hopped off my XR750 Harley straight on to the JPN, the Norton seemed extremely low and little—more like a 350 even than a 500, let alone a 750: what the monocoque-chassised machine must have been like with 2 in. less height in the front is impossible to imagine. The seat is extremely comfortable, and as I leant over the tank I found myself looking literally through the windscreen, which is a shal-

*Left* **After Peter Williams' accident (caused by the then one-piece seat/tank unit coming adrift), such secondary tanks were banned by the FIM, hence none fitted to this bike as later raced in the Spanish F750 championship (Author)**

*Above right* **With modern tyres, ground clearance becomes a problem on the last of the air-cooled Norton racers. The author at full lean in a Classic F750 race at Snetterton on the bike featured in this test (Masters)**

low piece of perspex much smaller than the conventional bubble found normally on racing bikes. The fully-enclosed handlebars are quite steeply inclined, and altogether I felt I was sitting in rather than on the bike, so completely enveloped did I feel both front and rear.

Noting with approval that Joaquin had just scrubbed in a new set of the excellent KR124 treaded Dunlops, I set off down the pit lane on what was for me a more than usually evocative ride: I'll never be another Dave Croxford (could there ever be a second one?), but it would be an unimaginative soul who wouldn't have admitted to a touch of Walter Mitty-esque sentiment, as my mind harked back to that murky day at Mallory in 1974 when Crox got the whole crowd chanting for him. My impossible dream had come true.

Out on the track I woke up with a start when a pair of Triumph triples interrupted my reverie as they overtook me one each side, before barreling into the Old Hairpin two abreast: it was

*that* sort of parade. Mentally recalling that by 1974 the JPN had the legs of the Trident, I set off after them—and immediately discovered the true charm of the Norton twin-cylinder engine: it pulls from practically nothing up to 4000 rpm, when the power really comes in, fairly suddenly but not with a great bang, however: in no time at all you're up to 7000 revs, and it's time to change gear on the right-foot, rod-linkage lever. To be fair, the Spanish Norton's gearbox had just had a rebuild and wasn't quite right, so that third and fourth were hard to engage at first when changing up—no bother coming down though—and called for very careful selection to avoid buzzing the engine if they hadn't quite gone in. Once on its way in the power band, however, the bike really flew, and what was specially reassuring was the way you could keep accelerating hard while laid quite far over at the start of the straight or on the way up from the Old Hairpin, for example. It would take a Williams or Croxford to explore the outer limits of this bike's handling, and if the monocoque really was so superior, it must have been a dream machine. As it is, I can quite see now how Croxford used to sail round the outside of his two-stroke rivals with such consummate ease.

But perhaps the best feature is the steering; the same identical front end is fitted to the 1974 bike as to the monocoque, and the result is positive, light controllability that belies the bike's weight and relatively long wheelbase. This was especially the case at the chicane, where the low centre of gravity (by the standards of most other machines!) and positive steering made getting through with the minimum of fuss easy to achieve. The rear units were set a little soft for Donington's billiard table surface giving a slightly imprecise feel on the uphill climb to McLeans especially, but otherwise the JPN's handling characteristics fully lived up to advance billing.

Riding this machine provided an interesting illumination on racer testing: no matter how competent the rider, unless you're in the very top grade, it's so very difficult to quantify that last little something extra which makes the difference between an outstanding machine and a great one. This 1974 spaceframe Norton was indeed an outstanding bike for its time—and my ride on it at Donington certainly proved that. Yet to imagine how the 1973 monocoque version could have been so much better still, as exemplified by the difference in lap times from one year to the other, is almost impossible unless you're a Williams or Croxford, in which case you regard the later bike, as Peter Williams evidently does, as a failure. For me, it was a superb machine—but then my level of comparison is scales lower than his.

Let Peter Williams—rider and engineer extraordinary—have the last word: 'The John Player Norton proved that a racing motorcycle really isn't just all about horsepower. Just like the Guzzis before us, or the 350 Yamahas when faced with the 750 Suzukis and Kawasakis, we demonstrated that a 78 bhp four-stroke twin

could be competitive with two-strokes producing 120 bhp and more—simply by ensuring a clear advantage in other areas than horsepower which, if you work on them hard enough, will eventually give you an edge. That's why I admire intensely what Honda have been doing with their NR500: it's simply a latter-day, high-technology version of the JPN, backed by a great deal more money than we ever dreamt of having, and good luck to them, I say. Look at Taglioni's 600 TT2 Ducati, beating RG500 Suzukis in open competition because it adheres to the same precepts that we struggled so long to uphold at JPN. If we eventually strayed away from them, that was our fault, and we deserved to fail as a result. Meanwhile I can live with the knowledge that results proved my ideas and designs to be correct.'

| Model | | John Player Norton |
|---|---|---|
| Engine | | Ohv twin-cylinder 4-stroke |
| Bore × stroke | | 77 × 80 mm |
| Capacity | | 749 cc |
| Power output | | 78 bhp at 7400 rpm |
| Compression ratio | | 10·5 to 1 |
| Carburation | | 2 × 32 mm Amal Mark 2 |
| Ignition | | Battery and coil |
| Clutch | | Dry multi-plate |
| Gearbox | | 5-speed Quaife |
| Frame | | Multi-tubular spaceframe |
| Suspension: | front | Norton |
| | rear | Girling |
| Brakes: | front | 2 × 10 in. discs |
| | rear | 1 × 9 in. disc |
| Tyres: | front | 3·50 × 18 |
| | rear | 3·75/5·00 × 18 |
| Weight | | 355 lb |
| Top speed | | 162 mph |
| Year of manufacture | | 1974 |
| Owner | | Joaquin Folch, Barcelona, Spain |

# 2 | Three is better?— *BSA-3* of 1970

**Dave Aldana (almost certainly riding the bike featured in this test) and Jim Rice accelerate away from the Mallory Hairpin on BSA-3s in the inaugural Transatlantic Match Races in 1971 (Nicholls)**

There's not much doubt which model takes the vote amongst classic bike enthusiasts for the best-sounding British racing motorcycle ever made. The haunting yowl of a BSA or Triumph triple in full flight on an open mega is one guaranteed to set the spine tingling and the memory racing back to those days at the start of the 1970s when Britain ruled the world in the then infant Formula 750 class.

Thanks to the success of the CRMC's F750 events in Britain today, you can still hear that fabulous sound: there are anything up to a dozen replica bikes taking part regularly in such races. To all but the hardened, knowledgeable Beezumph fan these machines might as well be the real thing—one of the 16 works chassis (eight 'highboys', eight 'lowboys', evenly divided between BSA and Triumph marques originally, though there was a lot of badge engineering later on) built by Rob North for the BSA/Triumph racing teams on both sides of the Atlantic. The five bikes which became so familiar in Britain at that time in the hands of Smart, Pickrell, Cooper, Jeffries and Tait are all still in the UK, but their track appearances are confined by their anxious owners to the occasional parade or demonstration, rather than outright racing. Pity.

However, on the other side of the Atlantic in sunny Southern California, believe it or not you can still hear the sound of a genuine works triple yowling its way to success 12 years after the factory's last major US win in the Ontario 200, courtesy of John Cooper. One of the very few genuine works BSA/Triumph triples in complete form in North America, the bike is the 1970 BSA-3 which Mike Hailwood rode at Daytona in March that year, before passing it on to then rookie road racer (and with Romero, one half of 'Team Mexican'), Dave Aldana. Over a decade later the bike won the So.Cal. CRMC's 1982 championship in the hands of present owner Greg Phillippi, an ardent racing triple enthusiast who's a walking encyclopaedia of facts about the US end of the Small Heath/Meriden factories' racing effort.

Greg found the BSA in 1980 after he'd heard about 'a weird guy out in the desert with an old three-cylinder Triumph racer sitting on his back porch'. Following the trail to its conclusion entailed a trip more in hope than certainty to a remote house out in the Mojave Desert: the man in question didn't have a phone. Once there, Greg found to his amazement that the tale was true: the man had bought the bike from a dealer in Van Nuys (a suburb of LA), tried to run it on the road once with lights fitted but got up to about 60 mph in second gear before hitting a cat which turfed him off! From then on the Triumph sat outside his back window, uncovered

and exposed to the elements so he could admire it without having to get up and take a cover off. Yup, that's California for you!

Already the owner of a road-going Trident, Greg managed to buy the racer, which was by now in a truly desolate state: apparently it took him two months and several layers of finger skin alone to remove the deep pitting from the total of 32 hand-made alloy parts, for example. But while carrying out a cosmetic restoration, he tracked down the Van Nuys dealer who'd sold the bike back in 1973, and in doing so discovered he was the owner of a very special motorcycle. That dealer was Jack Hateley, well known to Triumph fan Stateside as one of the most faithful exponents of the marque in dirt track and road racing competition alike, latterly with his son John riding. Hateley confirmed that he'd been given the bike by Triumph's American importers for John to race in the 1973 season, but that when he'd got it, it was decked out in BSA colours, having been raced for the previous one-and-a-half seasons by Dave Aldana as part of the BSA factory team. A later acquaintance with former chief mechanic, later BSA racing manager Danny Macias confirmed this to be the case:

The ex-Aldana BSA-3—back in the California desert again after being rescued from there by Greg Phillippi
(Dewhurst)

Macias was even able to point to places on the frame where the tubing had been hand-relieved to make the fuel tanks fit better. Even more to the point, Macias revealed that before passing to Aldana for his first race on the bike at Kent, Washington in 1970, it had been the machine which Mike Hailwood had ridden at Daytona in March that year, retiring after ten laps with over-heating problems which led to a burnt valve, after qualifying second on the grid. After that, it passed to Aldana who in May that year, in only his fourth-ever road race, defeated the might of the Suzuki, Kawasaki and Harley teams to win the Talladega 200 at the Alabama speedway, averaging no less than 104·59 mph to do so (making it the fastest 200-miler ever run in America at that time) and hitting the traps at 152·02 mph in doing so on the shallow banked oval.

Macias recognized the bike by its engine number stamped on the frame headstock: apparently the US customs wouldn't allow the normally unnumbered North-framed bikes into the country unless they were so adorned. So the engine in the bike is the one actually used in it then by Hailwood and Aldana, a fact confirmed by the letters MK stamped on various engine components which Macias revealed were the initials of Mack Kambayoshi, the BSA mechanic who looked after Hailwood's bike in 1970 at Daytona (and later became Dick Mann's tuner).

Aware that he now had a truly historic racing bike, Phillippi completed the restoration in BSA colours and with Aldana's AMA racing number '3' adorning the fairing entered it in a couple of bike shows. Then the racing bug struck. 'They'd started classic racing in California along the lines of the CRMC in England—one of your members called Peter Spencer-Hayes came out here to live and started things up. I'd always fantasized about going racing myself without ever plucking up the courage, but then after one of the shows I looked at the BSA and it looked right back at me and said "I don't belong in a beauty show: take me to the track!" So I did.'

To good effect, for after finishing 3rd on his first outing with the bike in the fall of 1981, Greg dominated the SoCal Classic Championship in 1982, in spite of blowing up the engine fairly disastrously when a main bearing went and broke the conrod. However he was able to repair the cases by welding them, and though his job as a dental photographer restricted his outings on

The distinctive 'letterbox' fairing improved top speed and resolved overheating problems when fitted for the 1972 season (Dewhurst)

*Left* 3-into-1 pipe gives one of the greatest-sounding exhaust notes in the history of road racing (Dewhurst)

*Below left* Primary drive is by triplex chain, with diaphragm clutch (Dewhurst)

*Below* Boyer ignition resolved many electrical problems on the ex-Aldana bike. Gearbox shell houses a 5-speed Quaife cluster (Dewhurst)

the bike in 1983, it was still the one to beat when he did bring it out for the odd classic event. It was also highly competitive against modern machinery in club racing at Riverside and Willow Springs. It was at the later track, located out in the baking hot Mojave Desert not far from where Greg found the bike, that I was able to achieve one of my personal ambitions and ride a factory triple for the first time.

To be truthful, riding Greg's bike conveyed a strong sense of *deja vu*, for the simple reason that I once raced an American-built BSA-3 myself in the UK between 1977 and 1980, when I sold it to Chris Allan: ex short circuit star Ron Chandler later rode it in CRMC parades. But my bike was a bitsa, built out of factory spares fitted to a US-made J&R aftermarket copy of the Rob North frame which was however gas-welded rather than brazed and had other detail alterations to North's original design which enable one to spot the replicas as opposed to the genuine works bikes quite easily. Though my old bike had quite a decent history (8th at Daytona in 1972 in the hands of Mike Ninci) it was a long way from being a factory machine, but at the same time once you've raced a Rob North-type triple, you never forget what great bikes they are to ride.

Remarkably, the engine in Greg's BSA was in excellent condition internally when he got it, and after cleaning up the electrics, changing the oil and plugs and hooking up a battery, it fired up first time after seven years' inactivity. A complete tear-down and rebuild for the 1982 season after his first two races revealed that the bike has all the Right Stuff inside, including hand-relieved gears drilled for lightness everywhere, including on the camshafts, oil pump and so forth. The crank had been beadblasted except on the journals, and as an additional safety check Greg had the rods Magnafluxed and X-rayed, as well as the pistons. Amazingly, the same triplex primary chain is still used that the bike was fitted with when he got it: constant checks reveal no stretching. The single-plate clutch has heavier

springs from standard, and a set of three 30 mm Mark 1 Amals are fitted, with the usual BSA/Triumph trick of a mechanical linkage controlled by a single throttle cable. The carbs carry the spun alloy velocity stacks designed by Jack Shemans which were apparently good for a couple more bhp. Gearbox is a 5-speed Quaife, as on most racing triples.

Greg acknowledges a debt of assistance to Jack Wilson of Big D Cycle in Dallas, still the foremost Triumph racing man Stateside, and it was Wilson who suggested fitting Lucas Rita ignition after Phillippi had experienced considerable problems with the points: sound familiar, triple racers? 'Switching to electronic ignition was the best thing I did,' says Greg. 'It gave me at least five more bhp and five times the reliability. We also saved weight by throwing out the battery, so the bike now weighs 380 lb dry—around 400 with oil and fuel.' Ignition advance is employed at 38 degrees, running on 115 octane racing fuel and using 12 to 1 compression.

After tracking down practically every member of the BSA/Triumph pit crew from the early 1970s, Greg was able to obtain from one of them a reprint of the test figures obtained from the team's dyno at the end of the 1971 season: these showed Mann's bike to be the most powerful, producing 71·4 bhp at 7800 rpm, measured at the rear wheel, against 69 bhp for the Aladana machine. Greg usually revs the bike nowadays to 8500 rpm, but on one occasion screamed it to 10,000 rpm for about 15 secs on the last lap of a race at Riverside to hold off a 1000 cc Kawasaki. No, the engine didn't blow up till three meetings later! Power comes in at around 4200 rpm with the works cams fitted to the bike.

The 'highboy' frame (so called because it had a higher headstock than the post-1970 'lowboys') was originally fitted with the early-type fairing without the distinctive 'letter-box' slot for the oil cooler. The latter was only fitted after the 1970 Daytona debacle, when all the bikes overheated; thereafter they were models of reliability and

In spite of a high-speed misfire, the Phillippi BSA ran well enough to show the advantages of non-period slick tyres as fitted to the bike (Dewhurst)

Mann's machine was reputed to have gone four races without having the head lifted. Aldana's ex-Hailwood machine was converted to a letter-box fairing for 1971, while retaining the earlier frame—hence the relieving of the frame tubes by Macias' merry men. Greg was fortunately able to acquire an extensive stock of fibreglass parts, which is just as well because three weeks before my ride he fell off the bike in a Willow Springs race and had to replace one side of the three-part fairing, as well as the screen. This is of the wrong type and too low to tuck under, as I found when after an exploratory couple of laps, during which the boom of the triple's exhaust echoing out over the empty desert seemed positively surreal, Greg came in to hand over to me. Sitting on the bike I immediately recalled how high-set the footrests are on a Rob North triple: they were definitely made for the Aldana-type stature rather than a Hailwood or Cathcart. The 56 in. wheelbase is compact for an early 1970s 750, and till you get used to the riding position there's a very real possibility of cramp in the legs. The big tank nestles nicely into your chest, and on a banked circuit like Daytona or Talladega the streamlined rear of the seat enabled the shorter riders to blend right into the line of the bike in

the interests of wind-cheating. In fact, the AMA did make the factory cut the seat down by a couple of inches because they claimed it was against the rules (translation: Harley thought the Beezumphs were too quick!).

The clutch action is really stiff, and so is the throttle—personally I could never race the bike myself the way it's set up and would certainly fit a softer return spring. There was also a great deal of vibration—more than I ever remember experiencing with my BSA-3 in the old days—and I'd have to question whether the engine's balance factor is correct: Greg had to install a new crankshaft after the blow-up and that might be the culprit. Again, too much vibration to make riding the bike hard for any length of time feasible for me. Half way round that first lap the question became academic anyway, as Joe Lucas, who ain't known as the Prince of Darkness for nothing, struck again and the bike spluttered to a halt out on the circuit. A connector had worked loose in the wiring above the engine and fried itself on the rocker boxes. Fortunately Greg was able to hitch a ride out to fix it, and eventually off we went again. Not really Joe's fault.

This time the BSA ran OK low down, but emitted a curious high-speed misfire that never quite disappeared completely in spite of various efforts to cure it. Still, it went well enough to give me an impression of the performance of a racing works triple, in spite of there being no revcounter fitted: the replacement Krober obtained after Greg's crash had been found to be broken on delivery. The power does come in with a rush at about 4000 rpm (by ear), and you better be pointing in the right direction when it does. However, the fact that Greg had fitted slicks to the bike (curiously, treaded racing tyres are very hard to obtain in California) removed most of the worries about having the back end step out when the throttle was cracked open laid over. 'Riding with slicks opened a whole new world to me,' says Greg. 'I found I could lean over ten degrees more at least, as well as get a much earlier drive from the corners.' True, but even though the North frame evidently has sufficient inbuilt strength to withstand the forces generated by such sticky tyres, I still prefer our British 'no slicks' rule as being more appropriate given the era of the bikes. Still, you know how the song goes: 'It Never Rains in Southern California'!

Braking is one of the BSA's fortes, thanks to the twin 10 in. Lockheed discs which were fitted up front in the 1970/71 off season to replace the Fontana drum originally used on the bike. Combined with the 12 in. Honda rear disc—yes, the factory team did use those back then—they gave superb stopping power at the expense of strong lever effort, and relatively little dip from the front forks: Greg's done his homework on the bike's handling, I'd say. S&W rear shocks are used. Just a thought: is the Rob North triple chassis the best-handling frame of the post-Featherbed classic era?

Riding Greg Phillippi's BSA, for all its misbehaviour on the day, brought back to me the delights of owning and riding one of these marvellous bikes, whether works original or replica. The howling exhaust note from the three-into-one pipe bays in your ear and reminds you that you're riding a real racing motorcycle;

the gearbox is sweet and the performance of the kick in the back type once the power comes in. Misfire and heaviness of controls apart, it steers like nothing since a Manx Norton and brakes on sixpence. And how good to see such a historic bike still being used for the purpose for which it was designed, rather than languishing in someone's garage or a museum. A winner in 1970 at Talladega, it was winning still 13 years later in the hands of its enthusiastic owner: classic racing fans have reason to be grateful to the likes of Greg Phillippi for ignoring the pundits and letting onlookers derive full enjoyment from seeing their bikes in action again.

| Model | | BSA Rocket 3 |
|---|---|---|
| Engine | | Ohv 3-cylinder 4-stroke |
| Bore × stroke | | 67 × 70 mm |
| Capacity | | 740 cc |
| Power output | | 69 bhp at 8500 rpm |
| Compression ratio | | 12 to 1 |
| Carburation | | 3 × 30 mm Amal Mk 1 Concentric |
| Ignition | | Lucas Rita electronic with capacitor |
| Clutch | | Single-plate Borg & Beck diaphragm |
| Gearbox | | 5-speed Quaife |
| Frame | | Duplex cradle |
| Suspension: | front | BSA |
| | rear | S&W |
| Brakes: | front | 2 × 10 in. Lockheed discs |
| | rear | 1 × 12 in. Honda disc with Lockheed caliper |
| Tyres: | front | 24.0/6.00 × 18 Goodyear (3.50 × 18) |
| | rear | 24.0/6.00 × 18 Goodyear (4.00/4.50 × 18) |
| Weight (dry) | | 380 lb |
| Top speed | | 156 mph |
| Year of manufacture | | 1970 |
| Owner | | Greg Phillippi, Manhattan Beach, California, USA |

# 3 | Four is faster?—
## *Yamaha TZ750*

**Richard Schlachter cranks the MacLean TZ750 round Druids Hill Bend at Brands Hatch during the 1982 Transatlantic Match Races (Author)**

If the 1950s was the era of the Manx Norton, then road racing in the 1970s belonged to the TZ Yamaha in all its various guises, ranging in capacity on the international scene from 125 up to 750 cc. Without the line of Yamaha's water-cooled production racers, grids would have been thin indeed not only for Grands Prix, but right down to club level all over the world: it's difficult to imagine how motorcycle racing could have developed to the point it has without the TZ.

Nowhere was this more the case than in the USA, where the largest capacity version of the Yamaha, the TZ750, dominated the AMA's National Road Race events for an entire decade. Even in 1983, four years after the last TZ750 was produced after manufacture ceased in the wake of the FIM's decision to scrap the short-lived World 750 cc Championship, four out of the first six riders in the AMA Formula 1 championship were mounted on what by then had come to be known as the TZ750 'dinosaurs' (copyright: R. Schlachter). And though Kenny Roberts won the Daytona 200 that year on one of the hen's teeth-rare 695 cc square-four Yamaha specials, it was the first time in no less than ten years that victory in America's most important road race had *not* been gained by a TZ750.

For a bike which was to become so popular, and competitive, for so long, the TZ750's debut could hardly have been more controversial: there was even talk at one time of having it banned. For when in spring of 1973 Yamaha engineers Naito and Matsui produced a 700 cc version of that year's factory 500 cc GP bike, as raced with success by the great Jarno Saarinen before his death at Monza in May, the class they were aiming at was Formula 750. With a minimum run of 200 machines required to meet F750 regulations, this had hitherto been a class reserved for racers derived from road bikes—like the BSA and Triumph triples, and Suzuki's TR750. But the new Yamaha changed all that, and though the competition protested mightily that F750 was *supposed* to be for road-based machines, the rules didn't actually SAY that, and in fact by the time the big TZ made its victorious debut in the hands of Giacomo Agostini at Daytona in 1974, no less than 271 bikes had been made, the majority for sale to the public.

That first TZ750 was actually only a 694 cc machine, achieved in essence by bolting two pairs of TZ350 cylinders to the crankcase of the works YZR500 GP bike. However, unlike the early 350, the TZ750 featured reed valves from the very beginning, and thus although the excess of power over anything previously available to privateers (around 90 bhp at 10,000 rpm) coupled with a rather flimsy tubular steel chassis with twin-shock rear suspension, made the handling somewhat lurid at times, the actual power delivery was always relatively smooth. In its first season the TZ750 completely dominated F750 racing, Aussie privateer Jack Findlay winning the FIM title on a customer version, and at the end of 1974 Yamaha effectively wiped out any chance Suzuki or Kawasaki might have had of catching up by taking the engine out to a full 750 cc, boring it out to measure 66·4 (instead of 64) × 54 mm. Cantilever rear suspension was added to the production bikes for the 1977 season, designed by Belgian engineer Lucien Tilkin and dubbed 'monocross' by Yamaha once they'd bought the patent, which featured a single long suspension running the length of the bike under the fuel tank and effectively linked the rear suspension to the steering head.

In this form the TZ750 continued to be made till 1979, when with the scrapping of the World Championship after only three short seasons there was no longer considered to be a market for it: Yamaha had dominated the series totally, works riders Baker and Cecotto winning in 1977 and 1978, and Patrick Pons scoring France's first-ever world title in 1979 with help from the local importer Sonauto, but on a production machine. The TZ750 had been too successful for its own good, and its total domination at world level eventually resulted in its demise. As well, the new generation of Yamaha production racers were to be made with variable port timing by means of power valves, and it was not thought worthwhile to redesign the TZ750 in this way.

By now the big TZ had become the privateer racer's favourite tool—fast, quite reliable and as easy to work on as any four-cylinder racer could ever be. Around 400 bikes in all were built, and though several were broken up mostly to provide engines for sidecars, a large number of them are still racing successfully today at all levels and all over the world. And especially in the USA, where no less than 36 TZ750s lined up for the start of the 1983 Daytona 200—nearly 50 per cent of the grid. So when the idea came to test a representative example of this flying dinosaur that doggedly refuses to become extinct, where better to go to find one? And who better to contact than Rich Schlachter, dinosaur devotee extraordinaire till he switched to the more exotic challenge of an RS500 Honda for the 1984 season, and US Road Race Champion in 1979 and 1980 on sponsor Bob MacLean's TZ750, one of the very last made of this dying breed, and almost certainly the quickest one around, having been trapped at over 170 mph on the Mistral straight at Paul Ricard in practice for the Moto Journal 200.

Sponsor, rider and bike duly awaited me on a crisp autumn day at Bryar Motosports Park, aka Loudoun, NH, scene of one of Rich's two National victories on his first full season on the bike in 1980

*Above* **Was there ever a meatier racing motorcycle? The TZ750 Yamaha packs a lot of motor into its 55½ in. wheelbase (Owens)**

*Above right* **Toomey pipes widen the powerband on the reed-valve engine, while a Schepp alloy swingarm improves handling and saves weight (Owens)**

*en route* to the US title. Second in two other races and 3rd in another, the only event he failed to place in that year was Daytona, but he made amends in 1981 by finishing 3rd in the Florida 200 after leading for several laps till an overstretched chain jumped the sprocket—a perennial problem with the TZ750—and he slackened off to be sure of finishing. Thereafter, Schlachter's successful but costly effort to break into GP racing in the 250 class meant the bike saw little use apart from as a consistent point scorer for the US team in the Transatlantic Match Races.

Rich had recently rebuilt the engine before my ride: 'We always fit new pistons and rings for each National,' he explained, 'it's just cheap insurance. Crank life between rebuilds is 700 miles, but you have to keep an eye on the reeds, which have a tendency to crack. We use stock heads with a 10 thou skim to raise the compression to 7·9 to 1, and the barrels have been ported by Kevin Cameron. The engine makes around 130 horsepower at 11,200 rpm on stock exhausts, but these pipes we run were made by Stuart Toomey in San Jose (California—where

else?) and give us power to 11,500 or even 12,000 if necessary. We run 20:1 mixture with either Castrol R or Yamalube: I can't remember the last time we seized a motor.'

So far, so encouraging, especially since the last thing I wanted to worry about while trying to tame this 130 bhp rocket ship was if I'd be quick enough on the draw with my left hand to avoid landing on my ear if the engine nipped up. Ignition is by standard Hitachi CDI, but the original Mikuni carburettors have long since been junked in favour of the 36 mm flat-slide Lectrons almost universally fitted to TZ750s by Stateside owners. At one stage these had to be strangled by the compulsory fitting of 23 mm retrictors for use in AMA competition, a contentious move allegedly on the grounds of safety after Cecotto won the Daytona 200 on his works bike with both tyres

worn down to the canvas, but equally so as to allow the four-strokes (meaning mostly Hondas) to become competitive in open class racing. The move was reversed a couple of years ago, much to the relief of the hard-pressed Yamaha privateers, who found that although the bikes were smoother to ride, the restrictors did knock off an appreciable amount of mid-range power. If he used the bike again, Schlachter was thinking of fitting power-valve Mikunis, which permit a finer degree of adjustment of the carburation as a whole over the Lectrons.

Power is transmitted through a large diameter 13-plate dry clutch to a 6-speed gearbox, with on this bike the usual Yamaha one up, five down left foot change. The chassis is the standard Yamaha tubular steel unit, but with a much stiffer and lighter anodized alloy swingarm made by Frank Schepp, which however still uses the standard Yamaha suspension unit. Yamaha 38 mm forks are fitted, without the modern luxury of any anti-dive system, with 18 in. EPM magalloy wheels front and rear giving a $55\frac{1}{2}$ in. wheelbase—pretty compact considering how much engine is packed into the available space,

as well as the bulky pipes. These originally ran under the engine together on the first 700 cc TZ, but the flats required to make them fit were not conducive to ideal engine characteristics, so the present system of two right, one left and the fourth pipe curving through the centre of the frame to end up on the right was soon adopted. Though the standard Yamaha 260 mm steel disc brake and caliper are retained at the rear, Rich has fitted twin 300 mm Brembo meonite discs up front which together with Lockheed calipers are a big improvement over the stainless steel originals. Dry weight is 342 lb, but add another 40 lb-odd for water, oil and a full load of premix in the 6·3 US gallon fuel tank (consumed at no less than 13 mpg!), and you have a motorcycle weighing just a tadge under 400 lb ready for the start of the Daytona 200.

Sitting on the TZ750 for the first time, the bike feels exactly the way you'd expect from looking at it: bulky and power-packed, yet at the same time lithe and wiry, it's a mixture of opposites. Rich is only slightly shorter than me, so the riding position was fine, except that you have to jack your feet up right high on to the footpegs, simply

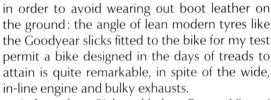

in order to avoid wearing out boot leather on the ground: the angle of lean modern tyres like the Goodyear slicks fitted to the bike for my test permit a bike designed in the days of treads to attain is quite remarkable, in spite of the wide, in-line engine and bulky exhausts.

A shove from Rich and helper George Vicensi and I was away—rather cautiously, I must admit, for not only was it my first visit to Loudoun (a sort of New England Brands Hatch but with seemingly twice as many corners) but the only other time I'd ridden a big Yamaha was on a 700 cc version which though in standard form and fitted with reed valves which supposedly softened the power characteristics, lit up like a firework at 8000 revs and sent the frame into a passable imitation of a belly dancer, with resultant adverse effect on the state of my nerves. I needn't have worried though—the

*Above* **Brembo discs and Lockheed calipers provide impressive stopping power (Owens)**

*Above left* **The four-cylinder engine produces around 130 bhp at 11,200 rpm (Owens)**

*Above right* **A nest of vipers: the Yamaha's 'stingers' (Owens)**

*Right* **Handling was surprisingly controllable and predictable around the tight Loudoun track (Owens)**

MacLean TZ750 was much better mannered, but in coming to terms with it I also got a big surprise.

Simply put, this was that the engine was far more tractable than I'd ever have imagined. That's not to say that once I got into the real powerband from about 7700 rpm upwards I

didn't have to exercise a great deal of effort to stop the front wheel pawing the air like a circus horse coming out of slow turns, or care to be sure the back wheel stayed in line with the front: you could get into a lot of trouble with one of these bikes if you started riding it carelessly. But the power comes in gradually rather than suddenly, and it's quite possible to ride the bike round slow turns off the pipe at about 6000 rpm, and then have it pick up cleanly when you accelerate hard once pointing in the right direction. It's really quite torquey and flexible, especially for a high-performance two-stroke, and I suppose this is down to a combination of the reed-valve design, Cameron porting, Toomey pipes and Lectrons, plus the expertise of an experienced topliner like Rich Schlachter in setting it all up together right. You can almost ride it like a four-stroke, it pulls so well from low down—and there's even a bit of engine braking into the bargain, or at least more than I expected, even if the superb braking power of the big twin Brembos made this largely redundant.

The handling was equally the reverse of what

I'd been anticipating, bearing in mind my previous ride on the older, twin-shock bike. The MacLean TZ behaved controllably and predictably around the tight Loudoun track which really isn't its ideal habitat. But while a flat-out blind like Daytona or much of Paul Ricard is where the Yamaha's scintillating top end performance really comes into play, that it's at home on the twisty stuff too is proved by the victories gained at tracks like Loudoun or the like. Rich has it set up to give really neutral characteristics, with just a hint of oversteer: only 97 mm trail on the front forks helps a lot here, and the bike was especially at home on the fast sweepers such as Turn 3, a 90 mph left hander which I could take hard on in fourth gear at 10,500 rpm, cranked right over without a trace of misbehaviour from the chassis. And then sitting up and braking hard, hard, hard for the tight right-hander immediately after, with a couple of bumps on the entry, showed that in spite of having no anti-dive system the front suspension still retains sufficient feel even under heavy braking provided you change the fork oil after every race, as Rich does. The brakes again were just fabulous: it seemed you could squeeze

**Making friends with a dinosaur (Owens)**

them as hard as you liked without coming to any harm. 'I've never ever locked a front wheel on this bike,' says Rich, 'It just stops—period. They're like power brakes without the servo!'

Switching on the power coming out of the last tight left before the pits was the only time the Yamaha got really out of shape: the front end would rise and wheel start to flap idly from side to side—just one lazy waggle in each direction before the standard Yamaha steering damper asserted itself. 'It's not adjustable like a Kawasaki damper,' said Rich, 'but it's really progressive and provided you change the oil regularly it works much better than anything else.' I'll go along with that. So tractable was the engine that I didn't have to slip the clutch even out of this tight turn, and except on Daytona gearing Schlachter doesn't need to normally either, nor does he normally use the clutch at all for upwards changes. I didn't either to begin with, but after a couple of near misses I decided to start using the clutch and had no problems after that, nor did I lose any revs: it felt much smoother, and the positive, light gearchange really came into its own. With the torquey engine I found that the hot tip was to short shift for the fast sweepers, which seemed to steady the bike up better rather than scream through at near maximum revs, but otherwise I ran the engine up to 11,200 in the gears, and noticed an appreciable extra dollop of power once I got above 10,000: from being merely breath-taking, the performance became electrifying above that figure.

After about 40 laps of the 1·6 mile circuit I decided I better stop wearing Bob MacLean's potent projectile out and pottered into the pits: playtime for dinosaurs was over. There was no doubt I'd had my eyes opened: now I know why the TZ750 is still the delight of so many topline privateers. For a start, provided you're meticulous about preparation, and learn the tricks of the trade like pre-stretching the chain and so on, it'll get you to the finish, and well up at that. Secondly, though the bike is undeniably power-

ful, and probably represents the most speed for the least dollars (or yen, or pounds, or . . .) that the motorcycling world will ever see, it's relatively easy for an experienced rider to go fast on, though I'd say it should be made illegal for novices! In other words, there isn't the quantum leap in machine behaviour over a TZ750, for example, that a GP 500 like a RG Suzuki represents, and in this respect I'd say the TZ750's latter-day successor is really the RS500 Honda—except that buying one of those (if you can get one) costs about the same as a brace of TZ750s and two years' running costs for each. But the Honda's smooth performance, aided again by the use of reed valves, is akin to that of the Yamaha. Rather a docile dinosaur!

| Model | | Yamaha TZ750 |
|---|---|---|
| Engine | | 4-cylinder water-cooled piston-port 2-stroke with reed-valves |
| Bore × stroke | | 66·4 × 54 mm |
| Capacity | | 748 cc |
| Power output | | 130 bhp at 11,200 rpm |
| Compression ratio | | 7·9 to 1 |
| Carburation | | 4 × 36 mm Lectron |
| Ignition | | Hitachi CDI |
| Clutch | | 13-plate air-cooled dry (6 steel/7 friction) |
| Gearbox | | 6-speed |
| Frame | | Twin loop |
| Suspension: | front | 38 mm Yamaha |
| | rear | Alloy cantilever with single Yamaha |
| Brakes: | front | 2 × 300 mm Brembo meonite discs with Lockheed calipers |
| | rear | 1 × 260 mm Yamaha steel disc with Yamaha caliper |
| Tyres: | front | 24·0/6·0 × 18 Goodyear |
| | rear | 26·5/8·0 × 18 Goodyear |
| Weight (dry) | | 352 lb |
| Top speed | | 172 mph |
| Year of manufacture | | 1979 |
| Owner | | Bob MacLean, New York, USA |

# 5 Endurance *et al* breeds four-strokes

## More money means more—*Honda's RS750 Interceptor and RS850R*

Strange how things often don't work out the way you expect. If at the start of the 1983 racing season someone had offered me a modest wager against Honda winning the US Superbike title, I'd have tried to persuade him to make it considerably less modest before taking him on. After their crushing 1-2-3 win at Daytona, spearheaded by World Champion-to-be Freddie Spencer, the VF750-based Honda Interceptors seemed a racing certainty for the first year of the 750 cc Superbike championship, aided by Honda's steamroller approach to winning the series that had eluded them for so long: a total of 11 complete bikes and 16 engines in all provided the basis for a team that included as many as eight riders, some forming part of a back-up 'support' squad. By mid-season it seemed all over bar the celebrations, with six Honda victories out of six events: yet thereafter things began to go terribly wrong, and by October we'd learnt that there is no such thing in racing as a certainty. Thanks to a series of crashes and rider injuries, including one fateful day at Willow Springs which saw no less than three Hondas destroyed in separate accidents, the Interceptors had to cede overall victory to Wayne Rainey's Kawasaki, running on a fraction of their budget and completely outclassed at the start of the season. It was one of the most surprising turnarounds in recent racing history.

At the same time on the other side of the Atlantic, Honda appeared to have little or no hope of retaining their World TT Formula 1 title, or of regaining the British crown, in the face of stern opposition from the works Suzukis. The same gloomy prospect overshadowed their chances of success in the World Endurance Championship, run to TT F1 rules, which saw 1983 as the final year of the 1000 cc top limit, before it dropped to 750 cc for the 1984 season. Honda decided to pin their hopes on an enlarged 850 cc version of the VF750 engine, suitably modified for racing and housed in a state-of-the-art racing chassis, in hopes that they might still retain sufficient competitivity to make a good showing against the bigger, more powerful full-size machines in 1983, and be a year's development ahead of the rest for 1984. A couple of months into the season, it seemed a horrible miscalculation: first of all the bikes were late arriving in Britain, then when they did it became rapidly evident that much of the development work remained to be done. Spares were in short supply, too, and all these factors combined to force Honda Britain to revert to the old in-line fours for a couple of meetings while they sorted out the troublesome new bikes. Meantime the works alloy-framed versions had debuted at the Le Mans 24 hours in April and encountered

numerous troubles before retiring from the first of only three endurance events planned for that season, culminating in the prestigious Bol d'Or in September.

Then it all clicked: hard work and countless testing miles made the bike into a winner at one of the races Honda wanted to win most, the Isle of Man F1 TT. Shortly before, Joey Dunlop was trapped at 171 mph on the 850 at the North West 200, and the speed deficiency allegedly evident at Le Mans was obviously no longer a problem. Back on the British short circuits, Aussie Wayne Gardner was proving the bike a winner too, scoring a string of successes culminating in a nail-biting victory in the Silverstone GP round after a fairing-bashing duel with the works Suzukis of Mick Grant and Rob McElnea that had strong men amongst the onlookers groping for support. Less than a second covered the three bikes at the finish, and in winning Gardner not only clinched a title for Honda that at the start of the season they could surely not in their wildest dreams have expected to win, but also proved on the fastest circuit in the GP circus that the RS850R could give away a fair bit of power, 150 cc and probably a couple of pounds to the opposition, and still win. When Joey Dunlop clinched the World F1 championship a couple of weeks later in Ulster, and a trio of French riders headed by Raymond Roche romped to emphatic victory in the Bol d'Or the following month on a 920 cc version, Honda's cup was filled to overflowing. Yet six months later it had all seemed so unlikely.

At the IoM TT in June I was favoured with an exclusive look at his factory data by Oshiro-san, the engineer in charge of the V4 racing project, coded NC9 inside HRC, as well as with a close examination of the bike and engine itself which, since it will certainly form the basis of Honda's

**Freddie Spencer cruises to an unchallenged victory in the 1983 Daytona Superbike race on the Honda VF750R Interceptor test bike (Author)**

four-stroke racing effort for the conceivable future, is of particular significance quite apart from its close relationship to their road motorcycles. And when later in the year I was able to ride Spencer's Daytona-winning Interceptor Superbike and Gardner's RS850R TT F1 title winner in separate test sessions 6000 miles apart, the result was a fascinating insight into how the world's largest motorcycle manufacturer goes racing with production-based machines. And in doing so in 1983 proved the principle of an old saying: Win some, lose some.

The 90 degree water-cooled dohc V4 engine used in both bikes first appeared in late 1981 on the shaft-driven Sabre road bike. For racing, though, a chain final drive was required, hence the introduction a year later of the VF750F (aka Interceptor in America) which not only incorporated this desirable feature but also a great deal of other Good Stuff besides. In short, instead of building a street bike and then sitting down to work out how to go racing with it, Honda engineers stood traditional Japanese design philosophy on its head and after close examination of the US Superbike and World TT F1 regulations, came up with a production motorcycle whose specification was determined with racing in mind. The result is not only a smash hit in the showrooms (try buying an Interceptor on either side of the Atlantic—if you can find one—and catch the salesman's reaction when you mention the funny word 'discount') but also the basis of a pair of racers surprisingly similar in mechanical detail to the roadster.

The principal difference is that the racing engines have gear drive to the twin overhead camshafts per pair of cylinders, compared to the road bike's chain drive. This necessitates not an entirely new crankshaft but one similar to production but with a pinion replacing the chain sprocket in the centre. Both US and TT1 rules require the standard stroke to be retained, which means that the only way of increasing the capacity is to overbore the 750's 70 × 48·6 mm cylinders to 75 × 48·6 for 858·83 cc, resulting in the RS850R engine. Honda aren't saying how they made the 920 version without cutting into the water jackets, and we may never know with the virtual end of 1000 cc four-stroke racing worldwide. A gallon of water is carried in a single radiator, compared to the two on the road bike, but a standard water pump is used.

Dry-sump oiling is desirable in competition engines, and so is an oil cooler, but the use of Pro-Link suspension makes fitting a separate oil tank in the conventional position impossible. Moreover, the plain bearing bottom end of the V4 engine requires a constant high-pressure supply of cool oil at 80 psi. These factors determined the Honda's unusual twin-pump, twin-sump system, which Oshiro-san calls a 'semi-dry sump' design, but which Udo Geitl, Honda America's racing team manager insists is a true dry-sump system. The area beneath the engine is divided into two compartments: oil returns by gravity to the front sump, where a scavenge pump transmits it to the oil cooler, mounted low down in place of the second water radiator on the road bike. From there, a high-output pressure pump feeds the lubricant to the engine again, before the whole cycle is repeated. This constant-pressure system ensures an uninterrupted high-pressure feed, permitting very close crankshaft big-end tolerances. The same oil also lubricates the 5-speed gearbox, essentially the same as fitted to the 1025 cc FWS V4 of 1982, the rolling testbed for the 1983 bikes from which their ancestry may be directly traced.

Ignition is provided by a Kokusan-Denko CDI generator, firing a single 12 mm plug per 4-valve cylinder: ignition timing is a conservative 37–42 degrees depending on the circuit. Induction is provided on both bikes by a set of four specially-made CV Keihin carburettors, made in weight-saving magnesium but otherwise similar to the street bike units: thanks to the curious World (meaning British) TT1 carburettor rule,

*Left* **VF engine produces over 120 bhp in 750 cc form (Dewhurst)**

*Below* **Standard frame and handlebar mounting points must be used in US Superbike racing (Dewhurst)**

Gardner's bike must run the same 32 mm size throat as on the VF750, while the US Superbike opts for 34 mm. The valves are all made of titanium, with 28 mm inlets and 25 mm exhausts (24 mm on the 850), set at a typical (for Honda) included angle of 38 degrees, using multi-rate steel springs after titanium ones gave trouble, and forged cam followers. Unlike on the road bike, where clearances are set by threaded adjusters, the RS's valve clearances are altered by fitting different-thickness caps over the end of each stem. The inlet tracts are curious at first glance, because while one heads straight for one of the twin inlet valves on each cylinder the other cuts off at an angle before curving back towards the other valve, with the presumed intention of creating a swirl effect. 'We doubted it was right, too,' says Geitl, 'but then we found with experimentation that the standard heads with very little alteration give all the flow the engine needs: we just open up the ports a little, that's all.'

Pistons are supplied to the American team as unmachined blanks from Japan, which enables them to employ different compression ratios for different circuits varying from 10·8 to 1 up to as high as 12·2 to 1; for Daytona they use 11·2 to 1, running

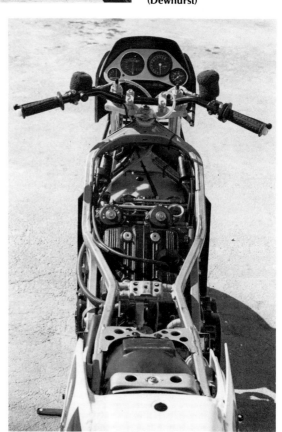

**From ten yards away the Honda Interceptor (*right*) looks like a stock street bike modified for the track. Up close (*above*), only a careful examination shows the external changes in this factory racer—like the Showa front suspension, 310 mm discs, oil cooler and so forth (Dewhurst)**

on 118 octane fuel as permitted under AMA rules. Honda Britain on the other hand employ 11·5 to 1 for the 850 regardless, using Avgas. Conrods are titanium, and surprisingly enough are manufactured in the USA to Geitl's specification for use in all racing V4 engines the world over: the Japanese accepted that doing it this way would result in a superior product. They're retained on the two crankpins by split end-caps, clamped by high-tensile steel bolts. The forged pistons carry short but full skirts: slipper-type pistons were not employed, according to Oshiro-san, because of the difficulty with a short-stroke engine of preventing the engine rocking in the barrel. Different philosophies are evident concerning the type of clutch fitted, which on the Superbike is a 13-plate all-metal dry clutch, but on the Gardner machine is a wet, oil-bath sort. Both are fixed units, after Honda America discarded the limited-slip sprag clutch fitted to the FWS and the road bike early in the season: 'We had a problem with high-gear starts like at Daytona,' says Geitl, 'where the clutch just wouldn't take the abuse necessary to get off the line with a high overall gearing fitted. We converted all the engines to fixed-clutch after that, and also air-cooled them all (the support team bikes were originally wet-clutch) because we had problems under racing conditions with the engines retaining heat from the wet clutch; the service life was much shorter with them, too. Now we have no concerns.' Yet Barry Symmons, Udo's counterpart at Honda Britain, claims no such problems with the 850, possibly because of the cooler British climate and torquier bigger engine. However, just to complicate things the engines fitted to the three Honda Japan bikes with alloy frames, on one of which Dunlop won the World title, had air-cooled clutches. Take your choice! Whatever the pick, standard hydraulic action was a constant.

The camshafts run in plain bearings, and thanks to their moderate lift by racing standards, plus the lowish compression ratio and the use of CV carbs as well as the intrinsic values of a 90 degrees V4 design, result in an exceptionally smooth-running engine with vast reserves of torque and practically no cammy effect. You can even ride it like a road engine, as not only the Honda Britain mechanics proved at the TT when they ran them up and down between the garage and paddock quite cheerfully, even stopping at traffic lights and taking off again without slipping the clutch, but as too did Udo Geitl himself at Daytona last March. How so? Well, Freddie's race bike needed a bit of running-in, you see, and the Speedway was closed, so ... well, anyway, he got caught with it out on Volusia Avenue by the local gendarmes, slick tyres, race exhausts and all. What got them interested in the look-alike racer? No licence plate!

The last time the Honda team had been to Willow Springs was the day their championship season fell apart. Team leader Mike Baldwin was badly injured, enough to put him out for the rest of the season and hand the Superbike title on a plate to Kawasaki's Rainey, while support riders Fred Merkel and Sam McDonald had also launched it in a big way, resulting in three totalled motorcycles and a proof that in racing you should never take anything for granted. Merkel made some amends, though, by winning the season's final race at Daytona on the bike Freddie Spencer had started out the season victorious on at the same track: a week later, mechanics Mike Velasco and Phil McDonald

**The Interceptor proved flexible but fast-steering round the Willow Springs track in the California desert (Dewhurst)**

(brother of Sam) returned to Willow with it for me to sample. It was also the bike on which Udo Geitl made the acquaintace of the Daytona Beach police department, and it *still* didn't have a licence tag. . . .

The 1983-model in-line Honda superbikes looked like stock FZ900s from 20 yards away, then lost five per cent of that similarity with every step you took towards them. Close to, they looked what they were: unabashed, tricked-out racing motorcycles based somewhat tenuously on their street ancestors. Approach the V4 Superbike the same way, and 20 steps later you'll still be amazed how close it looks to the stocker—and that's because it is. Partly that's because of a general tightening-up in the AMA rules, partly for reasons already discussed about the way the Interceptor came about: all the good stuff's already on the road bike.

So Geitl's men use the same square-tube steel chassis as the road bike, shorn of a few unnecessary lugs here and there and the sidestand, as well as the stock swingarm: they tried making special ones, but the standard one was better! The Pro-Link rear suspension employs a special Showa unit designed for the racing Interceptor and based on their design for the RS500 GP bike; naturally, it's adjustable in both directions as well as for ride height and spring preload. The front forks similarly are based on Showa's GP design, measuring 41·3 mm in diameter, except these are much longer to suit the taller road chassis. Again, they're two-way adjustable and are fitted with hydraulic anti-dive with external spring adjuster, coupled with a fork brace incorporating the mudguard mounting and carefully shimmed up so as not to load up the suspension. Steering head angle is 27 degrees—steeper than on the road bike by 2·2 degrees. The 16 in. front wheel carries massive twin 310 mm diameter discs, made from meonite after it was found that steel ones warped too quickly due to insufficient cooling at high speed when fitted to the narrow diameter wheel. The rear steel disc has been progressively reduced in size to only 190 mm: the riders claim to hardly need to use it. Front calipers are the excellent twin-piston Nissins as fitted to the GP bikes, which have differentially-

Joey Dunlop takes one of the three versions of the RS850R Honda built with an alloy frame to victory in the 1983 IoM F1 TT (Author)

sized pistons: the leading ones (i.e. those that meet the wheel first in the direction in which it rotates) are of 27 mm diameter, while the trailing ones are larger at 34 mm. Combined with oblong brake pads, this reduces the effect of gas build-up from the dissipation of the pads' material, as well as promoting more even wear of the pads themselves.

Wheels are extruded alloy bolted-up Comstar-type with magnesium hubs; wheelbase is standard, at 58·5 in. 'We tried carbon-fibre wheels,' says Geitl, 'but we really don't need them. The minimum weight for Superbike is 390 lb, we generally weight 398–400 with water and oil but no gas, and so we're very close. We can be lower yet, but since for most of the season we had a considerable horsepower advantage, it wasn't worthwhile.' How much horsepower? 'That we shouldn't discuss, but a lot.' More than 120 bhp, given that Oshiro-san's charts showed the 850 to be producing 132 bhp? 'Yes!' OK—thanks, Udo!

Once Mike and Phil had bumped the engine into life, the distinctive lazy-sounding flat burble

of the 90 degrees V4 began echoing across the Mojave Desert. On a hot 90 degrees day it didn't take long for the water temp gauge to hit the 85 degrees mark considered optimum for racing: 95 degrees is bad news, but unlike the RS850R I would try a couple of weeks later in much cooler conditions. Idling the engine didn't seem to cause the needle to start climbing off the clock. Sitting on the bike you'd swear you were on a roadster, even down to the dashful of instruments in front of you: the speedo is disconnected, though. . . . Flat, one-piece bars bolt to the top of the special yokes, contrasting with the street bike's adjustable clipons (or boltons, actually). In fact Spencer used the bike at Daytona with CB1100R clipons fitted, but Merkel prefers more leverage and had them changed after he took the bike over. The standard steel fuel tank is retained, by order of the AMA, complete with lockable filler cap which caused some excitement at Aldana's fuel stop in the Daytona 100-miler when he forgot he was supposed to unlock it with the key! The svelte standard instrument fairing is used, but no headlight fitted: Geitl tried

The Honda factory engines differ from those of the VF750 street bike by having gear drive to the four camshafts (Edge)

to persuade the AMA to let him run the bikes with the front number stuck on the front of the fairing without a separate plate, but no dice. Top speed is 159 mph on Daytona gearing, and 'to go any faster would require an awful lot of extra power,' says Udo, thanks to the substantial frontal area and commensurate drag.

Within the first 100 yards after accelerating away on to the track, I knew I was riding an exceptional racing bike. In fact, I had to mentally pinch myself to remember it was a racer at all: the power band is almost unbelievably wide, with usable revs as low as 6500, then real strong power coming in from 7500 rpm up. You have a sort of alarm call to remind you that this is about to happen, with a period of roughness at 7000 rpm which feels as if the engine's suddenly turned into a power drill but is in fact a sign that the camshafts are starting to work. Then everything smooths out and you get this feeling of lovely, liquid power right up to the usual rev limit of 12,700 rpm, though the engine is safe to as high as 13,500. However, there's no real point in screaming it to more than 12,000 because the closely-spaced gears, with a bit of a gap between third and fourth, keep you well in the powerband if you change even at 11,500, and the torque curve is so flat that the reading is almost the same at 7500 as it is at 12,500. Incredible.

The extreme tractability of the V4 engine was particularly useful in helping me to find my way round Willow Springs; it was the first time I'd ever been round the track, and all I can say is that if you think it's difficult to find the quick line round Silverstone's vast open spaces and featureless wasteland, wait till you try to navigate through Turns 8/9 at Willow. Going fast here without any markers and nobody to follow round requires Local Knowledge and practice: without either I was doubly grateful for the forgiving nature of the Interceptor's engine. On and off the throttle, on again when I remembered the line and stroking it into Nine's tighter apex before cracking it hard open for the run down

the finishing straight, the V4 engine took all this and more in its stride. No need to clutch it: just open the taps and let the power pour out. Downshift? Forget it—the engine'll pull you back to where you should have been on the rev counter. Race riding made easy, that's what the bike represents.

Of course, all this is very well if you just want to potter round and pick up place money, but these bikes were designed to go out there and WIN. And on the part of the track I did quite quickly get the hang of—roughly Turns 2–7 inclusive, mostly because I could see where I was supposed to be going—I was able to find out how well they fulfil that role. The combination of a vast torque band, pinpoint handling and superb front brakes (I hardly used the rear either: it's redundant) make the Interceptor one of the easiest bikes to start riding fast on through corners I've ever sampled. Mind you, given my European heritage of riding 'proper' race bikes with fairings and clipons and suchlike, it felt strange to be sitting there with the high, flat bars to hold on to and no fairing, giving the illusion of being a bit higher off the ground than usual on a race-track, but after a few laps even that disappeared and I began to feel complete confidence in the bike. Two places exemplified this: Turn 2 is a long, long uphill horseshoe with just a touch of off-camber. You go in there hard, lean the bike hard over to the right, and leave it there for what seems like an age while you hope you can catch the right moment to snap the throttle open without having the back end step out on you. The controls of the Interceptor are so light and responsive and the steering so perfectly balanced, without a hint of the understeer that would spell disaster if you didn't nip it in the bud, that after a while I was able to start taking it a gear higher than I'd been doing and let the tyres start earning their living. That's what inspiring confidence means on a bike. The other place was just a bit further on, the 3/4 complex that swoops up the side of the hill, turns sharp right, then

**The Honda Britain team machine on which Wayne Gardner won the 1983 British TT F1 title employed a steel frame. Dry weight was 376 lb (Edge)**

drops downhill again. Here the benefits of the 16 in. front wheel became readily apparent, because while braking hard for the entry to Three (and those brakes *are* fantastic, with lots of progression and feel) you have to turn into the corner quickly and start climbing the hill without losing momentum, all the while trying not to run off the edge where the road flattens out. Then at the top of the hill you have to flick over to the right to drop down again to Five. The bike felt so beautifully balanced and the steering so light and responsive that again after a few laps I could approach these corners with impunity, too. And under braking for Three the anti-dive really retained road feel and movement, rather than freezing the suspension as on other race bikes I've tried.

Anything I didn't like? Well, the front end felt a bit stiff (probably set up for Daytona's bankings), and at the end of the day I really didn't care that much for the riding position in race terms, but that's a question of personal preference and what I'm used to. Without another bike there to compare with I'm not sure about the Interceptor's acceleration against the opposition, but to have got a bike beladen with water-cooling so close to the class weight limit is a real feat that Honda should be proud of, especially since they've done it without *too* much exotic metallurgy. And their power output was certainly well ahead of the rest till Kawasaki caught up a lot at the end of the season. But then the Green Meanies closed their race shop, put riders and engineers on the unemployment line, and now we'll never know if Honda would really have got their own back in 1984. Though it was rumoured that Yamaha and Suzuki would both have a Superbike team in 1985, that still left 1984 as all the makings of a Honda benefit: you know—a racing certainty....

For those of us with any interest in the historical aspect of competition motorcycle development, the policy of the Japanese manufacturers towards their obsolete machinery is a source of constant disappointment: it's also ultimately short-sighted. Instead of retiring a championship winner to a factory museum, or even loaning it out on semi-permanent display elsewhere, they treat the bikes as being completely disposable, so that after it's done its job, the next appointment is with the crusher. That's disappointing because it means that successive generations will have no appreciation of that company's skills on the race track in finite terms, and short-sighted because they're passing up the chance of some great PR in later years: imagine if Luigi Taveri's five-cylinder 125 Honda hadn't by more or less devious means escaped being sent back to Japan—or the couple of 250 sixes that survived. Each time they appear, people who never saw them in action in their heyday can marvel and appreciate the engineering that went in to producing such jewels, to Honda's

undoubted advantage. If Yamaha could let us see and hear their 125 cc V4, or Suzuki the 50 cc twin, they too could reap similar benefits.

So what's that got to do with the RS850R V4 Honda that Wayne Gardner won the British TT F1 title with in 1983? Only that two weeks after my ride on the bike on a crisp and sunny November day at Snetterton, the bike was being broken up: the engine was being sent back to Japan to have a knife put through it, while the chassis was to be sold, presumably to a privateer to put a standard engine in for next season. OK, so the 850 cc version has fulfilled its task—but how sad that 15 years from now the next generation won't be able to appreciate it.

Thus thanks to Barry Symmons, team manager of Honda Britain, I was able to sample a bike that soon would be no more. And what made that even more regrettable to me personally was

**Fully flaired, the RS850R was timed at over 170 mph in the North West 200 (Edge)**

that it was unquestionably the finest racing motorcycle I'd ever had the privilege of riding up till then—and that included the current 500 GP Honda and its like. Obviously, such a sweeping statement has much to do with my own preference for big four-strokes, but viewed subjectively the RS850R was simply the most confidence-inspiring bike I've ever sat on. I rode it as hard as if I was on one of my own racers, just because it invited it, and was repaid with a 1 min. 13 secs Snetterton lap time seemingly without trying. The bike induces such faith in its own abilities that you find yourself going faster and faster and deeper and deeper into corners, still with absolute safety. I'd say this bike could be ridden fast by more riders who aren't in the top rank of racers than any other I know: it very nearly doesn't have a single vice, the engine like the Superbike has a vast power band with even more torque, and the handling is almost perfect. What else is there?

With its steel tubular chassis and wet clutch engine, the RS850R weighed 376 lb totally dry—without oil, water or fuel. The works alloy frame used in the World Championship and the Bol d'Or saved around 12 lb on this, but only three of the 25 RS750/850/920Rs made for 1983 boasted this feature, though the small batch of 750s made for sale to private teams for 1984 would have it; however, at around £20,000 each there unsurprisingly hadn't been a rush to sign cheques this big on the part of the relatively impecunious teams that made up the bulk of the TT F1 fields.

Like the Superbike, the RS850R's engine was rotated back in the chassis eight degrees to allow a steeper head angle (in this case 25 degrees) and shorter wheelbase (56 in.) for more manageable handling than would otherwise be the case. Even so, Wayne would have liked to bring the front wheel back a bit more, but there just wasn't the room to do it: the front camshaft cover gets in the way. Even so, compare the Honda's 56 in. wheelbase, with the 90 degrees V4 engine *and*

the extra bulk of the oil cooler/radiator with the 60 in. of the V-twin, air-cooled 900 Ducati and the feat of the Japanese designers becomes apparent. Water-cooling is the reason, for without having to worry about placing the rear cylinder where it'll get a good supply of cooling air, you can simply position the engine in the chassis where it'll result in the best handling characteristics.

Suspension was by means of a shorter version of the 41·3 mm Showa front forks fitted to the Superbike, and the same nitrogen-damped rear unit. Brakes were the same diameter up front, with a 220 mm rear, and all appeared to be made out of some esoteric alloy that had more than its fair share of cast iron in it: they rusted when wet! Steel nuts and bolts were used throughout, rather than titanium as in the alloy-framed specials, and the bluff-fronted, wind-tunnel tested bodywork bore a strong family resemblance to the NS/RS500's streamlining, with the sinuous pairs of twin exhausts exiting on the right side, that from the rear cylinders through the top of the seat. Instruments were confined to a rev counter and water temp gauge—the latter a vital fixture since much to my surprise it transpired that the engine overheated rapidly at idle, and once it hit 95 degrees you must shut down or risk serious damage—like a blown gasket. In fact, the bikes were kept waiting for so long on the grid for the start of the Assen World TT F1 round that Wayne's bike overheated so much the seat actually melted! Cracks about asbestos underwear need not be made. . . .

The riding position was a snug but comfortable fit, with the big 24-litre fuel tank nestling into your chest and providing a useful rest on long fast stretches. Bottom gear was very low, but even so with 11·5 to 1 compression it needed two people plus the rider firmly seated to bump-start from cold. Fortunately, the engine fired almost at once and settled down to a fast, easy burble, but solo push-starts would be out of the question, so forget about using the bike for British

Wayne's office. Temperature gauge on right must be closely watched to prevent overheating (Edge)

The RS850R's handling was awe-inspiring: here the author cranks round Riches Corner at Snetterton on a bike which invited to be ridden hard (Edge)

club racing! Once out on the track, I discovered that first is also much too low to use except for getting off the line, even at Snetterton's hairpin: before I managed to work this out I'd stalled the engine twice trying to change into the very notchy bottom gear. Fortunately, it restarted with momentum, but it also illustrated another feature of the engine: the flywheels have surely been reduced in size compared to the road bike, because their effect on engine braking is almost non-existent and the engine died immediately if you closed the throttle. As mechanic Dave Sleat neatly put it, it's a two-stroke engine in four-stroke guise. Except for one thing: that incredible power band. With the extra 110 cc and different camshafts the 859 cc engine was even torquier than the 750, if that were possible. Power came in at 6000 rpm, with normal peak revs at 11,500 though the engine was safe to 12,750 rpm. The rough patch was there, too, but this time higher up the dial at around 8200 rpm. But with the beautifully matched gear ratios you would never encounter it normally: second and third were 1700 rpm apart, to keep the bike moving right along under acceleration from a corner, then there was only 1300 rpm before fourth, and fifth very close to fourth indeed—only 1000 rpm difference: taking the left/right flick of Russells

meant just notching fourth on the way in, and driving hard up the hill to the start line before grabbing top for the run to Riches. Then back to fourth before coming down to second for Sear, then off down the straight. The smooth power delivery and exceptional flexibility of the engine really told in minimizing the number of time-consuming gearchanges. Slightly under-geared for the straight, I was actually seeing 11,900 on the clock before shutting off for the hairpin, and here the fabulous brakes really came into their own. After 15 laps or so I was able to brake from over 150 mph within the 200 yard mark (and I'm not kidding myself that Wayne didn't wait till even later!): the front discs responded instantly with maximum effect, and the back had lots of feel as well, while the anti-dive worked to advantage when negotiating the ripples at the end of the straight before heeling over into the left-hander before the hairpin. In other words, the suspension didn't freeze up. Lever action was light but not so light that it was possible to overbrake easily, and indeed all the controls—throttle, brakes, clutch—were feather light and positive: what a great bike to go endurance racing or round the Isle of Man with. As a heritage of all those production bike races he did in Australia, Wayne uses a one down, four up gearchange on the left, which took a bit of remembering, but the change itself was like butter and I didn't come close to missing a gear even riding as hard as I was.

The handling is literally awe inspiring. Though a big, relatively bulky bike the Honda changed direction precisely in the corners and steered lightly but positively through the swerves of Russells and the Bombhole: only at the former was there any trace of misbehaviour, with the front wheel starting to flap around as I crammed on the power while still cranked over: tightening up the steering damper a notch or two cured that. By ultra-critical standards the steering could be quicker, even with the 16 in. front wheel fitted, but there's no way to improve that without steepening the head angle further.

After a few laps of gradually picking up the pace, I settled into an easy rhythm on the bike in spite of the fast lap times: I could have gone on riding it all day. Sadly, after 25 laps or so the front wheel stepped out accelerating out of Sear and though I managed not to do a premature job in the crushing department and picked it up before I landed on my ear, playtime was over: the front tyre fitted was only an intermediate, and it was cutting up badly on the right side. With no slick on hand, it was time to call it a day after one of the most enjoyable rides I've ever had on any bike: 'I never thought you were going to ride it that hard, else we'd have brought a slick,' said Dave Sleat, while Barry Symmons just looked relieved that he still had a chassis to sell at the end of the day! But the RS850R was that sort of bike: it invited being ridden hard, and yet let you do so safely.

| Model | | Honda RS750 Interceptor | Honda RS850R |
|---|---|---|---|
| Engine | | Dohc V4 water-cooled 4-stroke | Dohc V4 water-cooled 4-stroke |
| Bore × stroke | | 70 × 48·6 mm | 75 × 48·6 mm |
| Capacity | | 748 cc | 859 cc |
| Power output | | Over 120 bhp at 12,700 rpm | 132 bhp at 11,500 rpm |
| Compression ratio | | 11·2 to 1 | 11·5 to 1 |
| Carburation | | 4 × 34 mm Mikuni CV | 4 × 32 mm Mikuni CV |
| Ignition | | Kokkusan–Denko CDI | Kokkusan–Denko CDI |
| Clutch | | 13-plate all-metal dry multi-plate | 15-plate all-metal oil bath multi-plate |
| Gearbox | | 5-speed | 5-speed |
| Frame | | Duplex cradle | Duplex cradle |
| Suspension: | front | 41·3 mm Showa | 41·3 mm Showa |
| | rear | Pro-Link with single Showa | Pro-Link with single Showa |
| Brakes: | front | 2 × 310 mm meonite discs with twin piston Nissin Calipers | 2 × 310 mm discs with twin-piston Nissin calipers |
| | rear | 1 × 190 mm steel disc with Nissin single-piston caliper | 1 × 220 mm disc with single-piston Nissin caliper |
| Tyres: | front | 12/60 × 16 Michelin | 3·50 × 16 Dunlop KR108 |
| | rear | 16·5/8·0 × 18 Goodyear | 3·85/6·50 × 18 Dunlop KR108 |
| Weight | | 398 lb | 376 lb |
| Top speed | | 159 mph | 171 mph |
| Year of manufacture | | 1983 | 1983 |
| Owner | | American Honda Motor Co. Inc., Gardena, California, USA | Honda Britain Racing Team, London |

# 2 | Well oiled but so strange—*ELF E*

**Christian Leliard gives the Honda-powered ELF its race debut at the 1981 Bol d'Or. It retired when a stub axle broke (Woollett)**

What do a 1902 New Werner and a 1984 model Honda VF1100 have in common, apart from the obvious fact that they're both motorcycles? Simply that they both employ the same relative features of engine, frame, fuel tank, wheels, front forks, rear fork and seat. In other words, basic motorcycle design has remained pretty static for the past 80 years: all that's happened is that engines have been developed to produce ever more power, while at the same time piecemeal changes have been made to the original motorized bicycle principle in an effort to make the chassis accept the additional horsepower. Telescopic forks for girders, swinging arm rear suspension for rigid frames, disc brakes for drums—all these are variations on a theme, because the basic concept of an ever more powerful engine sitting in a tubular chassis has gone relatively unchallenged down the years.

In the past couple of years the crunch has come: chassis development has been unable to cope with the fruits of the horsepower race amongst the Japanese manufacturers. Hence the controversial decision to reduce the top limit of TT F1 racing from 1000 to 750 cc for 1984, or the decision by the FIM, prompted by the Japanese companies, to consider reducing the 500 cc GP limit to 400 cc in the future as a means of reducing power, and thus speeds. But all this is stop-gap thinking of the worst kind: in a couple of years the 750s will be producing the same sort of power as the 1-litre bikes are now. Then what?

Don't imagine this problem is confined to the race track: the new generation of Japanese road-burners has proved that what appears on the circuits one year can be in the showroom in not too diluted form the next. So it's in the interests of all bike riders that a completely fresh look, which by any standards is long overdue, should be taken at basic motorcycle design.

Followers of the Endurance racing scene will know that that look has already been taken. During 1982/83, the radical ELF 'E' (for Experimental) Honda-powered racer was one of the front runners in the long distance classics, sadly without winning one so far, though coming close on a couple of occasions. When the chance came to ride the bike, which with the advent of the 750 TT F1 rules was now ineligible, due for retirement to life in a museum, I could hardly get to Paul Ricard quickly enough to try out the complete range of four all-but-identical bikes which the team constructed and raced in 1982/83.

The ELF's roots lie deep in the heart of auto-mobile technology, even though its concept was mirrored in a classic case of parallel development by the British Difazio/Tomkinson endurance racer—later to be known to one and all as 'Nessie'—which first appeared in Laverda-

engined form a year before the first ELF prototype was finally unveiled in 1978. There's no sugges-tion that one design copied the other—simply that two different people in two separate countries each decided at about the same time to work along the same lines to eradicate some of the more ingrained faults of motorcycle design.

The ELF's creator is 42-year old Andre de Cor-tanze, one of the original minds behind the Renault F1 turbo racing car and before that designer of the first-ever turbocharged endur-ance four-wheeled racer, the Alpine A442. He still works for Renault as a development engineer but, in an example of the sort of inter-company collaboration whose spirit helps explain France's resurgence as a competitive force on two and four wheels, is given leave to work on the ELF bike project by them.

A former successful enduro rider untill he broke his leg badly a few years back, de Cor-tanze's first brush with the motorcycle endurance world came when he designed the oddly-shaped but effective bodywork for the Japauto Hondas in the mid 1970s. But it was the ELF-sponsored Renault connection, rather than Total's Japauto, which led to the chance to design and build a racing motorcycle incorporat-ing many of the new ideas for chassis design which he had: in 1977 Francois Guiter, ELF's com-petitions chief, gave de Cortanze the money to produce such a bike, and the TZ750-engined ELF 'X' which appeared the following year was the result. Though it only raced once, Guiter was suf-ficiently impressed to offer de Cortanze a much bigger budget to build and develop an endurance racer: Ecurie ELF was born.

'From the very beginning I tried to rid myself of every preconceived notion of what a motorcycle should look like,' says de Cortanze.

**Herve Guilleux finds the limits of adhesion on the ELF during a wet Le Mans 24 hour race in 1983 (Edge)**

'I concentrated instead on how it should be. I had four principal aims: to lower the centre of gravity, incorporate 'natural' anti-dive and anti-squat suspension, reduce weight and eliminate the chassis completely. There were various secondary objectives too, such as to achieve a 50/50 weight distribution, reduce the frontal aspect and lower the drag factor, improve the braking, be able to change the wheels quickly and so on. I would say that I have achieved everything I wanted to with the current machine—for me, it's obsolete, so I don't really mind that the change in capacity limits will rule us out of racing with it in future. For me the next step is to increase the tyres' contact patch with the ground in all modes, which in turn requires much work to be done on the suspension, and so a completely new bike is in order.'

When the ELF first appeared at the Bol d'Or in 1981, powered by RSC Honda engines which the Japanese factory in an admirable display of bet-hedging had agreed to supply the team with after one of their testers rode the TZ750 version at Le Mans the year before and was reportedly highly impressed by it, onlookers were dazzled

by its design and execution. And when the bike, ridden by development riders Christian Leliard and four-time world champion Walter Villa, led the first two laps of the race and stayed in the leading bunch till the rear axle broke after eight hours, a breakthrough in motorcycle engineering seemed to have been achieved. While it's probably fair to say that since then the ELF's results have not lived up to either the hopes of the team or the expectations of outsiders, the responsibility for this must equally fairly be laid at the door of the year-old Honda engines, rather than at de Cortanze's design. Time and again the bikes were sidelined while well placed with one engine malady or another. However, though both entries retired from the Bol d'Or in September 1983, Ecurie ELF's endurance effort signed out with a flourish a week later when 250 GP stars Didier de Radigues/Herve Guilleux finished a superb third in the final round of the World Endurance Championship at Mugello, behind two works Kawasakis but ahead of the title-winning Suzuki team, while Villa/Leliard came ninth. The two bikes, plus one lightweight 'qualifier' and an 1123 cc version for use in the prototype class in

*Above* **A trio of ELFs—or should it be 'ELVES'? (Edge)**

*Left* **And now for something completely different—the ELF E devoid of its bodywork (Edge)**

non-Championship events, were waiting for me to try at Paul Ricard at the end of November that year.

The ELF's design is centred around de Cortanze's contention that telescopic forks are an engineering abomination: anyone who's ever seen or experienced them flexing or twisting under heavy braking or cornering, especially with the modern breed of sticky tyres, would have to agree. If you do away with tele forks, continues the de Cortanze philosophy, then there's no need for a chassis, which is simply a means of supporting a steering head from which to suspend the forks. The result is that the Honda in-line four-cylinder engine is in every way the heart if not soul of the ELF, for effectively the front end and rear suspension are hung on to it without anything remotely resembling a conventional chassis or subframe. True, there are dural plates, but these are only necessary, according to de Cortanze, because the engine is designed to be slotted in a conventional frame and has none of the cast-in mounting lugs that a purpose-built unit for the ELF would have.

The engine therefore acts as a fully-stressed member, F1 car-style, to which the 'one-sided' front and rear suspension and ancillary components are attached. At the front, hub-centre steering is employed with parallel swinging arms in the vertical plane, and suspension provided by a single specially-made Marzocchi unit with remote gas reservoir. The handlebars bolt to a block at the top of the steering column, which rotates in two ball races top and bottom, and transmits the rider's intentions via a pair of steering arms connected by an adjustable tie rod. Two large rose-joints (or spherical rod-end bearings, to give them their proper name) act as the pivots for the hub-carrier steering arm, which thus neatly does away with the need for a pivot within the hub and has the important side-benefit of enabling quickly-detachable wheels to be fitted. These are specially-made ELIA cast magnesium units which weigh a scant 3·2 kg, each, with single-bolt attachment front and rear that enables a full wheel change to be carried out in 18 secs thanks to the rear-end design which enables the wheel to be removed without disturbing the sprocket or chain. The front wheel only can be changed in the time it takes to add 23 litres of fuel and change riders—an astounding 11 secs: 'A little slow, but we lose two seconds having to open the flap in the nose which covers the filler!' explained head mechanic Alain Chaligne, de Cortanze's right-hand man for the past five years. Eleven seconds to change the front wheel, add five gallons of four star and swap riders is slow?

To help in lowering the centre of gravity de Cortanze placed the fuel under the engine, in contrast to the exhausts which now run up and over the top of the powerplant: fortunately the wind-tunnel tested aerodynamic all-enveloping bodywork is thick enough to prevent the rider's precious bodily parts from becoming over-heated. 'Empty exhausts weigh less than full fuel tanks,' says de Cortanze.

The team has only once ever had to change a chain even in the course of a 24 hour race, which is a great advert for the ELF's rear suspension design: this ensures constant chain tension by placing the pivot of the cast magnesium swingarm coaxially with the gearbox sprocket. Another special Marzocchi suspension unit sits inboard of the rider's right foot, working off the swingarm via a set of dural rocker arms, the whole attached to the rear of the gearbox via more dural plates.

Because of the qd wheels only a single brake disc can be fitted at each end, but here again the team broke new ground, having been the first in bike racing to use carbon fibre discs which weigh next to nothing and are made by the same French SEP company that manufactures the aircraft brakes for Concorde. A four-piston Lockheed F2 car caliper is used at the front, with a Golden Brembo rear. A problem associated with carbon fibre discs is that they hardly work at all when cold, a fact I almost discovered the hard way when I gripped the brake at the end of the Mistrale straight on my first lap on the bike and nothing happened! Back in the pits Walter Villa offered sympathy: 'The first time I rode it the same thing happened: what you have to do is

ride along for the first 200 metres with the brakes on—that warms them up'. Glad someone told me! Brake disc wear in 24 hour races is also a problem as is wet running when the discs obviously stay too cool, but all in all de Cortanze is happy he persevered with them: 'We and SEP have both learnt a lot, and while the reduction in unsprung weight is useful the main point of using them is that they offer a reduction in gyroscopic effect, which improves the handling'. Don't expect to see carbon fibre brakes on road bikes for a while though—apart from the other problems, it's also horrendously expensive: however, thanks to these and other weight-saving design touches the ELF scales in at a competitive 173 kg ready to race with oil but no fuel in 24 hour form i.e. with lights—the 'qualifier' is a mere 168 kg. This is not of itself remarkable—the Performance Kawasakis weighed the same last season—but where the ELF does have an edge is on top speed and fuel consumption, thanks to the distinctive tricolor-painted streamlining developed in the course of several laborious hours spent in the Renault wind-tunnel. Best-ever trap time for the bike on the Mistrale is

287 km/h in 1000 cc TT1 form (293 km/h for the 1123, which I sadly didn't get to ride as it had a camera fitted for movie-making), considerably faster than the competition. Its very low drag factor also results in better fuel consumption, an important factor in endurance racing, and at the same time de Cortanze was able to design the bodywork so as to achieve his targeted 50/50 weight distribution with the rider in place. The funny little flyscreen doesn't seem very aerodynamic, though: zapping along the Mistrale it felt more like riding a ten-times faster version of an unfaired Manx Norton than a modern racing bike, since there's no bubble to tuck your head under. 'Actually, it's only there for cosmetic purposes,' confided Walter Villa. 'Provided you mould yourself to the bike it makes absolutely no difference to the top speed. The coefficient of penetration is so good that if you tuck in behind another bike to slipstream it, you don't go any faster as you might expect to do.' Coming up behind another rider on one of the other bikes I tried to put this to the test, but instead discovered something else: the ELF is so slippery that it leaves a very small pocket of air behind

it, compared to a conventional bike, so in turn it's difficult for riders of slower machines to take advantage and get a tow themselves. Neat!

As far as assessing the ride is concerned I can do no better than quote Mr Villa again: 'First time you ride it, you think—hmm, not bad: not quite what I expected. Then the second time—well now, this is really something. And then the third time—you fall hopelessly in love! Any other bike seems inferior, because it won't do what the ELF does.' Leliard agrees: 'In the three years I've been riding this bike, I have yet to discover its cornering limits: provided you're prepared to accept that two-wheel drifts are not only necessary but even desirable, there seems no limit to the speed you can go into a corner at and still get round'.

Well, I can't truthfully say I became a two-wheel drifter, but in the course of the two days spent riding the ELF I gradually wound myself up to riding it about as hard as I've ridden any racing bike—in spite of a fearsome Mistrale wind that threatened to take the front wheel away from you on a couple of points on the track. The result was literally amazing: there seemed to be no limit to the bike's capabilities, only to my own

*Left* **Hub-centre steering permits use of a steering column, leading to a narrow riding position and reduced wind resistance (Edge)**

*Right* **Fuel tank under the engine, exhausts on top, single-sided rear swingarm with special Marzocchi suspension unit, cast magnesium wheels with carbon fibre brake discs— the ELF broke new ground in many directions (Edge)**

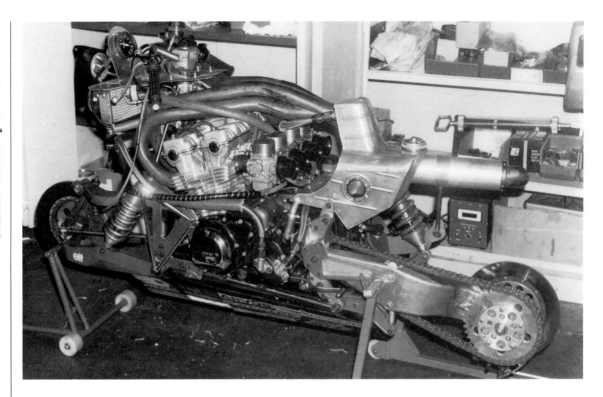

trust in them, and in mine too. In other words, the only barrier to going ever faster with the ELF into and round corners is a psychological one: what seems to be on the limit by the standards of other machines is in fact perfectly well within those of the ELF.

Take braking for example. On a conventional racing bike the ideal is to do all your heavy braking in a straight line while relatively upright, then flip it over and gradually apply the throttle to suit your cornering mode. Not so with the ELF. I found it possible to leave my braking seemingly suicidally late, then squeeze the front caliper for all it's worth, as well as stamp hard on the back stopper (which I hardly use at all normally). The front end dips ever so slightly, just enough to retain some feel to the suspension, and if you're still upright the bike stops dead level and flat— no dive. That's not so remarkable any more (except that it's achieved solely through suspen-

sion design, rather than an 'artificial' system of hydraulic valving or mechanical rods), but what is so is that you can bank the bike over as hard as you like while still braking hard, rushing deep into the turn way beyond where the braking mode would have ended on another bike. That in turn means you can brake yards later than the opposition: Leliard for example was braking at the 90 metre mark in practice for the Bol this year at the end of the Mistrale—that's from a terminal speed of over 280 kph!

To be honest I found out how good the ELF's brakes were accidentally: one lap in my second session a sudden enormous gust of wind caught me completely unprepared and blew me past my normal braking point. Oh God, I'm the only Anglo to ride this bike and here I am going to drop it. . . . I reckoned if I just squeezed tight and prayed that I could get round. . . . Five laps later I was braking an incredible ten yards further on.

*Left* The spare bike sitting in the pits for the 1981 Bol d'Or, ready to be wheeled out if necessary (it wasn't). Note the way in which the wheels can be removed without disturbing the brakes or final drive (Woollett)

*Right* Riding the ELF is an experience unlike anything else in motorcycling; is this the way ahead? (Edge)

The riding position is slightly unusual because the bars are close together to achieve a wind-cheating posture and you're leaning downwards a bit too. However it's perfectly comfortable, though low-speed manoeuvrability is poor, because it's impossible to exert much leverage on the bars. In fact, you're not supposed to: again I found out the hard way. Coming out of the corner by the pits on the first lap of the first totally dry session, I cracked the throttle open hard, drifting up on to the kerb as I and most other riders do at that particular spot at Ricard. As the 125 horses of the Honda engine chimed in together I was rewarded with a gigantic shake of the front end—if the tank was in the 'proper' place you'd call it a tank-slapper. Having sorted things out, I decided that maybe it was because I was riding the kerb, so in subsequent laps I took a tighter lane and everything was OK. Back in the pits Leliard and de Cortanze came up: 'I saw that,' said Andre with a grin. 'Do you know why it happened?' You guessed it—nothing to do with the kerb. 'You were trying to fight the front end—but the bike can react far quicker than the human mind. Next lap you were being much more careful, because you didn't know why it had happened, but really you were being much

more delicate, and that's the way to ride the ELF.' Didier de Radigues agreed: 'You mustn't grip the bars so tightly as with a normal bike: it's much more delicate a machine to ride than people think. Each command seems to be carried out just as you think it, rather than as a conscious action. You must just sit there and pretend you're driving a car with power steering—*doucement!*'

Compared to a conventional bike, the steering had a slightly remote feeling to it: I got the feeling that somewhere down there the wheel was turning in the direction I'd chosen, but you obviously don't get the same direct sense as with clip-ons bolted to the front forks. It did take a while to get used to, but after that I began to appreciate why riders from such completely different eras and backgrounds as Villa, Leliard and de Radigues rave about the ELF. It's so positive and neutral to steer: it goes where you want it with precision and immediacy, and that somewhere is much deeper into a corner than you could ever have dreamt of being able to go on two wheels while still braking hard. Part of the reason for this is the Dunlop tyres, specially developed in collaboration with de Cortanze especially for the ELF by the British company (Michelin weren't interested, strangely): the front in particular is unusual because it's much wider than usually fitted to a bike, to be able to accept the extra cornering and braking forces. The other main reason for the superb handling is de Cortanze's unconventional steering geometry. On a bike with a $56\frac{1}{2}$ in. (1435 mm) wheelbase, his steering head angle is a most unusual 29 degrees and the trail even more remarkable: 'I always tell people that it's a secret, but I will tell you that it's much, much less than other bikes. In fact, it's very, very close to zero!' And suspension defection is a mere 140 mm front and rear.

Streets faster than the opposition in a straight line thanks to careful attention to aerodynamics, the ELF's bodywork has also been designed to assist it in going round corners. The little handlebar fairings used to be adjustable for downforce till de Cortanze found the ideal position to impose maximum downthrust on the front wheel in the wind-tunnel and moulded them into the two-piece streamlining. As well, the rider is supposed to help by sticking his knee out—seriously! 'I used to ride in the classical style—knees in, bum on the seat,' said Walter Villa, 'Then I came to ride the ELF. Andre found in the wind-tunnel that if you sit off the bike and stick your knee out it not only has a positive effect on weight distribution but also means the knee acts as a wind flap—helps you spin the bike round the corner! Now I do it all the time!'

After my two days riding this avant-garde motorcycle in all types of conditions, wet and dry, still and windy, it was hard to escape the conclusion that this is indeed the way ahead for motorcycle design. All the riders were unanimous in believing this. Leliard: 'Dunlop's participation will pay off for them tenfold, because in five years' time all racing bikes will be like this. They have to be: the engines are now producing far more power than the present relatively primitive frames can handle, so the only possible way ahead is to concentrate on developing completely new concepts in

motorcycle chassis design. We already have such a bike'. De Radigues nodded agreement, but Walter Villa went further 'It'll be more than that: in 15 years from now all high-performance street motorcycles will have the same configuration as the ELF—it's as day follows night. This is the way of the future'. Tomorrow's motorcycle today.

| Model | | ELF E |
|---|---|---|
| Engine | | Honda Dohc 4-cylinder 4-stroke |
| Bore × stroke | | 71·6 × 62 mm |
| Capacity | | 998 cc |
| Power output | | 128 bhp at 8000 rpm |
| Compression ratio | | 10·5 to 1 |
| Carburation | | 4 × 33 mm Keihin |
| Ignition | | Kokusan–Denko CDI |
| Clutch | | 15-plate all-metal air-cooled dry multi-plate |
| Gearbox | | 5-speed |
| Frame | | Engine used as fully-stressed member, with front and rear suspension bolted on via dural plates |
| Suspension: | front | Centre hub steering with remote pivots and twin suspension arms. Single Marzocchi gas unit |
| | rear | Single-sided swingarm with single Marzocchi gas unit |
| Brakes | front | 1 × 300 mm SEP carbon fibre disc with Lockheed 4-piston caliper |
| | rear | 1 × 260 mm SEP carbon fibre disc with Golden Brembo caliper |
| Tyres: | front | 4·50 × 18 Dunlop |
| | rear | 3·75/6·50 × 18 Dunlop |
| Weight | | 173 kg with oil/no fuel including lights |
| Top speed | | 178 mph |
| Year of manufacture | | 1982 |
| Owner | | Société ELF, Paris, France |

# 3 | TT conqueror—
## *Suzuki XR69*

**Rob McElnea rounds Governors Bridge on his way to the first of a brace of victories (in 1983/84) in the Classic TT on the XR69 Suzuki test bike (Author)**

1983 was a watershed year in the history of motorcycle sport, for a variety of reasons, and in a number of ways. For while in Grand Prix racing the dawn of a new age arrived with Freddie Spencer's and Honda's first 500 cc title, and the subsequent retirement of 'King' Kenny, in the less rarified world of production-derived machinery, the end of one era took place, coupled inevitably with the start of another.

For at the end of the 1983 season the TT Formula 1 rules, which govern not only the World TT F1 championship run on road courses like the Isle of Man and Ulster, but also the World Endurance Championship, saw a reduction in the upper capacity limit from the 1000 cc mark in force since their introduction in 1977 to one of 750 cc. One year earlier, a similar move had taken place in the USA, where the Superbike class limit was reduced to 750 cc multis, and 1000 cc twins. The day of the brutish, ultra-powerful (and ultra-fast) 1-litre hyperbikes was over, except for a handful of races such as the Classic TT and Daytona 200 where this exciting but endangered species, the most powerful bikes the racing world has ever known, continued to be raced. And probably even there not for much longer.

All of this made Rob McElnea's victory in the 1983 Classic TT all the more significant, for it was achieved on a bike which when the history of the megapower 1000 cc racers comes to be written will almost certainly be regarded as the leader of the pack: the GS1000 Suzuki, known in its highly-modified works form as the XR69. Developed by Pops Yoshimura on behalf of the Japanese manufacturer, the XR69 not only won a host of races in Superbike form in North America for the Yoshimura team, notably four in a row in the Daytona 100-miler, but also enabled Suzuki to score a pair of World TT F1 titles in 1981/82 over their bitter Honda rivals, thanks in no small measure to the brilliance of Graeme Crosby. And when Croz moved on to the GP world with almost equal success, Suzuki's run of victories with the XR69 continued in 1982 with Roger Marshall, who dominated British short circuit racing with a pair of updated machines, winning the British F1, MCN Superbike and ACU British Road Racing titles with a series of victories that aptly earned him the nickname of 'Win-a-Week' Marshall.

A lucrative Honda contract enticed Roger away from Suzuki for the 1983 season, leaving his brace of 1982 model XR69s to be split up between veteran Mick Grant and newcomer to the team Rob McElnea; Grant was assigned a lightweight alloy-frame version into the bargain. But instead of the seasoned campaigner, it was the husky, good-looking rookie McElnea who posed Suzuki's greatest challenge to Honda's eventual World and British TT1 champions Dunlop and Gardner, winding up 2nd in both championships using just a single bike all season which was moreover, theoretically at any rate, inferior to his team-mate's. From the moment that Rob won the second British round at Thruxton in pouring rain, it was obvious that Suzuki had made an inspired choice, later confirmed for them by his superb victory in front of 160,000 people at Assen in the first World TT1 title round to be held in Holland. But two weeks beforehand McElnea had pulled off a prestigious triumph in the Isle of Man by registering a surprise win in the world's richest road race, the Classic TT, at a record average speed of 114·61 mph: it was, amazingly, only his second IoM TT year.

The machine which Rob used throughout 1983, and on which he scored that TT win, was retained by Heron Suzuki unlike most of its predecessors, which were returned to Japan at the end of their competitive life for an appointment with the crusher. Probably its last outing on a racetrack was in November 1983, a couple of weeks after Rob McElnea had taken it to victory in its final race in the last round of the British TT1 series at Brands Hatch, when it was brought back to the same circuit courtesy of Suzuki team manager Rex White for me to sample before it took up the sedentary occupation of museum life. Having ridden Wayne Gardner's British TT1 title-winning RS850R V4 Honda only a week beforehand, it was a unique opportunity to compare the two bitter rivals, one the epitome of the old 1-litre hyperbikes, the other the vanguard of the new wave of 750s.

Having first appeared in 1980, before the advent of the 16-valve GSX series, the XR69 is based on the older GS1000 8-valver—Suzuki's original four-stroke superbike. Though Yoshimura did obtain some appreciably higher horsepower figures from a GSX engine, attempts to run one in a Katana chassis in the 1982 US Superbike series with Wes Cooley aboard was not successful, primarily due to piston problems, and with the imminent reduction of the upper capacity limit to 750 cc, Suzuki persevered to the end of the 1-litre formula with the 8-valve engine. The in-line unit sits high in the XR69's tubular steel frame, essentially the same as when the model first appeared in Croz's hands in 1980, but with periodic detail improvements. For 1983 the principal modification made to the highly-tuned engine was the fitting of an 18-plate dry clutch in place of the wet multiplate unit used before, while the most obvious other external departure from the standard road bike engine is the fitting of dual ignition powered by a Nippondenso CDI unit. According to Suzuki's specialist F1 mechanic, Dave 'Junior' Collins, the twin-plug head transformed the engine,

The XR69 Suzuki was the
most successful design of
the 1000 cc TT F1 era. Note
the wide spread of the
handlebars, as favoured by
both Rob McElnea and
Graeme Crosby (Edge)

eliminating detonation, reducing flame travel and improving the carburation to the point where the engine was much more responsive at all revolutions. It allowed the team to run much leaner on jetting, as well as to reduce the ignition advance from 37 degrees advance with the single, offset plug, to only 25 degrees with the dual ignition—a considerable improvement.

Inside the engine Pops fitted oversize valves (39 mm inlet compared to the original 38 mm, and 37 mm exhaust as against 32 mm) matched to racing camshafts offering 10·3 mm lift instead of the street engine's 8 mm on the inlet, and 9·3 mm (7·5 mm) on the exhaust. 11·8 to 1 compression is used, but the Japanese pistons originally fitted were found to have a life of only 500 miles before cracking, causing Heron Suzuki to go shopping at Omega's in Britain for specially-made forged pistons which last four times longer; I wonder how the HB-Suzuki endurance

*Above* **The four-cylinder Yoshimura-developed engine produces 134 bhp at 9500 rpm (Edge)**

*Below* **Driver's eye view: strong men only need apply! (Edge)**

team that won the 1983 World title with the same engine mounted in an alloy chassis overcame this problem? A strengthened built-up crankshaft and tougher conrods are fitted, with the crank welded up to prevent it twisting and the end covers chamfered off to provide extra ground clearance. The 70 × 64·8 mm, 998 cc engine produces 134 bhp at 9500 rpm, measured at the gearbox sprocket, running on four magnesium-bodied 33·4 mm Mikuni smooth-bore carburettors whose choke size is dictated by TT Formula regulations. Peak revs normally used are 10,500 rpm.

The Suzuki's a big bike by any standards even just to sit on, though the 56·5 in. wheelbase is compact by the standards of big racing four-strokes and the dry weight of 160 kg (352 lb) a tribute to the extensive use of magnesium and other weight-trimming ideas: that's with a stainless steel exhaust and the steel frame, too, remember—the 1984 bikes with their alloy chassis and titanium exhaust scale around 8 kg less still. But thanks to the fact that Rob McElnea is a six-footer like me I found the riding position made to measure, though when getting on it for the first time I noticed at once that he has the clipons mounted very flat, sticking out almost at right angles into the airstream. Strange, I thought . . . but soon I would find out why!

Once encouraged into life the XR69 settled down to a fast idle even with the chokes off, and on a surprisingly warm autumn day the wet sump engine's oil supply was soon warm enough for me to venture out on to the track. While poodling round to get the hang of the bike, I found the 3000 rpm idle quite disconcerting: braking for Druids Hairpin was like having the throttle jammed open on you, and I doubt if Rob would have the carburation set up like that for rounding Governor's Bridge on the TT course. But at Brands once I started riding hard I even found it an advantage in that I could coast round Druids with just a whisker of throttle applied to keep the engine on song, before opening up coming out of the corner. Usable power comes in as low down as 4000 rpm, which with the 10,500 rpm maximum makes for an exceptionally wide power band—contrary to my expectations, I must admit—though there's a patch of megaphonitis around 5500 revs and real TT-winning herds of fire-breathing horses only arrive at 7000 rpm. But the Suzuki's far from the all-or-nothing monster I'll admit I'd expected to encounter, though it is VERY important not to crack the beautifully light throttle (as are the other controls: guaranteed sign of a works motorcycle) wide open coming out of a corner, else you'll land on your ear faster than you can spell disaster.

Needless to say, I found that out the hard way: after 15 laps or so of the 1·2 mile circuit, with its numerous off-camber corners with mean acceleration on a bike as powerful as the Suzuki must be treated with care, I'd grown confident on the bike to the point of trying a bit harder on it. Trying to get the maximum drive out of Clearways before the rush down the Pit straight, I applied just a touch too much throttle and was rewarded with a full-blooded slide as the rear Dunlop slick let go. Gripping the tank frantically with my knees, I fought the bars to regain control and somehow managed to succeed in doing so—but it had been a near thing. I realized then one reason McElnea has the bars spread so far on the bike, because though the handling is steady the steering is very heavy at the best of times, and the extra leverage of the wide bars must make it much easier to ride. Or rather, less difficult, because the combination of all that power and the bulky, in-line engine set high in the frame for necessary ground clearance makes for a top-heavy bike that requires a considerable degree of what American magazines call 'rider input': in other words, it's bloody hard work to ride at or near the limit! Suzuki have helped by steepening the head angle by special yokes for the 40 mm Kayaba forks, but it still requires a fair degree of effort just to flip the bike from side to

**Cracking open the throttle coming out of Clearways required care and delicacy if the rear wheel was to be kept in line (Edge)**

side as for example in the South Bank/Clearways esses. And because you're going so fast, the problem is exacerbated.

And fast you certainly do go, because the 130-plus horsepower shoved out by the factory unit propels the XR69 at incredible velocities for a road-based engine. Top speed of the bike is 170 mph on Isle of Man gearing (though it has been timed at 305 kph (189 mph) in testing in Japan), while even the 15/48 gearing fitted for Brands Hatch gives 156 mph at 10,500 rpm. I don't mind admitting that the best I saw on the rev counter before shutting off seemingly suicidally late for Paddock Bent was 9000 rpm, but even that's 134 mph, achieved on a stretch of road less than 700 yards long that on most other bikes is an undulating straight, but which on the Suzuki became a long, long right-hander with a short, straight entry to the right-hander at Paddock. The bike accelerates so fast and goes so quickly that straights turn into bends, and bends turn into hairpins. Compared to its V4 Honda rival, the Suzuki definitely has an edge on acceleration, even taking into account the Honda's deceptively lazy V4 gait.

Becoming gradually accustomed to the Suzuki's awesome performance, I discovered nonetheless that it's really a controllable bike at those speeds provided you're prepared to ride it on the throttle and really work at getting it round fast. The Kayaba suspension, matched at the rear to Suzuki's Full-Floater rising-rate design, was perfectly suited to my weight (about the same as Rob's, I suppose), and the XR69 was the only bike I've ever ridden round Paddock Bend at Brands on which I literally didn't notice the notorious and off-putting bump right on the apex: it rode superbly, and must have made a great IoM bike. The front end wasn't so good in a couple of places, though—notably when cranked hard over to the left sweeping down through Bottom Bend, when it chattered quite considerably, and again coming out of Clearways with the power applied when the front wheel started flapping once it ran over the ripples on the exit. On one lap this developed into a full-blooded tank-slapper that continued all the way down the pit 'straight': though it didn't really feel as if it was ever going to get out of hand, I decided to head for the pits to check everything was OK and inspect the steering damper mounted under the tank on the left. The consensus of opinion was that this was probably tired out, but now I know why a broken damper is a valid cause for retirement from a race on GP and works TT1 bikes when everything else is functioning perfectly: carrying on and making the best of things is probably the next best thing to writing your own hospital admission form.

Hauling the Suzuki down from its considerable top speed for corners was easily accomplished thanks to the massive twin 310 mm front discs, though the lever action for the RG500-type calipers felt a bit dead and the hydraulic anti-dive didn't retain as much feel as on the V4 Honda I rode. I hardly used the rear 220 mm disc, since when I did at the start of my ride I got a bit of rear wheel hop (probably simply through stamping on it too hard), and with all the engine braking on tap I really didn't feel I needed it. One nice feature was that I could go deep into a tight corner like Druids with the brakes hard on, without having the bike sit up and understeer on me as it would have done with a 16 in. front wheel fitted. On the other hand, replacing the 18 in. front wheel with a 16 in. one would surely have lightened the steering. In this respect I suppose the XR69 really belongs to a different generation than its Honda rival, which was certainly much easier and less tiring to ride hard. However, the Suzuki's power unit is almost as flexible as the Honda's even if the power delivery is rather more sudden, which does enable you to smoothen out some of the cornering problems. The close ratio gearbox has a nice spread of gears, even if the actual gearchange (left side, one up, five down) is a bit notchy and 'mechanical'. Allied to the tremendous torque of the engine it enabled me to short-shift coming out of Druids, for example, so as to be able to take Bottom Bend in fourth at about 6000 rpm, which lessened the impact of the front end chattering there, then hold fourth all the way along the back straight (just another long curve on the Suzy), running up to 10,000 rpm before braking and flicking the bike into South Bank, still in fourth, then coming down just one gear for Clearways which again made getting a good drive on coming out of the corner easier to obtain without the rear end breaking away TOO sharply.

After a total of 45 laps round Brands on this TT-winning bike, using the same engine that won Suzuki the 1983 World Endurance title, I can only say that my respect for the men who rode the XR69 to victory on the circuits of the world has only been increased. Unlike the RS850R Honda,

which almost any competent rider could go fast on with the minimum of practice, the Suzuki requires a real expert to wring the most from it, though the potential for someone of Rob McElnea's undoubted class to win with the bike is phenomenal. My session on the bike left me with arms and shoulders tired and aching from the sheer effort of riding it, seeking to assert my mastery over a fire-eating motorcycle that would cheerfully have spat me off soon as look at me. My best time during the day had been 52 secs—yet the TT1 lap record is in the 49 second bracket, which gives some idea of how far I still had to go before reaping the maximum potential out of the bike. Big, meaty, powerful and fast, the XR69 Suzuki represents a disappearing age in motorcyle competition, when muscle-bikes were just that, and only men of iron could ride them on the limit. Rob McElnea is one such man: now I know why his shoulders are as broad as they are!

| Model | | Suzuki XR69 |
|---|---|---|
| Engine | | Dohc 4-cylinder 4-stroke |
| Bore × stroke | | 70 × 64·8 mm |
| Capacity | | 998 cc |
| Power output | | 134 bhp at 9500 rpm |
| Compression ratio | | 11·8 to 1 |
| Carburation | | 4 × 33·4 VM Mikuni |
| Ignition | | Nippondenso CDI |
| Clutch | | 18-plate dry (9 friction/9 steel) |
| Gearbox | | 5-speed |
| Frame | | Duplex cradle |
| Suspension: | front | 40 mm Kayaba |
| | rear | Suzuki Full-Floater with Kayaba unit |
| Brakes: | front | 2 × 310 mm steel disc |
| | rear | 1 × 220 mm steel disc |
| Tyres: | front | 3·25/4·50 × 18 Dunlop |
| | rear | 3·85/6·50 × 18 Dunlop |
| Weight | | 352 lb |
| Top speed | | 170 mph |
| Year of manufacture | | 1982 |
| Owner | | Heron Suzuki GB Limited, Crawley, Sussex, England |

# 6 Battle of the Twins, or BoT

'The trouble with racing nowadays,' remarked Gary Bryan as we gazed at his superbly prepared RGB Weslake twin on a sultry day at Oulton Park in 1983, 'is that all the other classes tell you what you can't do, rather than what you can. Everything's so restrictive: you can't use carburettors more than this big, you can't alter the stroke, you can't change the castings, you can't use more than six gears—it goes on and on. They had the right idea in the old days—stick to capacity limits and a minimum weight rule perhaps to stop people producing bikes that are too flimsy, and then leave everything else up to the designers. That's why the Battle of the Twins is so good: OK, it's got a rule that you can't use more or less than two cylinders, and it's got to be a four-stroke, but that's only so that we all start off from the same point. After that, anything goes—and that makes it a perfect class for anyone who likes to use their own ingenuity a bit, like myself. I think the BoT is the best thing that's happened to road racing for years: it's brought back a wide variety of different bikes that sound great, don't cost a fortune to run, and give you unlimited scope to try out your own ideas . . . .'

Enthusiastic words, but only to be expected from the man whose bike dominated the early days of BoT racing on this side of the Atlantic in the hands of 1982 British Road Racing Champion Bob Smith—so tragically killed at Scarborough on his RG500 Suzuki later the next year. Invincible in Britain up till the time Gary kindly invited me to try the bike earlier that year, the RGB Weslake fared less well on its American sortie to Daytona in March 1983, when a succession of troubles resulted in Smith failing to start the final after lapping at speeds that would have assured him a midfield starting spot in the 200-miler itself, as well as running 4th in the BoT heat race before the gremlins struck. The chapter of accidents would have disheartened most men if spread out over a whole season, let alone one week, and included two broken primary belts (which had never given trouble before), a brand new battery which turned out to be a dud, an exhaust that broke off on the very first lap of practice, and to cap it all a mysterious misfire that appeared for the very first time in the warm-up area before the big race. Eventually traced to a minute particle of metal trapped in the pilot jet, the latter problem resulted in Smith non-starting after the team had travelled 4000 miles

and laboured in vain for a week. Back in Britain, though, the combination of Bob Smith and the RGB proved as invincible as ever in the Scarborough and Donington rounds of the inaugural UK Twins series, defeating a field led by Tony Rutter's works Ducati with ease.

Like most BoT racers, the RGB Weslake has undergone a lengthy process of continuous development over an extended period: there've always been new ideas to try out, new bits and pieces to fit in a quest for constant improvement. And for soft-spoken, likeable Gary Bryan, a former topline sidecar driver who's been confined to a wheelchair since a multi-machine pile-

*Below left* **Bob Smith and Gary Bryan ponder their problems during the abortive trip to Daytona in March 1983 (Author)**

*Below* **Bob Smith powers the RGB Weslake out of Turn 2 at Daytona on one of the few flying laps he managed there (Author)**

up at Oulton ten years ago in which two people were killed, the bike's present success in BoT and four-stroke events is plentiful reward for several years of endeavour with various riders tilting—often successfully—against the two-stroke windmill in open class races. As with any such machine, practically everything has been changed over the years on the bike, which dates back to 1975, when Stuart Jones rode it in Superbike races, using a wideline Manx Featherbed frame fitted with a 750 cc version of the Triumph-derived Weslake vertical twin-cylinder engine. 'The 700 Yamahas were just coming out then,' recalls Gary, 'and though they had the edge in speed, we could outbrake and outhandle them: Stuart finished 5th and 6th in a couple of the major races because of that.'

Next step was to increase the engine capacity to 850 cc, but at this point the power output—around 95 bhp in this form—began to prove too much for the standard Triumph Bonneville gearbox which Gary has used right up to the present day: the gear shifts simply fractured under load. Eventually Gary met up with John Rea, who's been one of his most faithful helpers since then and is a turner by trade. He made up an outrigger bearing to fit behind the clutch and support the mainshaft more rigidly: that did the trick, but didn't cure another problem which Bryan has had to live with all along, again as a result of the hefty power output. The Triumph box uses a woodruff key on the mainshaft to transmit the drive, and this has continually stripped over the years: Gary resolved this by fitting a modified splined shaft off a Quaife, and at Triumph's suggestion gave it to them back in 1982 to have a small batch made. Over a year later he not only hadn't had the promised supply, but after months of trying he still couldn't get his original pattern back! R.I.P.

This transmission problem only really surfaced after 1979, when two things happened: Bob Smith started riding the bike, in doing so exploring the frontiers of its performance for the first time, and Gary Bryan began to pop up the power output to well over 100 bhp with an oversize 950 cc version of the Wessie engine. The result was a TZ-beater, Smith for instance lying 2nd in the British Open Championship round at Scarborough in 1980 when he grounded the fairing and came off. With such a hard and competitive rider now aboard, Gary decided to capitalize as well on Smith's small stature and fit a more modern, lighter chassis, which he duly commissioned from fellow Welshman John Caffrey in the winter of 1981/82, just in time for the advent of the Battle of the Twins: the rest is recent history. Gary Bryan's RGB Weslake is now the most powerful air-cooled British four-stroke road-racer ever produced, and thus in many people's eyes the ultimate British racing motorcycle.

The most immediate impression you get on seeing the RGB for the first time is how small and low it is. Designed for the 5 ft 4 in. Bob Smith, the nickel-plated Caffrey frame has a seat height of only 25 in., which in turn makes for a low centre of gravity and an easily-flicked, chuckable machine which changes direction very readily. It also encourages the vintage style of riding in which the bike is pushed in towards the apex of the corner while the rider leans outwards, just because it is so low-slung, but ridding myself of such fanciful notions I found that Bob Smith's knee-out style was better suited to the grip available from the wide Dunlop slicks, mounted on Dymag magnesium alloy wheels: these are 18 in. diameter front and back. The bike not only steers well, it handled superbly over Oulton's bumps, the combination of twin gas Girlings and a long box-section swingarm at the rear, and front 38 mm Spondon forks making the now very

*Above right* **Lean and muscular, the RGB Weslake is in many ways the ultimate British twin-cylinder racing motorcycle (Sloane)**

*Right* **Caffrey-built frame wraps snugly around the mechanical components (Sloane)**

bumpy ripples coming out of Cascades, or the near-potholes on Island Bend a cinch to ride over even with the power turned fairly hard on. The front forks could be damped with air pressure only, but experience has found that this makes them stiff, so hydraulics are used on the RGB, which makes for a really nice, progressive fork action, coupled with Bryan's own design of mechanical anti-dive linkage, similar to the Spondon type fitted to the works Honda TT F1 bikes and employing a system of rose-joined rods and plates to transmit braking forces to the bottom yoke of the forks. I found that this actually doesn't completely eliminate front-end dive under braking, as a similar system fitted to the works Garelli 125 I tested had done, but instead slows it up, however hard you grab the front brakes. This is in many ways the most desirable point to aim for, since you still retain both feel and damping effect in the front forks, which don't 'freeze' as can happen under racing conditions with some of the hydraulic anti-dive designs.

Two enormous fully-floating $12\frac{3}{4}$ in. undrilled brake discs are fitted to the front end, with Spondon calipers, while at the rear there's a smaller drilled disc with a Lockheed. Part of the reason for this seeming overkill on a four-stroke weighing only 295 lb ready to race is that to save imposing undue reverse loads on the fragile transmission, Bryan asks his riders to use as little engine braking as possible, so that riding the bike like a stroker imposes that much more pressure on the braking system. I tend to use a lot of engine braking myself, which meant having to rethink my approach to riding a four-stroke, but even so I felt after the end of my ride on the bike that it's definitely over-braked; using only one front disc would save a useful 10 lb into the bargain.

Finished patriotically in red, white and blue (though with its Welsh heritage I'm sure some of my fellow-countrymen will feel the third colour might well have been green!), the RGB uses

an abbreviated fairing and small, sturdy seat which carries the battery that sparks the twin 6v coils feeding the Boyer ignition. An oil cooler sits behind a mesh grille in the nose, with a Krober rev counter and oil pressure gauge squeezed into the space behind the top crown: oil reading when hot is 70 psi. The dry sump system employs a double relief valve design, with the small, carefully shaped tank under the seat. To those cynics who expect that this ultimate

*Above* **Girling rear units helped to give positive handling over Oulton's bumps (Sloane)**

*Above left* **A belt drive primary conversion has been fitted (Sloane)**

*Top* **Seat height is only 25 in. Forks are Spondon units, with mechanical anti-dive on the right leg (Sloane)**

British parallel twin should leak oil as a matter of course, I can report that a more spotless bike after 20 minutes round Oulton Park could not be imagined. Thanks to a conversion to QPD belt-drive primary, the standard Triumph clutch runs dry; I found it extremely stiff to operate, thanks doubtless to the heavy-duty Norton springs fitted to stop it slipping under the extra power. There are five fibre and six steel plates, and Gary says he plans to convert it to hydraulic action over the winter: wish he'd done it before my test—then my left forearm wouldn't have seized up after about five laps! The original primary belts were 30 mm wide, and were replaced every two meetings when the bike was in 850 cc form, running on lower compression. Daytona's experience, when the teeth ripped out of one belt after just four laps, prompted Gary to move to a 40 mm belt with the bigger engine, and he's had no trouble at all with it since then.

The cause of all this aggravation is the 103–105 bhp churned out by the 80·5 × 91 mm 927 cc 8-valve engine, which uses a one-piece Nourish nitrided 360 degrees crankshaft stroked from 88·5 mm in 850 cc form to obtain the extra capacity. Weslake pistons, valves and rods are fitted to the plain-bearing pushrod engine, which runs on 11·5 to 1 compression using 50/50 Avgas and 4-star. Weslake's own 320 road racing camshafts permit a wide spread of power throughout the rev range, but of course you don't get a parallel twin to produce that sort of power without some pretty canny internal modifications about which Gary Bryan was understandably reticent. He did admit to having opened out the inlet ports to 40 mm to match the choke size of the Mk 2 Amal carbs, as well as modifying the Weslake spec exhausts slightly: next step was a two into one exhaust, as the left one used to ground sometimes with Bob Smith riding—but not with me aboard!

Riding the bike a couple of weeks after Smith's last victory on the bike I found it still set up for him, which meant that I couldn't squeeze my head under the screen at all with a helmet on—it's that compact a machine. Otherwise things felt just fine as I burbled round the first lap to get the feel of things, apart from the Charles Atlas-spec clutch action. But then as I began to open the engine up, I started to encounter all sorts of problems. Firstly, though there's power from as low down as 3000 rpm and a strong pull from 4000 revs up to the 8000 rpm maximum, I found the vibration which sets in very forcibly as soon as you go over 6000 rpm so bad that it was difficult to concentrate on braking and

Built around the short-statured Bob Smith, the RGB is low-slung and short, but vibration proved intense at high revs (Sloane)

finding the right line round corners. It wasn't so bad that it blurred my vision or anything so dramatic, but it made riding the bike at those engine speeds so uncomfortable that your mind subconsciously urges you to ease things down a bit till you get to the smoother waters of six grand and below. With all the heaps of torque on offer and the nicely spaced ratios of the 5-speed Triumph gearbox, there really doesn't seem much point in exposing oneself to this sort of torture unless absolutely necessary, which would be fine on a British short circuit perhaps, but impossible on the wide open reaches of Daytona, for example, where over half of every three-mile-plus lap is spent flat out at peak revs. My fingertips tingle at the very thought of it! Interestingly, I encountered exactly the same sort of problem on the 975 cc Big D Triumph that I rode previously, which buzzed like mad at anything approaching peak revs, where its smaller 750 cc brother did not: punching the engine out to these extremes would seem to alter the balance factor adversely.

Not being able to get flat on the tank was a bit of a disadvantage round Oulton's hills and dales, where you like to get as much weight over the front wheel, especially at places like Deers Leap, to stop it pawing the air. Thanks to the engine location, 2 in. further forward in the Caffrey frame than it had been in the Featherbed one, this never really became a problem even in the semi-upright position dictated by the screen. But what I was less able to cope with was the uncertain action of the Triumph gearchange. I don't think a single complete lap went by without my missing at least one change: nothing to do with the lever position, which was fine, so into the pits I went for a talk with Gary. Told that I had to keep my foot on the lever till I felt two clicks, which would indicate that the gear was home, I went out again, and though things were slightly better I can't pretend I felt really confident about swapping cogs on the bike. Fortunately, there's so much torque that you can cut

out much unnecessary gear-shifting but even so I'd need a lot of practice before I'd feel at home with the gear change. At the end of my second session I returned to base, where a possible cause of the problem was diagnosed. The woodruff key on the main shaft had gone: the Trimph box's perennial problem had raised its head just in time for me to sample it on the test.

Gary Bryan's RGB twin is a mean, lean (only 15 in. wide at the engine cases) and powerful motorcycle; years of development have been aimed at making it more purposeful rather than refining it, and it's a bike that would scare the pants off a novice rider who tried to exploit its amazing performance to the ultimate. I've ridden a few big, powerful four-strokes in my time, but I have to admit it even daunted me: when Bob Smith used to get on it, it did the same to the opposition!

| Model | | RGB Weslake 925 |
|---|---|---|
| Engine | | Ohv twin-cylinder 4-stroke |
| Bore × stroke | | 80·5 × 91 mm |
| Capacity | | 927 cc |
| Power output | | 103 bhp at 8000 rpm |
| Compression ratio | | 11·5 to 1 |
| Carburation | | 2 × 40 mm Amal Mk 2 |
| Ignition | | Boyer electronic with battery/two 6V coils |
| Clutch | | Dry multi-plate |
| Gearbox | | 5-speed Triumph |
| Frame | | Duplex cradle |
| Suspension: | front | 38 mm Spondon |
| | rear | Girling gas |
| Brakes: | front | 2 × 12¾ in. discs with Spondon calipers |
| | rear | 1 × 10 in. disc with Lockheed caliper |
| Tyres: | front | 3·50/4·50 × 18 |
| | rear | 3·75/5·00 × 18 |
| Weight | | 295 lb |
| Top speed | | 150 mph |
| Year of manufacture | | 1982 (in this form) |
| Owner | | Gary Bryan, Gresford, North Wales |

# 2 | Lucifer's Hammer—
## *Harley-Davidson XR1000R*

**Gene Church en route to victory in the 1984 Daytona BoT race on Lucifer's Hammer—still fitted with 16 in. front wheel (Petro)**

Lucifer's Hammer, according to an old Irish legend, was a comet sent by the Devil to destroy a village which had been invaded by foreigners who were so evil they made Lucifer himself jealous. How apt therefore that the bike bearing the hellfire red and black colours of the American Harley-Davidson factory which destroyed the Italian machine domination of the USA's Battle of the Twins series in 1983 should be so named.

The first Milwaukee-built V-twin to carry the factory's colours at Daytona in ten years, Lucifer's Hammer scored a convincing victory on its debut appearance there in March that year in the hands of dirt-tracking great Jay Springsteen, an expert road racer into the bargain but one with only four such races under his belt in the previous seven years. Fastest in practice, easy winner of his heat race, and quickest through the speed traps on the banking at 158 mph into a 7 mph head wind, Springsteen dominated the 50-mile race, defeating reigning Twins champion Jimmy Adamo's Ducati by 24 seconds, easing up. A week later at Talladega, Springer was half a minute in front of Adamo when he unloaded on someone else's oil on the last lap, while on his next ride on the bike at Elkhart Lake the engine seized when a camshaft bearing broke up, sending him on his ear again. But at Loudoun in June, Jay rode the bike to a superb 13th place overall in the Formula 1 race against the might of Honda and Kawasaki, as well as the horde of TZ750 Yamahas, earning himself some valuable

*Left and below* **Two views of the factory Harley-Davidson XR1000 roadracer with and without the fairing. Note the oil tank beneath the engine, termed a 'semi-dry sump' system (Petro)**

*Right* **Fairing is a modified Wixom-designed XR750 unit (Petro)**

National title points into the bargain. Thereafter his dirt-track commitments precluded his using the bike again last season, but Dave Emde took it over to register a couple of second places behind Adamo, before Gene Church was entrusted with it for the final race of the season at Daytona in October, where he won after a thrilling three-way Battle with the Ducatis of Adamo and Joey Mills. Lucifer's Hammer had routed the foreigners again!

As a keen supporter, and competitor, in the Battle of the Twins on both sides of the Atlantic, the chance to ride the factory Harley was even more of a treat for me: Harley's participation really put the BoT on the map Stateside. But at the same time the class did help the factor to publicize their XR1000 street bike, a descendant of the legendary XR750 and together with it the progenitor of the BoT racer, as I found out when I met up with Lucifer's Hammer at the pic-

prototype street bike in the Twins race at Daytona in October '82,' Don recounted. 'The bike went real well, so Dick got management approval to get back into road racing with a full-race version, provided we could have it ready for the March Daytona race and stand a strong chance of winning it. By the time that came through that really only left us with not much more than a couple of months to develop the bike, but Peter had already done most of the ground work so we were in good shape. As you know, we made the deadline!'

Yes indeed, and in doing so created an amalgam of XR750 and Sportster components that is a fascinating mixture of old and new. The chassis is the ex-Mark Brelsford one which was involved in the fiery and spectacular crash at Daytona in 1973, then sat around the race shop till last winter, when Resweber set to to update it for use with modern slicks by adding a triangulated backbone brace, stiffening up the steering head and swingarm pivots with extensive box-gusseting, and constructing an entirely new box-section swingarm. Forcelli Italia 40 mm forks with adjustable damping and magnesium sliders were used with fabricated H-D triple-clamps and a Kawasaki steering damper, with a pair of Fox shocks at the rear and Campagnolo magalloy wheels. The latter were originally 18 in. front and rear, but for Church's Daytona outing a 16 in. front was tried for the first time, and was still fitted when I rode the bike. Two large 300 mm diameter fully-floating meonite Brembo discs are fitted up front, with a fixed single, smaller rear: Golden Brembo calipers are used all round. Wheelbase is a trim 56 in. with the 16 in. front wheel.

While Resweber was building up the chassis, Habermehl worked on an engine configuration which similarly combined something old, something new, something special.... Using XR750 cases with an oversize left hand main bearing, iron Sportster barrels coupled with XR heads and rocker boxes, special flywheels made from XR

turesque Blackhawk Farms track on the Illinois-Wisconsin state line. Also on hand was Don Habermehl, who together with chassis specialist (and four-time National champion racer) Carroll Resweber, and designer Peter Zylstra was one of the select team inside the H-D race shop who under the guidance of the legendary Dick O'Brien was responsible for creating both road and race versions of the XR1000.

'It all started after Dave McClure rode the

forgings but with the Sportster stroke, an XR caged roller crankpin and short rods, he built a unit that gave 90 or so bhp quite easily, compared to the 70 bhp of the street XR1000. Then came the hard work, wringing a couple more brake horses here, another one there, with the aid of lengthy and patient experimentation on the dyno with a variety of exhaust systems, ignition timing, camshaft profiles and carburation. Retarding the ignition to only 17 degrees of advance in combination with twin-plug heads yielded the greatest power increase, and combined with 42 mm smoothbore Mikunis and some experimental cams which had lain around the race shop for quite some time, eventually produced 106 bhp at 7500 rpm. Lowering the rev limit in the interests of reliability meant that in the form I rode it Lucifer's Hammer was giving an honest 104 bhp at 7000 rpm, measured at the gearbox output shaft, running on 10·5 to 1 compression and 110 octane Union 76 racing fuel.

Starting the bike up from cold, especially on a crisp 55 degrees Midwest fall day, requires patience and care. The two quarts of R40 castor oil live in a fabricated oil tank bolted to the underside of the crankcases and incorporating a flywheel scraper to improve scavenging by employing a gravity drain to assist the conventional Harley timed breather. It's what you might call a semi-dry sumped system, but it's vital to get the oil good and warm before moving off, and because of the complex system the engine must be warmed up slowly and carefully. This means a plentiful supply of batteries is called for, because the total-loss system feeding the twin Accel coils isn't good for much more than 35–40 minutes before the engine starts misfiring although work has been done on an alternator system as a cure.

As I rode the bike it had literally only been checked over after Church's Daytona victory, so gearing was way off for the tighter, twistier Blackhawk Farms track. However, the couple of laps it took me to deduce this also displayed the XR's trump card: its incredible reserves of bottom-end torque and wide power-band. While I was getting used to the bike, grossly overgeared as it was, it seemed irrelevant in what gear and at how many revs I went into a corner: that powerful, smooth engine just pulled away from almost nothing. A Harley smooth? But of course—45 degrees V-twins don't have to shake, rattle and roll if they've had the benefit of a wave of the O'Brien magic wand. There's no real sense of vibration, only of real push, rather than kick, in the back power rushing you unhurriedly but deceptively quickly to the next corner. The engine's lazy but brawny beat belies its considerable performance.

Adding five whole teeth to the rear sprocket made all the difference to the gearing and, already beginning to feel at home on the bike, I went out for a more protracted session. The riding position is nice if meant for someone a bit shorter-legged than I, but the oversize tank fits snugly into your chest, with its scalloped sides providing good leverage to push the bike into long, sweeping turns while keeping flat under the wide, all-enveloping screen. The fairing is actually a Wixom-designed XR750 with alloy wing extensions for the big screen. In spite of the twin throttle cables and considerable suction effect from the massive carbs, the throttle action is firm but smooth, and not stiff. The left-foot gearchange is very positive but requires a firm foot on the pedal, for while nothing like as clunky as that on my old (1972 ex-Pasolini) XR750, the dogs are so widely spaced and the gears so large that there's inevitably a click to convey mechanical awareness that you've just swapped a cog. But with only four speeds, one of which (bottom) is largely redundant, you don't have to do so that often, thanks to the wide spread of power. A triplex primary chain is fitted: the team had a belt drive conversion all designed up till they found it would mean spinning the XR750 road racing transmission too fast and thus risk overloading the gears accordingly. The gearshift has

**2-into-1 exhaust, 16 in. front wheel and Italian forks are some of the external modifications to the original period XR750 chassis (Petro)**

a very short throw, however, and downshifting without blipping the throttle was no problem even into bottom.

The engine is superbly torquey and responsive: it pulls quite well from as low down as 2000 rpm before really coming on fire at exactly 4000 rpm up to maximum revs of 7000, without any sign of megaphonitis from the two into one exhaust. But it's controllable power at all times—cracking open the throttle doesn't unhook the rear tyre as was the case with Britain's champion Twin, the Bob Smith RGB Weslake which I rode a couple of months before the Harley. That had a comparable power output and weight (Lucifer scales 285 lb with oil but no fuel, around 50 lb lighter than a Rayborn-era XR750 with its all-alloy

engine, a remarkable feat), but a much less manageable powerband as well as horrific top end vibration in best parallel twin style. The XR1000 couldn't have been more different.

What *did* unhook the rear on the Harley was the ultra-hard compound of the rear Goodyear slick, designed to run at top speed for extended periods on Daytona's bankings in 30 degrees warmer weather. It just never even came close to heating up at Blackhawk Farms, and some lurid slides resulted, one of which had photographer Bill Petro wishing he'd chosen another spot to take leaning away pictures! Even after 35–40 laps of the 1·8 mile track with its 2400 ft straight the centre of both tyres was barely warm, in spite of dropping the pressures by 4 psi. Pity.

The brakes are simply fabulous though, even disregarding the considerable assistance available if needed from the longstroke 81 × 96·8 mm engine (compared to the XR750's 79·4 × 75·7 mm). Don has been working on an air anti-dive system for the front forks similar to that employed on Harley's street bikes, and had hoped to have it ready for me to sample on the test, but without success. Personally I really doubt whether it's needed because the Italian forks retain such excellent damping characteristics even when all three brakes are being squeezed tight that the suspension doesn't freeze up. The Brembos haul the bike down from speed so incredibly quickly and effectively that when you add in the engine braking ingredient I can quite see how Springer was able to dazzle other riders (me included!) at Daytona with his ability to go barrelling into the turns so deep—with both wheels drifting, I may add. Maybe *that's* why they use such hard-compound tyres—just to make those dirt-tracking good 'ol boys feel right at home!

So far so great—but now for the one thing I definitely didn't care for on the bike: the handling. It just felt decidedly odd. Strangely it's not the problem I had expected after talking to Carroll Resweber at Daytona, when he lamented the limit to how much it's possible to beef up a ten year old frame to cope with today's tyre technology: 'All you're doing is shifting the forces somewhere else,' he said, shaking his head. 'They've got to work themselves out somehow, so all you're doing is putting the hinge in the middle rather than up front or out back. Once Jay really starts switching 'er on, we may have to go to a new chassis.' So far that hasn't been necessary, and the hard tyres prevented me finding out exactly where the hinge is located at present. The problem I experienced instead was a strange feeling of instability, as if the bike's top heavy and wants to topple over into a turn rather than drive into it. Partly I think this may be caused by the newly-fitted 16 in. front tyre which really doesn't suit the bike that much: the chassis wasn't designed for it and I don't feel the modifications to the front end made when it was fitted

have been entirely successful. Firstly, Lucifer definitely didn't like being flicked from side to side on a trailing throttle, as on Blackhawk's Turns 2 and 3, before the heavy braking for Turn 4: the front end starts gyroing even with the steering damper adjusted well up. Then when you get to Turn 4 the old bugbear of 16 in. fronts becomes apparent when the bike sits up under heavy braking and tries to understeer straight on. Then when you do persuade it to lean over into the corner it just sort of flops suddenly into it without any feeling of progression such as, I might say, I get on my own XR750 (with 18 in. front tyre). 16 in. wheels are all very well if the chassis is designed around their use: Hondas have proved that with their VF750 road bike for all to try. But sticking a smaller diameter front wheel on a bike designed for an 18-incher (and retaining the bigger wheel at the rear) may give quicker steering response and enable you to run a wider rear tyre, but it can bring concomitant problems in its wake even if you adjust the front end geometry to suit, because you're upsetting the whole balance of the bike's chassis. I think that's what's happened with Lucifer, because I can't believe that Springer rode the bike so hard and well at Loudoun with the chassis handling like that. If Church's Daytona outing had been the only test so far of that new configuration, most probably that's the reason, because the Florida track does not make great demands on a bike's handling compared to a road circuit like Loudoun or Blackhawk. More work needs to be done on this area, I'd respectfully submit, and I'd even question if a 16 in. front is really necessary. Better I'd have thought to try to lower the whole bike, which *is* rather upright by modern standards, and that would seem to indicate a new chassis, as Resweber intimated.

*Above left* **Lucifer felt top heavy in corners, but had superb engine response (Petro)**

*Left* **Don Habermehl poses proudly with Lucifer's Hammer and the author at Blackhawk Farms (Petro)**

Hard tyres and iffy handling notwithstanding, my overwhelming impression after a day in the company of Lucifer's Hammer is of that lovely, smooth, torquey and powerful engine and the reassuringly positive gearbox, as well as of the excellent brakes. That and the numerous clever touches abounding on the bike, from the fabricated oil tank to the oil pressure gauge plumbed into the crankcase (4 psi when hot) where the rider can't see it but the mechanic can! Almost everything on the bike is a one-off component, made specially for this motorcycle by true craftsmen with one aim in mind: winning. It would take quite some doing by the band of foreigners to stop Lucifer's Hammer doing just that in 1984.

| Model | | Harley-Davidson XR1000R |
|---|---|---|
| Engine | | Ohv V-twin 4-stroke |
| Bore × stroke | | 81 × 96·8 mm |
| Capacity | | 998 cc |
| Power output | | 104 bhp at 7000 rpm |
| Compression ratio | | 10·5 to 1 |
| Carburation | | 2 × 42 mm Mikuni |
| Ignition | | Total-loss 12v battery and twin coils with two spark plugs per cylinder |
| Clutch | | Multi-plate oil bath |
| Gearbox | | 4-speed |
| Frame | | Single-loop backbone with triangulated subframe and duplex cradles |
| Suspension: | front | 40 mm Forcelli Italia |
| | rear | Fox gas |
| Brakes: | front | 2 × 300 mm Brembo meonite discs, fully-floating |
| | rear | 1 × 250 mm Brembo steel disc, fixed |
| Tyres: | front | 22·5/6·5 × 16 Goodyear |
| | rear | 26·5/8 × 18 Goodyear |
| Weight | | 285 lb (claimed) |
| Top speed | | 165 mph (estimated) |
| Year of manufacture | | 1972 chassis/1983 engine |
| Owner | | Harley-Davidson Motor Company, Milwaukee, Wisconsin, USA |

# 3 | State of the art— *Ducati 600 TT2*

**Tony Rutter leads Donny Robinson's Yamaha round a wet Dundrod circuit in the 1982 Ulster GP en route to a second TT F2 World Championship for himself and Ducati (White)**

It was the Monday before the World Cup soccer final, and Italy—the future champions—were playing hot favourites Brazil in a quarter-final game that nobody expected them to win. Even so, it seemed the entire population of Italy were engrossed in watching the match: every cafe with a TV set had people spilling on to the roadways to peek a long-distance view; factories shut down in the face of massive absenteeism; streets were deserted of traffic, and even the carabinieri were nowhere to be seen.

And yet here I was mounted on another kind of World Champion, lapping the Misano GP circuit in total solitude in the 90 degrees F heat of the Italian summer. I was aboard the works 600TT2 Ducati, one of the five factory specials that in 1982 had repeated their success of the previous year by winning the World TT F2 title with Britain's Tony Rutter in the hot seat with the backing of Sports Motor Cycles, and the prestigious Italian TT2 series in the hands of works pilot Walter Cussigh. In each case the little Ducati achieved a grand slam of its respective championship, both riders winning every round convincingly against far from negligible opposition, which in Rutter's case included thinly- (or un-) disguised TZ350 Yamahas.

Boxing fans like to pick the fighter who pound for pound they rate as best in the world irrespective of weight. On the same basis, the 600TT2 Ducati, practically invincible in its class, must have had a strong claim to being the king of the racing bike world regardless of capacity or formula. Before you dismiss such comment as the preposterous ravings of a hopeless Ducati freak, consider this: a sleeved down version ridden by last year's Italian TT2 champ Massimo Broccoli finished 7th in the final round of the Italian 500 series at Mugello in October 1981, ahead of two dozen assorted RG500 Suzukis and OW Yamahas ridden by the likes of European champion Leandro Becheroni. Not convinced? Well, then there was Jimmy Adamo on a stretched 750 version finishing 13th in the Imola 200 in April that year and passing RG500s and Honda superbikes for speed down the straight. Still not? Then you must look at Tony Rutter's amazing new IoM TT F2 lap record of 109·27 mph as he won the 1982 TT at a speed which would have given him 3rd place in the 1000 cc F1 event—incidentally flying through the speed traps at 144 mph, compared to the 152 mph of the factory Hondas with 40 per cent larger engines.

The bike I was riding was Cussigh's machine, on which he'd just clinched his title at Misano the previous day with a flag-to-flag win; factory racing boss Franco Farne—himself a former works rider of some distinction, and for long the right-hand man of legendary Ducati designer Ing. Fabio Taglioni—was on hand to supervise my test session and fill me in on the background to the bike, and its heavily oversquare 81 × 58 mm engine.

'We use standard 600 Pantah cases with a bolt-on magnesium casing for a hydraulically-operated dry clutch,' Farne pointed out to me, 'Inside the engine is so close to the standard road bike it's unbelievable. We only port the heads, fit racing camshafts, high-compression pistons for 10·4 to 1 compression ratio as compared to the 9·5 to 1 of the standard engine, and oversize valves: we use a 40·5 mm inlet (the road Pantah has a 37·5 mm one) with 35 mm exhaust (33·5 mm). Valve timing is 67 open/90 close on the inlet, and 101/58 exhaust. Included valve angle is 60 degrees, as standard, compared to the 72 degrees on the older 900 V-twins, which also have expensive and noisy bevel shaft drive to the sohc desmodromic valve gear. That on the Pantah is by silent toothed belt, which on the TT2 we leave exposed to the elements, the belt cover having been jettisoned to save weight.'

Ignition on the TT2 was by Bosch electronics, firing Champion L81 plugs which were used for

One of the four 600TT2 Ducatis built initially in 1981 in the Bologna factory, together with a brace of experimental Pantah road bikes from which they were derived (Author)

*Above* **Cussigh's title-winning bike awaits the author at Misano (Moretti)**

*Above right* **A dry clutch with magnesium outer cover is the principal external hallmark of the works, as opposed to customer, 600TT2 Ducatis (Author)**

both warming-up and racing. The factory ran 32 degrees of ignition advance, and the whole system used a quite hefty battery mounted in the seat, a far from ideal location which raised the centre of gravity but was, unfortunately, unavoidable. 1981 saw the use of a small dry-cell battery which proved inadequate even with a generator fitted; solution was to fit a bigger wet-cell unit which couldn't be squeezed anywhere inside the tight-fitting frame.

And it was the multi-tube chassis, made by Verlicchi in Bologna, which was the heart of the 600TT2. Heavily triangulated especially round the steering head and balance point of the bike just above the rear cylinder, the chromemoly unit weighed a scant 7 kg including the single-shock cantilever swinging arm. A Marzocchi rear unit was fitted to the bike I rode, with magnesium 35 mm front forks from the same manufacturer with magnesium sliders and Campagnolo

wheels. Cussigh used a 16 in. front wheel, with specially-wide forks yokes to accommodate the wider tyre, whereas Rutter always opted for the larger 18 in. rim and narrower cover as providing better steering on road courses.

Other differences became apparent when I came to try the bike for size. Cussigh prefers a TZ Yamaha type left foot change with reverse pattern one-up, four-down configuration. But there were other idiosyncracies I needed to come to terms with before I could begin to ride the 600TT2 at even eight-tenths of its potential. The first thing was its size. Having become

accustomed to the rangy (and that's the polite word!) 61 in. wheelbase of the big 900 Ducatis in the course of my Battle of the Twins racing on Syd Tunstall's bike in the USA, I could hardly believe how little the 600TT2 was. Out with the tape measure: 55 in. wheelbase, a riding position like TZ Yamaha, dry weight of 128 kg including the heavy generator and electric starter required by Italian TT2 regulations (lose 10 kg straight off if you remove them as Sports M/cs' Steve Wynne did on Rutter's bike), and what do you have? A four-stroke racing motorcycle with road-based 600 cc engine with a similar power to- weight ratio to a TZ 250 Yamaha or Armstrong, and a 5000 rpm rev band. Was this not really my ideal racing motorcycle, I began to ask myself . . .?

The sculptured alloy fuel tank sat inside the spaceframe, allowing you to tuck your knees around it: Cussigh is only 2 in. shorter than I, so I found the riding position almost ideal, if a little cramped. The ultra-slim fairing allowed the bike to present a very narrow profile, undoubtedly a factor in its amazing straight-line speed, but you had to be careful to squeeze those knees tight into the tank on the straights, else precious mph were lost in increased drag. It's not a tall person's bike any more than a TZ is, but you can make do. I did!

Farne fired up the 90 degrees V-twin engine using the self-starter with the aid of a slave battery; the Italian TT Formula rule that you have to have the original means of self-starting fitted as on the road bike on which the bike is based is a good one, since it rules out the use of racing engines such as TZ Yamahas and Aermacchis. On the other hand, there's no carburettor rule, so 'my' bike was fitted with 40 mm Dell'Ortos as compared to the 36 mm units Tony Rutter had to use. After warming the engine up for just 2–3 minutes on such a hot day, Farne gave me the all-clear after testing the oil temperature with a hand on the oil cooler mounted in the nose of the fairing. I notched first gear on the standard road gearbox, and set off.

Accelerating out of pit lane I noted at once the wide power band and precise gearchange; you must count the gears since once in top the gearlever doesn't go floppy to let you know you're there, and a couple of times to start with I found myself stabbing for a non-existent sixth gear. The engine is amazing: it pulls cleanly from zero revs, with no hint of megaphonitis from the 2-into-1 open pipe. By the time the white-faced Veglia rev counter hits 6000 rpm the cams are beginning to do their stuff, and there's good strong power all the way up to peak revs of 11,000. Maximum torque is produced at 7500 rpm, and peak power of 78 bhp at the rear wheel at 10,500. It's truly an exceptionally easy bike to ride, though it was noticeable that once I got the engine buzzing at around 9000 it was almost like sticking it in overdrive—there seemed to be an extra dollop of power at the top end of the rev range.

These characteristics make the 600TT2 Ducati a bike for all circuits. On a road course like the IoM or the Ulster you can use the engine's flexibility and drive through sections in the same gear, concentrating on the corners and giving the motor an easier time over the bumps. But come to a purpose-built track like Misano, and you can gear it like a stroker to keep the engine buzzing at or near peak revs for maximum performance, as I'd observed Cussigh doing the day before in winning his race comfortably. At first I tried to ride the Ducati the same way, but could only pull 9500 rpm down the main straight, which is one reason he's a TT2 champion, and I'm not!

Then I realized that all the gear-changing I was indulging in was probably unnecessary, and started using the torque and wide powerband of the Bologna twin to full advantage. Reducing the number of gearchanges and squirting the bike between corners not only made for easier riding but also cut down my lap times. As Norton's Joe Graig once said: 'All the time you're changing gear, you're not going anywhere'. The 600TT2 proved him right, but it required mental effort to keep reminding myself not to change gear, and let the engine do the work between corners.

The multi-tube frame complemented the engine perfectly, providing safe, sure handling through Misano's twists and turns. The monoshock rear suspension wasn't really tested except over the joints of the resurfaced sections, but must have been a joy to ride over the Isle of Man bumps with. Braking was superb, the twin 280 mm floating front Brembo discs hauling the bike down from 9500 in top down the back straight—around 135 mph—from within the 200 metre board for the second gear left-hander at the end. I did find it difficult to use the rear brake though, for the simple reason that the lever was tucked in too close to the frame on the right side for easy access by my size nine boot.

The only really negative factor surrounded the use of the 16 in. front wheel. Going into a corner a fraction too fast, I grabbed the front brake to knock off some more speed, and had the bike sit up on me and understeer straight on. Having sorted out the ensuing moment I deliberately did the same thing the next lap, with similar results. Having been designed for an 18 in. front wheel, the frame doesn't take kindly to use of the smaller diameter rim, and the works bikes have since been converted back to the original spec. With such good weight distribution and steering, the bike doesn't need the smaller wheel.

*Above right* **Handling on the Misano sweepers was impeccable (Moretti)**

*Right* **The tubular spaceframe is made in chrome-moly steel by Verlicchi. Belt-drive covers have been jettisoned to save weight (Author)**

**Only drawback on the test bike was the fitting of a 16 in. front wheel, which promoted understeer under heavy braking. Tony Rutter insisted on an 18 in. wheel being fitted to his bikes (Moretti)**

Otherwise the 600TT2's handling was pretty well impeccable; coming out of the slow chicane before the pits it'd shake its head briefly as full power was applied and the front wheel got light. But a combination of the frame characteristics and adjustable Paoli steering damper tucked close into the tank soon sorted out the wiggle. And rushing into the next right-hand sweeper after the Pits straight, the Duke powered its way round hard on in fourth gear without the trace of a wobble, in contrast to the big TT F1 multis the day before which had tied themselves in knots on this demanding curve.

After 20 laps or so aboard the 600TT2, I'd come to respect it for what it is: almost certainly the best all-round racing motorcycle in the world of its day. A languidly-waved chequered flag from Franco Farne signalled the end of my test session, but as I trundled gently into Pit Lane after a slowing down lap, the place was deserted. Resisting the temptation to ride off into the sunset so as to hang on to the bike permanently, I went looking for people. Just then there was an uproar from the trackside office; peering inside I found a flickering TV set and a dozen ecstatic Italians embracing each other. You guessed it: Italy 3, Brazil 2!

| Model | | Ducati 600 TT2 |
|---|---|---|
| Engine | | Sohc V-twin 4-stroke with desmodromic valve gear |
| Bore × stroke | | 81 × 58 mm |
| Capacity | | 597 cc |
| Power output | | 78 bhp at 10,500 rpm |
| Compression ratio | | 10·4 to 1 |
| Carburation | | 2 × 40 mm Dell'Orto |
| Ignition | | Bosch BTZ electronic with battery |
| Clutch | | 14-plate dry |
| Gearbox | | 5-speed |
| Frame | | Multi-tube spaceframe |
| Suspension: | front | 35 mm Marzocchi |
| | rear | Monoshock cantilever with Marzocchi unit |
| Brakes: | front | Twin 280 mm Brembo discs with Brembo calipers |
| | rear | Single 260 mm Brembo disc with Brembo caliper |
| Tyres: | front | 3·25/4·50 × 16 |
| | rear | 14/68 × 18 |
| Weight | | 128 kg (dry) with generator and electric starter |
| Top speed | | 145 mph |
| Year of manufacture | | 1981 |
| Owner | | Ducati Meccanica SpA, Bologna, Italy |

# 4 | Fastest in the west—
# *Big D Triumphs*

'Triumph spoken here': home of the Big D specials
(Author)

Is there anyone with a TV set who hasn't heard of Dallas, Texas? Thanks to the fortunes of the Ewing family and the guy we love to hate, J.R., it must be the most famous place in America— yet in the motorcycle world Dallas has meant only one thing for the past 25 years: the home of the fastest British bikes in the world. Surprised? Read on.

'Big D' Cycle in Dallas is the home of Jack Wilson—Triumph tuner supreme. Wilson's Triumph credentials are impressive. A dealer in Meriden products since the early 1950s, he tuned the 650 engine which powered Johnny Allen to a new outright world speed record mark in 1956, thus giving Triumph's most famous model its name: the Bonneville. Since then, he's reaped a host of other world marks at the Salt Flats with his machines—often riding them himself—and still holds 14 world class records set there. His new 'double triple' drag racer is the latest in a long line of successful straight line machines; Gary Nixon was just one of the many topliners who rode Wilson-tuned twins to success on dirt-track ovals in the 1960s; and son-in-law Jon Minonno is only the most recent of many riders to road race Big D Triumphs to one victory after another, winning up to three US National class titles in a single season in the late 1970s against the best that Japan could offer.

When the kick-off for the US Battle of the Twins in 1980 coincided with the imminent arrival of the 8-valve head for the Triumph twin,

*Above* **Jack Wilson (right) and Jon Minonno pose with the original, standard-framed Big D Triumph in front of the Travellin' Texan transporter after another championship victory (Author)**

*Top* **Jon Minonno delights British admirers on the 'sitter' at Donington Park in 1982 (Francis)**

*Right* **Standard forks mate with magalloy wheels, slicks and Brembo discs to produce the fastest Triumphs in the West—or East (Author)**

Wilson knew he had to get involved. Prising the factory's development hack loose from Meriden's clutches, he received the engine only two weeks before the 1981 Daytona event—too late to make the very tired unit reliable enough to face the rigours of the banked Speedway. But a week later at Talladega, Minonno romped to 3rd place overall and an easy win in the Modified Production class: Jack Wilson knew he had a potential race winner. 'That was the only good result we had all year, though,' said Jack in his Texas drawl as we sat sipping coffee in the February sun at the little Oakville Raceway track near the Texas-Louisiana border. Freddie Spencer's home circuit, where he cut his racing teeth, it was the venue for my chance to try out the fastest Triumph road racers in the world today— an honour indeed, since nobody but Jon

Minonno had ever sat astride them on a race track. First though, we had to give the track staff a chance to clear off the evidence left by a substantial herd of Lone Star state's biggest asset after J.R. and oil—'steak on the hoof'!

'We were doing development work that first year we ran the BoT,' said Jack 'That li'l ol' 8-valver's a fine engine, but it never got used for road racing before. We had to be the competition R&D department for Triumph with it'.

To good effect, since on returning to Daytona a year later—still with the bike in 750 cc form— Minonno ran through the traps at 155 mph on the banking and scored an easy victory in the

**The basically stock Triumph frame is seen here to advantage in the Daytona pits (Author)**

Modified Production class. Amazingly, not the slightest effort to capitalize on this noteworthy success was made by the parent factory, even in advertising, a fact which ruffled even Jack Wilson's ingrained loyalty to the marque: 'Seemed like nobody knew or cared what we were trying to do out here,' he remarked, 'and as for getting spare parts out of them—well, it was like pulling teeth. I was even prepared to pay the dealer price just to have them, but it wasn't a bit of good. Without parts we couldn't run the whole series—else I know we could have won the MP title easy'.

So lack of vital spares restricted the team's outings in 1982—that plus the distance of Dallas from most of the BoT rounds, coupled with the fact that the entire racing effort is funded out of Wilson's own pocket. 'Daytona's our nearest event,' says Jon Minonno, 'and that's an 18-hour drive each way. We drove 32 hours straight to get to Laguna Seca, and Loudoun—well, that was 48 hours each way just stopping for gas and to change drivers.' Nevertheless, the longest journey was the highlight of the season, when Wilson and Minonno brought the high-barred Triumph 'sitter'—now with engine punched out to no less than 975 cc—over to Donington to represent the USA in the first international BoT at Donington in August 1982. After problems with low octane British fuel 4th place still made the trip worthwhile.

But for Daytona '83 Wilson decided to go for broke—and outright victory in the BoT. The first bike I tried at Oakville was his latest machine, only completed the night before and fitted with a hack 750 8-valve engine for our initial trials. It was one of the US-built J&R copies of a Rob North frame for the racing triples made ten years ago or so, with which Minonno won the US Unlimited road race title in 1978 at WERA events, using a three-cylinder motor bored and stroked to 1020 cc! The 750 twin sits in the chassis with room to spare, the whole clothed in a Yamaha TZ750 fairing whose windcheating properties

Wilson enabled Jon to break the 160 mph barrier on the Florida banking on the lighter, lower bike compared to the bulkier, unstreamlined 'sitter'.

Jon Minonno's a good 6 in. shorter than me, and the 'twinple' was tailored to suit him. That meant even jacking my legs high enough to plant my feet on the high-set rests a major problem, let alone changing gear or riding the bike hard. The $56\frac{1}{2}$ in. wheelbase offers fast steering, aided by the 16 in. front wheel which also permitted a fatter tyre profile. Paired with the hefty 16/70 × 18 rear—the swingarm had to be specially widened to accept the massive rear slick—the use of a 16 in. front wheel ensures Minonno will have all the tyre he needs to get maximum drive out of the infield turns at Daytona. Even in 750 cc form I found that torque was the Big D Triumph's middle name—the 5-speed gearbox was almost superfluous, so wide was the spread of power. Interestingly, Wilson uses the standard Meriden box, having found that Quaifes are unable to transmit the substantially increased power without breaking up. But you don't need close-ratio gears with an engine that starts to pull hard from 3500 rpm up to peak revs of 8000. Point it and squirt used to be the maxim with the 'sitter': with the new bike you didn't even need to have it pointing straight before you cram on the power, as my ride showed.

A dozen laps was my ration for the day on the latest Big D Triumph, since sorting it out for Daytona was the main priority. It would be unfair to criticize a bike that had never turned a wheel till that morning, but it's a tribute to Jack Wilson it worked so well straight away. Only real problem appeared to be with front damping: changing springs in the 35 mm Ceriani forks hardened them up and improved things greatly. I found the riding position really awkward, though—but not so the armchair-like 'sitter'!

Accelerating out on to the bumpy Oakville track on Jon's older bike was the difference between chalk and cheese. Fully sorted, it's a proven class winner which being an MP bike uses

*Above* **Minonno (in go-faster, unbearded form) and Wilson fettle the new Rob North-chassised machine at Oakville Raceway (Author)**

*Top right* **The Triumph 8-valve cylinder head was originally a Weslake component, much modified by Jack Wilson (Author)**

*Above right* **Riding position on the 'sitter' was comfortable apart from the high-rise bars, which however gave excellent leverage round the twisty Oakville track (Wilson)**

the standard Triumph frame, heavily reinforced and covered with a single coat of $1\frac{1}{2}$ thousand E-nickel, and consequently provided me with all the room my lanky limbs required. Riding it was a revelation, for not only was the braking and steering literally impeccable, but the massive torque and superior top end of the 975 cc engine showed me why the bike had become so hard to beat in Stateside BoT events. Wilson planned to fit the big engine in the Rob North frame for Daytona, and I could see why: the almost 25 per cent increase in capacity accounts for an even greater difference in performance. The Big D

*Above* **ARD magneto and a belt-drive primary are just some of the modifications made on the Big D Triumphs (Author)**

*Left* **750 engine was originally fitted in the 'sitter' till Wilson had a long-stroke crank made to produce the 975 cc engine (Author)**

*Top* **The twin-cylinder engine fits neatly into the North chassis originally designed for a triple. Note the 16 in. front wheel and large diameter disc (Author)**

Handling of the Rob North chassis was excellent—but riding position very cramped (Wilson)

dyno—'Old Scrooge' as Jack Wilson calls his conservatively-reading engine brake—claims 86 bhp at 7000 rpm for this engine, but it feels like a whole lot more, especially low down. 'Power comes in anywhere you want, don't it?!' grinned Jack after I returned enthusing from my first extended spin on the bike—and so it did. Surprisingly, the big engine was also a bit smoother than the 750, though both vibrated a good deal; Minonno put much of this down on the newer bike to the short, stubby exhausts which actually terminate inside the full fairing, causing some resonance. The secret is more likely to be the hand-made 360 degrees crank in the 975 motor, turned locally from a solid steel billet in a single piece, a job which set Jack Wilson back over $1200 alone. Puma barrels sit on standard cases, with Venolia pistons and a Weslake head fitted to each bike, as is an ARD magneto belt-driven off the exhaust cam at half engine speed: the resultant saving of 15 lb achieved by junking the coils, condensors, battery etc. is well worthwhile: 'We only got three wires on the whole bike,' says Jack proudly, 'two plug leads and the kill switch!'

Similarly, both bikes are fitted with a QPD belt-drive primary which is cleaner, more reliable and saves a further 8 lb. It also cushions the gearbox drive and allows the clutch to be air-cooled. 36 mm flat-slide Qwiksilver carbs—a later development of the Lectron unit—are fitted, but on the 'sitter' the throttle kept sticking open slightly on slow turns. This is apparently a perennial problem, caused by the slides getting slightly sticky from an additive in the exotic 125 octane H&H Blue racing fuel which Wilson uses. No wonder he had trouble with Donington's 97 octane 4-star especially with an 11 to 1 compression ratio on the 975, and 12·5 to 1 on the smaller engine! Honda-type positive action throttles on the new bike cured the sticking problem.

The Rob North chassis had had its oil cooler moved from the nose to the side of the fairing: Wilson uses Valvoline 20/50 lubricant. On the 'sitter' the oil was contained in the frame, which has had the steering head altered to give three degrees less rake and $\frac{1}{4}$ in. more trail. The resultant 54·5 in. wheelbase is one reason I found the bike steering so perfectly, aided by the high bars which gave plenty of leverage in Oakville's tight turns.

One of these was almost my undoing, as I had

by now started to enjoy myself hugely on the big-engined 'sitter'; coming out of the Paddock hairpin one lap I switched on the massive reserve of torque too soon while still laid over, and got a full-blooded rear wheel slide for my pains. 'Guess you just found out why we needed the new frame,' smiled Jack at me as I returned sheepishly to the paddock the following lap. 'We can't fit a wide rear tyre to the bike the way it is, and Jon kept doing what you just did. Glad you found out for yourself!'

Both bikes braked exceptionally well: on the sitter, standard Triumph 35 mm forks mate to a 13 in. Kosman disc and Grimeca caliper. You have to use the brakes hard on this bike because engine braking puts too strong a reverse load on the gearbox for it to withstand the strain on the 975 engine. The gearbox too requires strong and positive lever action; I found you have to be very precise in changing gear else the box will slightly mis-select and then 'uncorrect itself' back into the gear you just came from. There were no such problems with the 750 though: there my main difficulty was simply reaching the lever with my size nine.

Britain is fortunate indeed to have so deeply committed a pair of ambassadors in the USA as Jack Wilson and Jon Minonno. Money couldn't buy the sincerity with which Minonno defends the Triumph name, for example: 'I get madder 'n' hell when people look down their noses at Trimphs,' he burns. 'They're still the best darn scooter you can buy, and I aim to prove that every time I go out on the track.' Brit bike fans everywhere will be crossing their fingers for him and Jack Wilson in their future efforts on behalf of the newly constituted Triumph maufacturing company.

| Model | | Big D Triumph<br>BoT GP class bike<br>(Rob North frame) | Big D Triumph<br>BoT MP class bike<br>('sitter') |
|---|---|---|---|
| Engine | | Ohv pushrod twin-cylinder 4-stroke | Ohv pushrod twin-cylinder 4-stroke |
| Bore × stroke | | 76 × 82 mm | 81 × 95 mm |
| Capacity | | 740 cc | 975 cc |
| Power output | | 82 bhp at 7800 rpm | 86 bhp at 7000 rpm |
| Compression ratio | | 12·5 to 1 | 11 to 1 |
| Carburation | | 2 × 36 mm Quiksilver | 2 × 36 mm Quiksilver |
| Ignition | | ARD magneto | ARD magneto |
| Clutch | | Dry multi-plate | Dry multi-plate |
| Gearbox | | 5-speed Triumph with belt-driven primary | 5-speed Triumph with belt-driven primary |
| Frame | | Duplex cradle | Backbone-type duplex cradle |
| Suspension: | front | 35 mm Ceriani | 35 mm Triumph |
| | rear | Fox | Fox |
| Brakes: | front | 13 in. single disc with 4-piston caliper | 13 in. single disc with 2-piston caliper |
| | rear | 8½ in. single disc | 8½ in. single disc |
| Tyres: | front | 3½ × 16 in. rim | 2¾ × 18 in. rim |
| | rear | 3½ × 18 in. rim | 3 × 18 in. rim |
| Weight (with oil but no fuel) | | 283 lb | 312 lb |
| Top speed | | 160 + mph (estimated) | 155 mph (with 750 engine) |
| Year of manufacture | | 1982 (as tested) | 1976 |
| Owner | | Jack Wilson, Dallas, Texas, USA | Jack Wilson, Dallas, Texas, USA |